10/9

Joel
242½ North La Peer Drive
Beverly Hills, California 90211

Howard Hughes

HOWARD

HUGHES

by John Keats

RANDOM HOUSE

New York
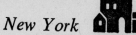

Contents

Foreword

This book is, hopefully, merely an interim report. But it is a time now for summing up the tale to date, for appraising insofar as we can the meaning and works of a man who sometimes seems at this writing nothing more substantial than a rumor on a guarded hilltop.

It would be difficult to find a subject for biography whose life more outwardly resembles the most improbable Grade B spectacular in glorious Vistavision. It also seems possible to suggest that Howard Hughes represents a kind of apotheosis of the very ordinary American who lives an apocalyptic version of the American Dream, for his life would seem to recapitulate very nearly all of the popular legends so dear to Americans.

One legend, bound up in the national worship of youth and optimism, pays honor to the poor orphan who, called before his time to man's estate, nonetheless plays a man's role. Howard Hughes unquestionably acted out this drama. Despite his wealth he somehow suggested Tom, the Honest Bootblack, when he stood before the judge and asked permission to rule, at the age of eight-teen, one of America's great industries.

Another legend presumes there is something good about being a Texan. The Texan we like to imagine is tall, dark, handsome, truthful and unpredictable; he pushes his luck and plays a lone hand and women love him and men respect him. In a great many ways Howard Hughes is a satisfactory Texan.

The legendary American is a mechanical genius and a sharp bargainer. He can build himself the machine he needs, even if he never did go to school. In fact, he is somewhat suspicious of book larnin', and he is quite able to show those professors and Eastern city slickers a thing or two. Howard Hughes seems to have met the basic requirements.

A legend many of us like to believe is that a private citizen, all by himself, armed only with justice, can defeat the machinations of the politically powerful. Unquestionably, the nation applauded when Howard Hughes stood right up to those Senators and told them where to head in.

We also like to believe that anyone can strike it rich; that this is still a land of opportunity from can-see to can't-see, and that the frontier is still wide open. Howard Hughes struck it very rich indeed. Granted that he began with a shoelace big as a hawser, he still built a struggling airline into a giant; he did establish an industry worth hundreds of millions; he did push at the frontiers of flight and fling them farther back.

A legendary figure in America is the wealthy man who is just plain folks; to whom new cars and fine clothes mean very little; who—because of his honest lack of concern for fripperies—could go to the most fashionable restaurant in the world wearing old tennis shoes and not feel at all ill at ease. Howard Hughes would be a leading candidate to fill this bill of particulars.

But legend, in its contrary way, also celebrates the man who, at a snap of his fingers, can command mansions, aircraft, yachts; who has chefs waiting on twenty-four-hour duty just for him at fashionable hotels; who is so utterly freed by his wealth that he can have virtually anything he wants. Once more, Howard Hughes would seem such a man.

Then there is the universal dream of mankind to possess "the Most Beautiful Woman in the World." In point of fact, Howard Hughes has appeared in public with a high proportion of the world's most beautiful women on his arm.

Finally there is the legend, so fervently believed by women, that says the man who can have any girl he wants invariably marries the one who plays hard-to-get. So it would have seemed in the case of Jean Peters and Howard Hughes.

That sundry aspects of Hughes-as-legendary-hero are contradictory is neither here nor there. Rather, contradiction is intriguing. If much about the life of Hughes seems the stuff of dreams, if not the stuff of maudlin melodrama, there is even soap opera's favorite question to be asked at the end of it: Can money buy happiness? One thinks of the guards in their old Chevrolets parked about the secluded house of a man who once flew faster than any man, who circled a world and who lived like a fire in the world—and one wonders. What moves him now? What dreams has he? What dreams has he dreamed; and if this is the end of it, is the ending anything he had ever imagined? If you had a billion dollars, what would you do with it? And if you lost it all, what difference would it make?

This is what Howard Hughes did:

He flew airplanes. He flew them very well.

He made motion pictures. Most of them were popular.

He designed aircraft. He had inspired help; but there is agreement that Hughes is a competent mechanic, a shrewd questioner and an original thinker. He was more responsible than anyone else for designing the largest aircraft in the world.

He created an inter-continental airline.

He also made the decisions—and put up the money—that called into being one of the world's great scientific centers where developmental work was done on missile systems, lasers and communications satellites.

So Hughes ran a fortune up into more than a billion dollars and he did a great many things with his money. But in all candor, he seems not to have ever had a plan for his life. Rather, it resembles a picaresque adventure, as if to demonstrate, on a canvas most highly charged, the proposition that most human lives are never planned but merely ricochet from one thing to another.

Nowhere in an examination of sources is there the slightest suggestion that Howard Hughes ever read widely or deeply or took any part in the life of the mind as such a life is understood in colleges of the liberal arts. Nowhere in the record is there evidence that Hughes' life was filled with warm friends. He seems to have had few of these, but a great many servants. Perhaps more strikingly than anything else, Hughes' life points out the power that money has over the minds of a great many of us, for the record is replete with examples of men and women of all conditions doing the most preposterous things because Hughes paid them to.

The dark side of the record shows Hughes as capricious as Caligula and just as self-centered, surrounded by a kind of Praetorian guard that admitted sycophants to the Presence and transmitted impulses to puppets that danced at the ends of telephone wires.

And now, what is at the end of it all? Hughes' pleasures were never carnal; he was ascetic with respect to food and drink; he pushed himself through staggering working hours. His one great pleasure seems to have been flight. Two personal aircraft, a dusty DC-6 and a Convair, stand waiting at Santa Monica airport. They have not been flown for years. Young men sit in old automobiles beside them night and day. Other young men sit on the porches of bungalows, and outside the fences of sundry houses of incredible opulence, and yawn. They wait for Father to return from San Limbo, not really believing that he ever will.

Perhaps Eddie the barber said all that anyone can really say about Howard Hughes. Eddie has left him now, and he said, "Looking back, I have no complaints. It was unusual, sure, but Hughes was always a courteous, polite, well-paying customer, and more than that, a good friend. I know he has his problems; don't we all. He just operates a little different from the rest of us. Who's to say who's wrong?"

part i Sonny

1

His family called him Sonny or Junior. To the rest of Houston he was Young Howard or Little Howard. He was six feet, three inches tall, but he would never be Big Howard. Big Howard was his father, who was now dead. There was a question in Houston business circles as to what Little Howard would do when he came of age, because the lives of a great many people were predicated on the success of the Hughes Tool Company, in which the boy had inherited a majority interest. It was an immediate question, because Young Howard did not wish to wait. Not yet nineteen, he had come into a Texas courtroom, asking Judge Montieth, an old friend of the family, to declare him a responsible adult. If the judge should sign such a declaration, nothing could prevent Little Howard from voting his stock as he wished. The family view of the matter was that Sonny's request should be refused. The family held all the rest of the stock.

The boy came into the courtroom carrying himself with that slight stoop that so often is the attempted apology of the excessively tall, or which in his case might have represented an adolescent fear of being conspicuous. To many people he seemed somewhat hard of hearing and terribly shy. He had attended seven schools and was the distinguished graduate of none. He was trained for no trade. He liked to tinker with mechanical contraptions, to drive fast cars, fly airplanes, and had spoken of wanting to play the saxophone in a jazz band. One of his father's business associates knew the boy as "this thing, a sort of nocturnal varmint type, six feet tall and a hundred and four pounds, sitting up in bed in a hotel room, playing the saxophone. No tune, just blowing." Sonny sel-

dom smiled; the melancholy cast of his features was enhanced by
his somber clothes. Despite his fidgeting, there seemed an old world
courtliness about him, a sort of understated politeness perfectly
matched to his soft Texas drawl. All he wanted, he told the judge,
was something he was going to get anyway. He just wanted it three
years early. Judge Montieth said he would take the matter under
advisement until he could learn what there was to be known about
the spindly orphan who wanted to be called a man.

The evidence was sketchy; not all of it favorable. But one fact
was immediately, brilliantly obvious: There was little in the boy's
life that could be called average or normal. Even the date of his
birth seemed singular. Howard Robard Hughes was born on
Christmas Eve, 1905. His mother was a dark-eyed beauty of
French descent; his father was a Harvard lawyer who dressed like a
dandy, practiced no law, lived on his wits and his luck and spent
what he had whenever he could get it. Big Howard had spent the
years between his Harvard graduation and his marriage at the age
of thirty-six chasing the ends of rainbows across the Texas plains,
sometimes finding them and sometimes not—an activity that often
had him sitting down at a dinner table in evening clothes, but just
as often required his sweating in Levis and rough boots as a day
laborer at an oil rig while he accumulated enough money for another, hopefully more fortunate, gamble. He was a wildcatter and a
speculator in oil leases, wheeling and dealing his way through an
oil boom. In the year of his marriage, good luck attended him: he
bought and sold leases on land that actually proved to have oil
under it. So he took his bride and $50,000 to Europe for a honey-
moon, returning several months older and exactly $50,000 poorer.
To spend such a sum so quickly in that simpler time required a
certain ingenuity. But Big Howard's ingenuity at all manner of activities was most remarkable, as no few of his business associates
rather bitterly observed.

When the son arrived, Mr. and Mrs. Hughes were living in a
small frame house that stood at 1402 Crawford Street, next to Fire
House Station Eight in downtown Houston. It was a rented house
on a dirt street, but it was the first home the young couple had

known in two years of peripatetic marriage. Sonny was born at home, and he was to be their only child.

By the time the boy was three, two facts about him had already attracted adult attention. First, the firemen who played cards at Station Eight remarked that he was an unusually quiet and lonely child. The world of 1908 believed that children should be seen, not heard, and judging by this standard one of the firemen said that Little Howard was "just about the nicest kid who ever came to visit us." Second, the boy's interest in machinery of all sorts was rather more than merely noticeable. His view of the world around him was such that, as his mother said, "I think he thought a puppy dog was a machine of some sort." At the age of three he was already taking pictures with a box camera given him by his indulgent father.

Big Howard's indulgence of his son was to burgeon as the means came more to hand, and, in 1908, it seemed that the family was on its way to stable wealth. Big Howard was something of an inspired tinker, and he brought this talent to bear upon a problem.

The problem was that the oil drills of 1908 were incapable of penetrating the thick rock shale of southwest Texas, beneath which, geologists said, lay enormous deposits of oil. So far, it had been only the easy oil, lying close to the surface, that had been reached. Understandably, many oilmen were frantically trying to devise a drill bit that could cut deep through rock. Big Howard came across a promising idea for something called a roller bit. The trouble was it didn't work. It looked as if it should, but for some reason it didn't. Big Howard, laboring with pencil and paper on the dining-room table of his rented house, came up with a revolutionary drill bit that had 166 cutting edges, and he worked out a method of keeping the bit constantly lubricated as it tore at rock hundreds of feet below the surface. He took the plans almost as far away from Texas oilfields as he could possibly get—to a tool shop in Massachusetts. A pilot model was made, and Big Howard promptly covered it with patents in his own name. Then, together with his partner in the leasing business, Walter B. Sharp, Big Howard established the Sharp-Hughes Tool Company for the manufacture of roller bits. The partners refused to sell their devices, prefer-

ring the far more lucrative scheme of renting them for short periods
to drilling companies. A bit sold was a bit gone, but a bit could be
leased to a company at a fee of $30,000 per well, dry hole or
gusher, and then be leased again.

Development of the bit and production of the first models took
place in a small workshop during the three years the Hughes family
lived on Crawford Street. So quickly was the invention accepted by
drilling companies that in 1908 the partners were building a factory on a seventy-acre site east of Houston. The same year they
moved their families to substantial houses in Houston's most fashionable part of town.

Moving from the familiar to the unknown was no doubt as much
of a shock to Young Howard as it always is to any child, but he
was to find certain compensations. Instead of his friends the firemen he now had a playmate—Dudley Sharp, the son of his father's partner. There was also a workshop behind the Hughes
house. Here the boy was allowed to amuse himself for hours on end
with bits of wire and metal, inventing those curious objects to
which only a child's imagination can give meaning, but which, in
that imagination, are just as real as the inventions of the father.
The boy had the freedom of the workshop on one condition: that
he keep it spotless. Big Howard came often to inspect it, and a
smear of oil, a rag or a tool out of place would mean exile from
the workshop for a week.

The picture that emerges of Young Howard at this time is that of
an only child, tall and thin for his age, sometimes playing with his
one friend, but spending many more lonely hours puttering by himself in the dim quiet of a room that smelled of oiled metal. He was
the observer from a distance of the teas, the garden parties and the
lawn dances which his mother, the descendant of Huguenots and
the granddaughter of a Confederate general, staged for the delecta-
tion of Houston's society.

Another picture emerges from these years: that of a boy creeping
like a snail unwillingly to school. Sonny was first enrolled in a kin-
dergarten kept in Christ Church Episcopal Cathedral in downtown
Houston. Next came a private elementary school, Professor Pros-

so's Academy, then South End Junior High School—a public school. The boy took very little interest in any of them. An aunt, Mrs. F. R. Lummis, said "I wouldn't say he was studious, except in the courses he was interested in." He did well in arithmetic and seemed bored by everything else. His school days were unmarked by noticeable popularity or by academic success. He attended school, and that was that.

Between the ages of ten and thirteen, Sonny's principal energies were spent in the workshop, where his inventions were no longer precisely childlike. He built and operated a ham radio set. He asked his father for a motorcycle, but Big Howard said no. Days later, Sonny was scooting down Houston streets on a motorcycle. He had built it himself, devising a power plant for his bicycle out of a storage battery and a self-starter motor taken from one of his father's automobiles. Big Howard, whose own great hobby was speed and who fancied himself an amateur racing car driver, was too pleased with his only son to punish him. He said Sonny could keep the battery and the starter.

It was during these same gawky, gangling years when the boy was crossing the threshold of puberty that he discovered the witchery of the night. He had known its solitudes while sitting up late at his ham set talking with wireless operators aboard inbound Gulf freighters, but the first time the world became aware of his predilection occurred on a Boy Scout expedition to the San Jacinto battleground. The Scoutmaster heard strange moans coming from a tent in the pre-dawn hours. In the tent, under a blanket, there was Sonny playing his saxophone. The boy's punishment—which may not have seemed a punishment to him—was to stand guard the rest of the night. In the morning he was made Troop Bugler, and later his mother was to wonder if Sonny could not invent a muffler for his bugle.

It was Big Howard's wish that his son attend Harvard, just as he had and his father before him. Fearing that a Texas education would hardly prepare a boy for admission, the father took Sonny out of South End Junior High and packed him off to the Fessenden School in Newton, Massachusetts. Fessenden remembers Howard

Hughes as awkward, shy, lonely and homesick for Houston and his tool shop. The boy, well dressed, good-mannered and remote, kept his monastic room immaculate, made no real friends, sat in silence at the rear of the class and underwent stammering agonies of embarrassment when called upon to recite. He tried to correct this deficiency. Like many schools of its time, Fessenden obliged its students to recite poetry from memory, and in some desperation the boy took himself off to the gymnasium after hours to shout his poem at the silent, echoing walls. A teacher found him practicing there and commended him for his efforts. His grades for conduct were excellent.

The most massive experience in Sonny's life at Fessenden occurred in the spring of his fourteenth year, when Big Howard came to visit and took him to the Harvard-Yale boat races. If Harvard won, his father said, then he would buy Sonny anything that Sonny wanted.

Harvard did win, and the delighted father wondered what his boy would ask. He probably suspected it would be a sailing canoe, inasmuch as the boy had been talking about little else since Big Howard had arrived. But it seemed that Sonny had seen a flying boat moored on the river. It interested him more than the races had, and had driven sailing canoes out of his mind. More than anything else, he wanted a ride in that seaplane.

In 1920 flying was hardly one of the least dangerous forms of amusement, albeit the most glamorous. In those days, youth wanted wings, and perhaps those who felt the pull of flight most strongly were boys who had been too young for the recent war, but whose special heroes had been the well-publicized young duelists in goggles and leather who had fought for possession of the French skies. In any event, Sonny had named his choice, and his father had given his word.

The flying boat roared heavily downriver, gathering speed until it fell lightly upward into the vacuum created over its cambered wings. It swung through the air on a flight that might have seemed hours long to the father waiting below, but which would have been only an inadequate instant to an excited boy. During the flight,

Sonny shouted incessant questions to the pilot, and by the time the craft splashed down onto the water, he had an elementary grasp of the mechanical principles of flight.

On his return to Houston that summer, Sonny discovered that a barnstorming pilot was selling flying lessons. Without telling his parents, he enrolled in what was apparently the first course of instruction that he had ever really wanted to take. He paid for the lessons out of his allowance, and he kept his experience and his new knowledge secret. That summer, flying, tinkering with his father's new Locomobiles and Stanley Steamer racing cars, and operating his ham radio in the midwatches of the night commanded the major part of Sonny's attention. Little else impressed him. He lurked in corners at the debutante parties he was made to attend. He took more interest in the automobiles parked outside the club than in the girls who arrived in them.

At this time of the boy's life, the father was spending increasing amounts of time and money on parties, automobile racing and travel. One of Big Howard's amusements was to charter a railroad car, fill it with friends, and roll to and fro between California and New York. He dressed his beautiful wife in high fashion, maintained a yacht, cut an elegant figure and was one of the most popular men in Houston. He spent so freely that his executives protested his cash withdrawals from what was now, since the death of his partner, the Hughes Tool Company. (Widow Sharp had inherited her husband's half of the concern; was advised by bankers to sell it. She did, but the purchaser, alarmed by Big Howard's lavish spending, feared the company would collapse, and he sold his interest to Hughes.) Perhaps to show his executives exactly how much attention he would pay to their advice, he then withdrew $75,000 in cash from the firm. There seemed to be no limit to the earning potential of Hughes Tool so long as men would hunt oil. Big Howard held the patents to the best drilling bit in the world. He had bought out his closest competitor, who marketed a very similar bit, and already a majority of United States oil prospectors were leasing Hughes bits. So many men were drilling in California that Big Howard opened a branch of Hughes Tool Company in Los An-

geles. He began to spend longer periods of time away from Houston, tending to his California business and cultivating a growing
circle of Hollywood friends. If this fortunate man suffered from
any disappointment, it might have been the realization that his son
would never go to Harvard. He took the boy with him to California
in the fall of 1921, and instead of returning him to Fessenden,
enrolled him in the Thacher School at Ojai, California. According
to one California educator, Thacher's reputation was that it was
not unduly challenging.

In the spring term of that school year, when Sonny was sixteen,
Mrs. Hughes entered a Houston hospital and died on the operating
table.

To Sonny, the news was as abrupt as it was unexpected. The
effect that any mother has on any boy's life is always a matter of
conjecture, but the opinion of friends and relatives of the Hughes
family was that Sonny had always been more his father's boy than
his mother's. After the mother's death he was wholly in his father's
hands, and after a conventional period of mourning, Big Howard
introduced Sonny to a pace and style of life that might best be
described as existentialism-with-money.

Soon after the mourning band disappeared from Big Howard's
arm, Hollywood actresses appeared on it. He began to give parties
lavish even by Hollywood standards, and proudly brought his sixteen-year-old son into a tinsel world compounded of hotel suites,
games of chance, evening clothes, Prohibition whisky and flash
money; a world largely nocturnal and generously populated by
breathtakingly beautiful women. Such a world and such a life con-
stituted an education of a sort; it served as a kind of finishing
school for a basically introverted boy who was never to complete a
formal education.

The principal lesson that such a world would teach might be that
wealth was one means to satisfaction of one's whims. Here was Big
Howard, a glittering figure, one of the best-dressed men in America, singularly popular, doing what he pleased, a freewheeling
spender in what would become the tradition of the Texas oil man,
the frequent companion of Mae Murray, an actress known to the

nation as "the girl with the bee-stung lips." It might have seemed to Sonny that there was a direct relationship between his father's purchases of jewels from Tiffany's and Cartier's and the friendship of Miss Murray and of sundry other young ladies upon whom these baubles were bestowed; another relationship between his father's open-handed generosity and the willingness of people to serve him. Money certainly made possible Sonny's own pursuit of pleasure at the golf courses and behind the wheels of fast cars. It made possible additional flying lessons—and California flyers said that Sonny enrolled in three different flying schools, one after another, always as a beginner, never telling his instructors he had flown before, carefully dissembling his knowledge. Pilots wondered why. Was it because the boy wished to check each instructor's theory of flight against the others'? Was it that a lonely boy, attending the only kind of school that he really seemed to enjoy, badly wanted the praise that his instructors were quick to give?

Meantime, the money poured in. Rumor had it that the Hughes Tool Company was then worth between seventeen and eighty million dollars; that Sonny, when he turned seventeen, had an allowance of $5,000 a month; that Big Howard would draw $10,000 a month for himself from the company, and if he had anything left in his pockets at the end of the month, would give it to the first man he met. And money made further education possible. After Sonny had spent an undistinguished year at Thacher, Big Howard made an anonymous donation to scholarship funds at the California Institute of Technology, in return for which the Institute allowed Sonny, not yet of college age, to take special courses to prepare him for entrance to Rice Institute. The following year, Sonny earned fair grades at Rice—except for his course in mathematics, in which he received the highest possible mark.

There was every evidence that the boy had a mind as intricate as his father's. The apparent problem was that Sonny was unwilling to apply it to that which bored him. Given his fortunate circumstances, there might have seemed to him no reason why he should. Yet beneath that shyness and apparent apathy, there was a streak of stubbornness and a smoldering spirit of revolt that the adults of

Sonny's acquaintance seemed not to have suspected. But boys con-
fide to one another, seldom to adults, and Sonny's one close friend,
Dudley Sharp, had this to say: "He seemed to have an absolute
mania for proving himself. He didn't want to stay in Houston in his
father's shadow. I think he even disliked bearing his father's name.
He wanted to get out and find something he wanted to do. He
didn't know exactly what, but nothing was going to stop him."

Nothing, perhaps, except an uncertain adolescent's inability to
compete with a splendidly omnicompetent father.

But then in January, 1924, at the end of Sonny's first semester at
Rice, the father died as abruptly as the mother. There was even less
warning. Big Howard was striding back and forth in his office, discussing business with a fellow oil man. In mid-sentence, he gasped,
clutched at his chest and fell to the floor, dead.

There is apt to be a difference between freedom granted and
freedom won. Like a nation successful in revolution, a man who
has fought for his freedom most usually has a definite idea as to
how to employ it; an adolescent boy, like an adolescent nation, is
most often confused by the gift. Hughes was not. When the solicit-
ous aunts and uncles gathered round the newly orphaned Sonny,
they discovered the boy was not at all backward in stating what he
wanted. He had very little use for their well-meant advice. His father's will contained this passage: "I desire and request that my
son Howard be given as good an education as possible to fit him for
such business or profession as he may desire to enter, and particularly request that if possible, a part at least of such education be
given him in the university of the state in which he may expect to
make his home."

The will, written eleven years earlier, left half the estate to Mrs.
Hughes; one-fourth to Sonny; and the balance to Big Howard's
father, mother, and brother. Since Mrs. Hughes had died before her husband, her half went to the son. And since Big Howard
had owned all the tool company's stock, Sonny now held three-
quarters of it; and he would be able to vote that stock as soon as he
came of age.

The total value of the estate, including real property, stocks, bonds, notes, accounts and personal property, was appraised for tax purposes at $871,518. An appraisal for tax purposes frequently does not approach reality, however. For example, the assets of the Hughes Tool Company were listed in the appraisal as being worth $750,000, but the company could not have been purchased for ten times that amount if its stock had then been offered for sale.

Of course there were certain debts against the estate. It seemed that Big Howard had left a number of unpaid bills behind. For example, there was a Brooks Brothers bill for six suits, three overcoats, fifty shirts, several pairs of knickers and assorted hose and vests; in all, $2,258. Another New York tailor, James Bell & Son, sent a $500 bill for two tuxedos and four vests. Cartier's was owed $3,252, and the jeweler's account included a $2,250 diamond ring and $690 for a set of sapphire cuff links. There was $3,500 due for a grand piano, and the Parker Music Company of Houston sought to collect $99 for saxophone reeds, a saxophone, and a $2 Ludwig whistle. A Los Angeles tailor wanted $225 for a riding habit. But this is only a partial accounting. In all, Big Howard's unpaid bills totalled $258,000.

So, on paper, the value of the estate dropped to $613,518, but Sonny understood the major fact very well: three-quarters of it was his, and the tool company was potentially worth millions. He apparently was not satisfied with his share. Perhaps he remembered his father saying so often, "Never do business with partners." In any case, he immediately suggested that his grandparents and his uncle sell him their one-fourth share of the tool company stock. The soft-drawled words fell into a pool of silence.

Hastily the lawyers explained that Sonny could not, at the age of eighteen, make a contract. The aunts and uncles and the grandparents wanted him to reconsider about going to college. Wouldn't he, or didn't he feel a need to go to school to learn how to handle his future responsibilities?

Apparently Sonny didn't.

Shortly after this funeral scene Mrs. Walter Sharp, widow of Big Howard's former partner and mother of Sonny's friend Dudley, announced that she was going to Europe. In the implacable way of a

Southern gentlewoman who will not be gainsaid by mere males, she said she was taking Sonny and Dudley with her. She said the trip would do them all good, and particularly Sonny, because it would give him time to think and get him away from all those lawyers and relatives; and besides, every young boy ought to see Europe. Anyway, she said, she was going, and she needed escorts, and Sonny and Dudley were her choice, and that was all there was to it.

The boy was glad enough to leave even without such persuasion, and the ensuing trip was chiefly remarkable for three events. First, on arrival in England, Sonny convinced Mrs. Sharp that they should all fly to the Continent instead of taking a Channel steamer. In later years Dudley said he still had no idea how young Hughes ever managed to induce his mother to fly for the first time in her life; not only to fly, but to fly across the Channel.

Once on the mainland Sonny seemed to care little for the museums and cathedrals of the conventional itinerary. He was fascinated instead by the Brussels casino. He watched the roulette table with a mathematician's eye. At last one night he placed a $5 plaque on red to win. Red won; the boy let the $10 ride and won again. He began to switch between red and black, consistently winning. As the pile of plaques before him mounted a crowd began to gather. The tall young Texan with the dark eyes and the somber features seemed almost contemptuous of good fortune. There was $1,000 worth of plaques before him; $2,000; $4,000. At $8,000 he reduced his bet and slowly built again until his winnings totaled $10,000. For a long moment he wondered whether to bet it all. At length he picked up just one plaque, worth $10, and placed it on red. The wheel spun, the ball jittered among the slots and came to rest on black. Without a word the boy scooped up the $9,990 that remained. He felt his luck was starting to change, and that it was time to quit.

The third event which impressed Sonny upon the memory of others occurred on the passage home. When the steward showed the two boys to their cabin, Sonny objected. It was a first-class cabin, but a small one. The boy stalked off to see no less a person than the captain, demanding to know who had been placed in the biggest and best cabin on the ship. The passenger list was checked. The cabin had been reserved by a prominent physician. Money changed hands; the doctor's accommodations were changed; the two boys were moved in. It was an imperious act, not without portent. The impressive fact seemed to be that money talked—not age, nor courtesy, nor precedent, nor wisdom, nor social condition, nor reputation. Just money. Given sufficient money anyone could get whatever one wanted, no matter if one was only eighteen years old.

Back again in Houston, Sonny spent money on lawyers. Through them he learned of a seldom-used provision in the Texas law. It seemed that if a minor could convince the court that he was mentally an adult and capable of handling his affairs, the court had authority to declare him a legally responsible adult. So it was that Sonny and his lawyers appeared before Judge Montieth, who began by asking the boy a series of questions about the Hughes Tool Company. It turned out that Sonny had done some homework. He knew the company's financial standing, the extent of its obligations, the roles of its key personnel, its plans for the future. It was at this point that Judge Montieth undertook his investigation of the boy's background, education and general reputation in the community. Against the boy were ranged his youth, his lack of experience in any business and the wishes of his relatives. In his favor there was the fact that he had legal counsel, had a demonstrable interest in and ability at the operation and design of things mechanical and enjoyed in the Houston business community (which largely knew him as the frequent member of a golfing foursome of Big Howard's friends) a better reputation than his father. Questioned by the judge, Houston businessmen said first of all the company was so good it could run itself anyway, and besides, they said, Sonny was a right good golfer.

There was also a quality of decision about the boy that was impressive in itself. It might not have been manifest before, but it was obvious enough now, despite his uneasy fidgeting. Finally, it might have appeared to Judge Montieth that, if he granted Sonny's request, he would be doing nothing that the passage of about three years would not do automatically.

After due deliberation the judge declared that Sonny was legally a man. He had only one suggestion: that the youth seriously consider returning to Rice Institute to finish his education.

Sonny quickly moved to buy his relatives' interest in the Hughes Tool Company. His offers were at length accepted. The sums he paid have never been disclosed, but in later years there was a feeling in the family that they should have held out for more. The important fact was that a boy, at the age of eighteen, closed his fist around one of the most profitable businesses in the United States. He had all the freedom that a man could ask, and it now remained to be seen whether he understood the obligation to others that freedom entails. In short, it was time for him to stop being Sonny. But who would he be, and what would he do?

One of his first acts was to visit the tool company. Older workmen still remember that visit. One said, "I remembered him as a little fellow, banging away with hammers and anvil iron in a back shop. Now he shook hands like a man, strong, and he looked us right in the eye and called us by name." Leaving the factory floor, Young Howard settled himself in Big Howard's office and studied company charts and plans. It seemed as if he would take his ownership quite seriously. If he had a mechanic's interest in the tools the company made, he also had an analytical interest in what made an industrial corporation work. The answer seemed to be that people were its moving parts, and despite his tender years, his awkward nervousness, his look of abstracted melancholy and his somewhat lonesome life, the youth was a rare judge of people. He was not at all shy about hiring and firing men thrice his age. To be sure, it was his company, but this activity bespoke something more than sheer whim, for his choices proved excellent. At this stage of his life the boy capitalist not only had the knack of sensing the right man for the job, but he had the wit to stand back and give that man room to work.

Of all his appointments none was more fortuitous than his en-

gaging a tough, brilliant accountant namd Noah Dietrich. Mr. Dietrich had answered a Hughes Tool Company newspaper advertisement. There was very little he did not understand about corporate
finance or about the oil business. In all that was to follow, it was
said the work was "eighty percent Noah Dietrich's genius and
twenty percent Howard Hughes' gambling blood," but however
this may be, it is also true that the whole is the sum of its parts.
Both the eighty percent and the twenty percent, if this is the way it
was, were absolutely essential to each other. In Dietrich, Young
Howard found precisely the man to entrust with the day-to-day
operation of his affairs. Their relationship was to continue for more
than thirty years.

The already prosperous company leaped ahead under its new
owner. Whether this was because of his efforts or despite them, it is
impossible to say; perhaps, as Houston businessmen said, the company was basically so strong and the market so good, it would have
made money no matter who was running it. In any event, Young
Howard's interest in it soon diminished to a narrow concern for the
profits it produced. Money had meaning to him only if it was being
spent for something; otherwise, a pile of banknotes might as well
be a heap of wastepaper.

At this time—it was now his nineteenth year—it was plain to
Houston that the boy was no longer Sonny, but it was just as plain
to him that he would never stop being Young Howard so long as he
remained in Houston. Houston's memories were too long, the city
was too small and Big Howard had been too big for that to happen.
The young man's attention turned outward, seeking for something
that he could indeed call his own and so become in his own right
Howard Hughes. And that year he took two steps in the direction
of full manhood. He married, and he moved to California to begin
a career of his own.

His bride was Ella Rice, a dark-haired, high-spirited daughter of
the family that gave Rice Institute its name. She was some months
older than he, and had beaux who were years older. The young
people had known one another for years, for tradesmen like the
Hugheses, the Sharps, the Rices and the Carters, a family whose for-

tune had been made in lumber, formed the axle round which the wheel of Houston's society turned. They had met at debutante parties in the past, and Howard had sometimes written letters to her when he had been away at school. There now ensued a courtship, and on a stifling day in 1925 Ella and Howard were wed in a rose garden. It was the most fashionable event of the Houston summer season; but to anyone who might have had Dudley Sharp's insight into the secret vehemence of Young Howard's rejection of Houston and of Big Howard's shadow, the marriage may have seemed inexplicable or at least contradictory.

How, after all, does one reject Houston by marrying one of its most prominent daughters, whose associations will naturally center in Houston? How can one reject a formal education at Rice Institute and marry a Rice? How is it a rejection of one's father if one does precisely what the father did in marrying a Texas aristocrat? How does one break away from home by marrying, as it were, one of the family? If a young man wants his freedom above all else, why would he rush into matrimony at the age of nineteen? To be sure, matrimony is something men engage in, but one wonders whether in this case the young man wanted a wife to prove himself a man, or whether he wanted a mother.

The same kind of questions hover about Young Howard's choice of a career. Together with his bride, he set out for Hollywood to make motion pictures. The idea came from a former Hollywood actor then resident in Houston, who had been one of Big Howard's close friends. In fact, he had been so close a friend that Big Howard had once told his son, "After I'm gone, if you can ever help Ralph Graves in any way that's economically feasible, I want you to do it. Men like that are rare."

Meeting Graves in Houston following Big Howard's death, Young Howard was reminded of his father's request.

"There is something," Graves had told him. "I have a story that will make a hell of a movie. It's about a Bowery bum who adopts a baby. I'd like to produce it and act in it . . ."

Young Howard asked how much that would cost.

"We could bring it in for $40,000, I think," Graves guessed.

The actor said Young Howard replied, "You got it, provided you'll let me watch."

It is interesting to speculate as to the emotional appeal such a motion picture story might have for a nineteen-year-old orphan; as to why the boy that Dudley Sharp knew should wish to venture off to one of his father's stamping grounds under the aegis of his father's friend. But it may be more profitable to consider that ontogeny recapitulates phylogeny, inasmuch as all that Sonny had done the man who was to be Howard Hughes would do again. The box camera would become the motion picture camera; the love of speed would bring forth new speed records; the ancient flying boat would call forth the greatest flying boat the world has ever seen; the ham radio would lead to an electronics industry. Other parallels could be drawn, for it might be said that every man, in essence, recapitulates the boy he has been.

part ii The Camera and the Sky

2

In 1925, motion picture actors flashed their eyes, moved their lips and hugely exaggerated the gestures of pantomime to be sure that nothing of their make-believe would be lost upon the millions of illiterate theatergoers who would be unable to read the words flashed across silent screens. So it was a time for posturing; and since it was also the Jazz Age of coonskin coat, hip flask and flapper, it could be said that not all the posturing occurred in Hollywood, although Hollywood seemed to set a national pace in this regard. On Hollywood locations the uniform of the day for directors ran to whipcord riding breeches, polished boots, open-throated check shirts cut in military style with two buttoned breast pockets, and monocles. Cameramen affected a similar costume, adding visored caps worn backwards. Very much a part of the Hollywood scene, but splendidly conspicuous, was a bareheaded lanky boy who tilted back in a director's chair wearing a soft, woolen V-necked sweater, a wide-collared white shirt with silk tie, plus fours, gaudy Argyle stockings and white sneakers. On the back of his chair he hung an Army webbed belt with canteen attached. This was Howard Hughes, living out a dream of himself as a brilliant young producer. Hollywood's view of him was that of a woolly lamb with an endless supply of fleece.

He had hired one hundred electricians; no one had told him that ten would have been enough. His were the highest salaries for the least talent in town. One story went that Howard Hughes, on first arriving in Hollywood, asked Louis B. Mayer, "How do you go about getting into the picture business?" and that Mayer had replied, "Well, you find yourself a studio, get some stars, a script, and you just start shooting." Whereupon, the story went, Hughes asked, "How much do you want for MGM?" Everybody laughed, and then set to work trying to sell the young Texan almost everything else but Mr. Mayer's property. The estimated $40,000 production cost of Ralph Graves' film *Swell Hogan* had quickly been exceeded. Costs ran past $60,000, then past $70,000. It was certain they would exceed $80,000 (and this in a day when the dollar was still as good as gold), and it was equally clear to Hollywood gossips that every penny of it would prove wasted; that *Swell Hogan* would prove to be a frightful failure artistically as well as commercially. But young Hughes seemed neither to know nor care. He just went on signing checks, interviewing pretty girls hopeful of screen tests (turning down Clara Bow, who later became the It girl), speeding in his Stanley Steamer to the Los Angeles airfield for an afternoon's flying, mingling with the movie people in the night clubs, playing golf. He hired a camera crew to film him as he played golf. Then he studied the films—to learn what he was doing wrong, he said; to correct his swing. The town smiled. Hollywood was full of actors who, found watching their own films, would claim they were studying their faults. But the town may have missed the point that young Hughes was methodical and meticulous, and was merely among the first—if not the first of all—athletes to use motion pictures as a training aid.

On coming to the Los Angeles area, Hughes had bought a two-story house of Spanish style on Muirfield Road adjacent to the Wilshire Country Club grounds. As Ella Hughes discovered, motion picture people lived there; ladies and gentlemen lived in Pasadena. Ella's acquaintances were in Pasadena; she began to miss her Houston friends. She wished that Howard would spend more of his time at home, but of course Howard had his work.

Howard's career was, of course, made easier by the Hughes Tool Company, which hovered in the background like a fairy godmother waiting to be called on at need. Back in Houston, Hughes Tool was steadily improving its position in the absence of its owner. The company manufactured tool joints used to couple sections of drill pipe; it was developing four hundred different sizes of bits, pioneering new oil rigging and conducting research into the heat treatment of metals. Meantime, in Hollywood, under the guidance of Noah Dietrich, Hughes was making certain purchases for Hughes Tool.

He bought 51 percent of the stock of Multi-Color, Inc., a concern trying to develop high-quality color film for motion pictures. He bought an experimental laboratory where he assigned technicians the job of trying to marry the best features of the steam and gasoline engines, for use in automobiles. He bought a major interest in a chain of 125 motion picture houses, so as to be able to show his own movies in his own theaters, thus saving distribution costs. Dietrich helped him establish these enterprises as companies substantially held by Hughes Tool.

Dividing his attentions among these projects, now showing up at one, now at another, golfing, appearing at his movie studio and then jetting off in his steam car for the airfield, Hughes seemed as busy and as happy as a five-year-old let loose alone in a toy shop at Christmastime. His curiosity was as remarkable as his passion for detail. On one occasion he was discovered by the studio night watchman in the projection booth. He was all alone, sleeves rolled up, surrounded by neat groups of bits and pieces of the projector. When asked what he was doing, Hughes replied he was taking it apart. He said if he was going to be in the movie business, he would need to know how everything worked, including the cameras and projectors. He worked through the night, perhaps from time to time pausing to eat bacon and avocado sandwiches from a brown paper bag and to drink from a quart bottle of milk. Just before dawn, he had the projector back together again and in working order. When the day's shooting began some hours later, there was Hughes, back at the studio to watch the action, to peer through the cameras and ask the cameramen technical questions, to ask the actors how they went about the business of bringing interpretation to the roles. Then he was off to see how things were going with the development of color film, or to check the progress on the gasoline-steam engine at the workshop.

Hughes' incessant sort of random Brownian movement was a source of conversation and perplexity in Hollywood. That is, he

was talked about, particularly by those who complained that whenever his decision was wanted Hughes could not be easily found.
For example, it was not always easy to reach him at home, for
Hughes had begun to live according to what he called his "awake
periods." He would work at one thing and another for forty hours
at a time, eating only when he was hungry and apparently not car-
ing a great deal what it was that he ate. He carried no watch and
seemed oblivious to the fact that other people kept to times and
schedules. He was a man who wanted something when he wanted
it, and if this meant calling a man out of bed at two o'clock on a
Sunday morning to come at once to the workshop with a bottle of
milk, a can of beans and a willingness to tinker with a sleeve valve,
there is no record that Hughes ever considered such a request to be
an imposition. At the end of an awake period, Hughes would fall
exhausted into bed—at home, if that was near where he happened
to be when he decided he was sleepy. These habits of her husband's
were somewhat disconcerting to Ella Hughes who, whenever she
invited her Pasadena friends to supper or to parties, could never
know whether Howard would appear or not.

Worse, Howard took little interest in her friends, and she found
it difficult to pretend that she was interested in his Hollywood acquaintances. She tried to interest herself in his enterprises, but he
would tell her little about them. When he was at home, he spent
most of the time on the adjacent Country Club golf course. Whenever he disappeared for days on end, Ella had no more idea than
anyone else as to where he was. When he reappeared, he would
offer no explanation. In all probability, he had merely been at the
studio office, or off on a cross-country flight, or had spent a night
talking with mechanics in a garage, but Ella never knew, and had
no way of knowing. One thing she did know was that Hollywood
was filled with stage-struck girls, and her husband was a motion
picture producer. It was borne in upon her that Hughes ran his own
life in his own way, and neither wanted nor would accept interfer-
ence in it from anyone.

Meantime, production of *Swell Hogan* proceeded under the general direction of Ralph Graves. It was completed behind schedule

at more than twice its estimated production cost, but at last Hughes was able to see what a wonder his money had wrought. He saw the first showing in a studio screening room.

The script had not the slightest literary merit. Hughes, however much a newcomer to the theater, nevertheless had a sense of staging and effect, but here again *Swell Hogan* was lacking. The film simply could not be shown as it was. Something must be done. Hughes hired the best cutters and editors in town, but this proved to be an exercise in throwing good money after bad. Hughes put the can of film on the shelf and never released it. To show there were no hard feelings, he made Graves the present of a new car. Yet he was not quite through spending money on *Swell Hogan*. Under terms of his lease of the General Service Studios for the purpose of making his film, it was specified that any sets left behind became the property of the studio unless the lessee was willing to pay to have them destroyed. Now Harry Cohn, another producer and next to hire the General Service facilities, planned to use the *Swell Hogan* sets. This was not an unusual practice in Hollywood, but apparently the idea that another man could capitalize on something he had built sent Hughes into a rage. He immediately paid $2,500 to have the sets destroyed. Thirty years later, in a Las Vegas night club, comedian Red Skelton dropped by the table where Hughes was being interviewed by the magazine writer Stephen White. Skelton said he needed a vulture in a picture he was making.

"A real vulture," Skelton said, "with beady eyes."

In the softest of voices, Hughes replied, "Get Harry Cohn."

If such was Hughes' mood thirty years after the event, one can imagine his feelings at the time. He decided to wind up his affairs in Hollywood and return to Texas, but something happened to change his mind. His family called to give him their advice. Among those present were his grandmother and his Uncle Rupert, and they pointed out there were dangers in show business; that a novice could and did lose his money, and besides, the wild living and scandals of the movie town discredited anyone who lived there. The family conference was not a success.

"I was actually through with making movies until that little powwow," Hughes confided to the director Lewis Milestone. "But my family made it a challenge. I had to prove me right, and them wrong."

He promptly put $150,000 into a film called *Everybody's Acting*. There was nothing amateurish or experimental about this project. The film was made by Marshall Nielan, a director with a record of success. Hughes stayed in the background during the making of the film, contributing the necessary money. When *Everybody's Acting* appeared, even the critics were kind—"a rather clever exercise in fun," the critics said. Perhaps even more important to Hollywood, and certainly to Hughes, the public loved it. The new film made so much money that it not only covered its production costs, but enabled Hughes to recover those of *Swell Hogan* as well, and to pocket $100,000 besides.

So much for the advice of relatives! Director Nielan may have made the film, but Hughes regarded the success as vindication of his own judgment. He may have taken a disastrous fall with his first effort, when he was only twenty; but he had come back, at the age of twenty-one, with a solid hit. It was time to give the wheel another spin, this time betting with the profits from the last. And just at this point he received a windfall from Hughes Tool.

Caddo Rock Drill Bit Company, a Hughes Tool subsidiary, won a half-million-dollar judgment against a competitor, Reed Roller Bit. With Dietrich's help, Hughes used the money to set up the Caddo Corporation, a film-making company. Hughes Tool advanced Caddo films the half million dollars, thus becoming Caddo's largest creditor. But since Howard Hughes owned all of the tool company's stock, *he* thus became Caddo's principal creditor as well as being Caddo's principal stockholder. Meantime, Hughes signed Milestone to a three-year contract to make Caddo films.

The first was a slapstick farce about two American soldiers taken prisoner during the First World War. It was called *Two Arabian Knights,* and two relatively unknown actors, Louis Wolheim and William Boyd, played the leading roles.

When the shooting began Hughes began to haunt the set, silently watching the action, returning late at night, to the astonishment of the watchmen, to inspect the equipment; to sit in the production office, proofreading the silent film's flashed-on titles. When the film was finished, Director Milestone carefully cut and edited it, and when he was satisfied, retired to nearby Lake Arrowhead for a deserved vacation. He was startled out of his retreat by a Sunday morning telephone call. A friend wanted him to know that Hughes had been seen recutting Milestone's picture. As Milestone later told the story, this is what happened next:

Milestone slammed down the phone, ran out of his house, jumped into his car and sped to Los Angeles. He burst into the studio; and there was his boyish employer sitting on the floor, film festooned around his shoulders and spilling about him as he held a length of it to the light.

"Dunderhead!" Milestone shouted. "Artistic dunderhead!" Who was he to recut a Milestone film? Was he going to wreck months of hard work? Throw away all that money?

He said that Hughes gazed mildly into this storm of Slavic exasperation and murmured, "Calm down, Milly."

If there had been something to throw at Hughes, Milestone said, he would have thrown it. Instead, he demanded, "What in hell are you doing to *my* picture?"

"You're still not calm enough," Hughes said. "Let's go for a drive."

So they went for a ride in Hughes' Stanley Steamer—blasting out of the studio lot, careening through Hollywood, and whistling along the highroad with the speedometer needle teetering toward a hundred miles an hour until Milestone, terrified, yelled, "All right! Stop! I promise! I'm calm!"

Whereupon, Milestone said, Hughes slewed to a stop at the side of the road. Milestone said Hughes smiled, and explained, "You see, Milly, fortunately or unfortunately, I happen to be a very rich man. Because of the wealth I control, I permit myself the luxury of doing things that may look stupid to others. But they make good sense to me. Take what we were just talking about. You thought I was recutting your film. I wasn't recutting your film. That's your job, and you did it well. Your film, as you cut it, is already on its way to New York for distribution. I wanted to learn about film cutting, so I had another print made from the original. I have to teach myself these things."

Milestone shook his head at the memory.

"Hollywood was Howard's classroom," he said. "He was learning about movies. He was the type of person who could never accept anything as the truth unless he had learned it or experienced it personally for himself. He would not take anyone's word. He had to do it, then store it away in that genius mind of his."

Genius was not the word most often used to describe Howard Hughes at the time of *Two Arabian Knights,* however. But when the picture appeared, it most certainly increased Hughes' stature in the film colony. It brought Hughes a 100-percent return on his investment, made stars of Boyd and Wolheim, and it won the 1927 Academy Award for comedy. This at least raised the question as to what word might best describe a wealthy amateur who, at the age of twenty-two, had financed two successful comedies, one of which won the highest award Hollywood had to offer. What might be the *mot juste?* Lucky? It could hardly be genius because Hughes' successful films were largely the work of his directors, and besides, the films were not original. They were simply two more Hollywood comedies, more successful than most, but derivative.

The second Milestone-Hughes picture was likewise derivative. It was called *The Racket.* Gangster pictures were becoming a vogue. *The Racket* was another of them, commercially successful. The Hughes record now stood at one failure and three hits. Caddo film company stock looked to be an excellent buy on that record; young Hughes seemed to have a Midas touch.

Encouraged by success and apparently confident that he had learned all he needed to know, Hughes now moved to stage center in proper person. It seemed as if nearly every studio in Hollywood was making airplane pictures as well as gangster films and comedies, and airplanes happened to be something that Hughes knew even more about than film making. Instead of Milestone, Hughes looked for a director who shared his enthusiasm for flight, and seized upon Luther Reed of Paramount films, who had been aviation editor of a New York newspaper before becoming a Hollywood director. But Reed and Hughes soon violently disagreed over casting, shooting sequences, and over the frail script which Hughes himself had written with the aid of two writers who lacked screen credits. Reed departed, and Hughes announced that he, Howard Hughes, would both produce and direct *Hell's Angels*.

The plot was trivial to the point of vapidity. It concerned the competition of two handsome young British pilots for the attentions of an English society girl. It was just a story of sorts to provide Hughes with an opportunity to portray a far more exciting and believable competition aloft—that of British and German airmen fighting over France. The boy who had been too young for the war was now going to show how men lived and died at speed among the clouds.

Hughes signed Ben Lyon and James Hall, popular stars of the moment, to play the pilots. For leading lady, he secured the services of Greta Nissen, a blonde Norwegian who spoke very little English but who, in the days of silent pictures, could have recited Norwegian pastry recipes before the camera for all it mattered. Miss Nissen had only to stand between the camera and the background and open and close her mouth and look beautiful. The leading men had to do little else, because the real stars of the show would not be the actors, anyway. The stars would be the aircraft. To Hughes the story was almost nothing, but the aerial combat, everything.

This picture would be real, he said; it would therefore have real aircraft—the types that had actually snarled across European skies, and not just whatever airplanes could be found in California and painted to somewhat represent the fighting aircraft of 1918. It would, he said quite seriously, be the greatest motion picture ever made. Whereupon, he set out to buy greatness.

Specifically, he began to spend what would eventually amount to $562,000 to buy and recondition for flight eighty-seven World War I fighters and bombers, and another $400,000 to rent or build airfields in the Los Angeles area. One field was constructed at Van Nuys and christened Caddo Field after the film company. A field at

Chatsworth was built to resemble a German air base; one at Ingle-wood became a simulated British flying school; fields were con-structed at Santa Cruz, Encino, San Diego, Riverside, and far up-state, at Oakland. Hughes needed a Zeppelin to burn, and bought one. Needing an army to fight a ground battle, he hired 1,700 ex-tras. Needing pilots to put his squadrons in the sky, he hired them at $200 a week each. Needing a German Gotha bomber to shoot down and learning that the man he had sent to Europe to purchase warplanes could not find one, he realistically compromised with necessity and leased a Sikorsky aircraft touched up to resemble a Gotha.

Shooting began on Halloween, 1928. The first scene on the call sheet demanded a muddy, rainy night in London. Hughes, de-lighted by the fact that it was actually raining on his simulated London street in Los Angeles that Halloween, announced that the scene would be shot as indicated by the script—at night, and in the rain. Why rig up sprinklers and night lighting effects, when one could use real darkness and real rain to simulate reality? The stars were furious. Hughes was calm and a little hard of hearing. The shooting began. It lasted all night. The sneezes, curses and grum-blings of the sodden stars and camera crews did not matter; this was a silent film. The expressions of the actors were eloquent of people standing all night in a rainstorm, losing an argument with a deaf man.

When it came to shooting the interior sets, the novice director demanded retake after retake. One scene of a grand ball took more than a week to shoot. Production began moving over budget and behind schedule. But the time taken with the terrestrial scenes was as nothing compared to the time and care spent upon the aerial scenes.

Hughes devoted hours to diagraming on paper the dogfights he would film. Then he constructed three-dimensional models of the weaving flight paths with toy airplanes, studying the camera angles. He spent days explaining to his pilots exactly what he wanted them to do. To be sure that all went as planned, he said he would be flying the camera plane, hand-signaling directions. When all was set in train, Howard Hughes' version of the Royal Flying Corps took off to battle Howard Hughes' representation of Von Richthofen's Flying Circus over the Pacific Ocean's simulation of the English Channel, only to be defeated by the weather.

The trouble was the weather was good. There were no clouds. How, Hughes wanted to know, could you fight a photogenic war against a cloudless sky? Not only were clouds desirable to form a dramatic background that would give the audience some fixed points of reference to emphasize the speeds of the darting aircraft, but the nature of war itself was grim and foreboding—it really demanded clouds to help create a mordant atmosphere. Who could imagine a bright, sunlit war?

Hughes began to rise early—or to stay up all night—to watch for an opportune dawn. If, unfortunately, the sun rose bright and clear over Los Angeles, then he and his squadrons would take off to search elsewhere for cloudy skies over Southern California. If weather reports indicated the likelihood of a dull day over, let us say, Oakland on Tuesday, Hughes and his pilots would fly to Oakland on Monday to be ready for Tuesday's probably filmable weather. If there were no clouds to be found anywhere, the entire Hughes air force would be kept on standby at full salary.

The pilots whiled away the time with jokes. Someone produced a sign that said, "Today's War Postponed: No Clouds." Hughes took to riding a motorcycle about his airfields, zigzagging over the grass as his pilots threw cow chips at him while everyone, Hughes included, laughed. They called him Sonny, Kid, Skinny and Punk. And such was the degree of permissible camaraderie among fliers that they played practical jokes on one another. For example, it was Hughes' custom to begin each day's activity by patronizing a flimsy outdoor privy built on location. One morning he greeted the pilots as usual, looked up at the cloudless sky, and, as usual, excused himself. A moment after the door closed a pilot started the engine of a de Havilland two-seater parked just behind the privy. The propeller wash struck like a storm; a shower of toilet paper burst out of the suddenly-blown-open door; Hughes came stumbling after it, struggling with his trousers, just before the whole structure collapsed. It was all good fun, and one day when Hughes crashed on landing his airplane, the pilots made a joke of that as they ran to the wreck. They told one another they sure hoped Skinny hadn't busted the arm he used to write checks.

Fortunately, he had not; he walked away from the wreck relatively unhurt. But the pilots' hope concerning Hughes' check-writing abilities was most certainly not shared by the Hughes Tool Company's executives. The expenses of *Hell's Angels* were running to $5,000 a day; whatever Caddo films had earned or was earning on its other films was nothing compared to what was going out. Nor was this all. Paul Talbert, then general manager of Hughes Tool's California division, told a meeting of company executives that every other enterprise of Howard Hughes was turning sour. The experimental laboratory was producing nothing; Multi-Color had yet to come up with an economically feasible motion picture color film, and the theater chain was in trouble. Mr. Talbert, who years before had been worried about Big Howard's spending, was appalled by the son's.

"I understand he's lost a million dollars on his steam car, two million on color film, and he's losing a hundred thousand a month on his theater chain," Mr. Talbert was reported to have said.

Another officer told the meeting that he had heard Hughes had gone to New York to borrow three million dollars against the tool company, to finance his Hollywood activities.

"For Christ's sake," a third executive complained, "can't somebody talk some sense into this kid's head? He's wrecking a solid business."

When Hughes heard the complaints, he said, "It's my money I'm spending."

This was, of course, absolutely true. In the event of disaster his corporate officials might lose their jobs, but Hughes would lose his fortune, and no one was more conscious of this than the slender young Texas gambler. Like any good gambler, he took what seemed to him to be good calculated risks. He believed in himself and in his luck. So he continued to play golf, appear at night clubs, fly about looking for clouds and sign checks. Meantime, production of *Hell's Angels* continued to dance attendance upon the weather.

During the filming men died.

One pilot parachuted over Hollywood when the engine of his Fokker pursuit plane failed. The plane swooped down to dig itself into film magnate Joe Schenk's well-manicured lawn—the propeller sailing off into adjacent Hollywood Boulevard while the pilot drifted to earth beside a swimming pool—but others were not so fortunate. Ferrying an airplane from one part of Los Angeles to another, a pilot struck a high-tension wire and burned to death. Another, flying a British pursuit plane up the California coast, ran into a storm and died. A young mechanic who either would not or could not take to his parachute when the Gotha was deliberately crashed died in the wreck. In addition, there were at least half a dozen mid-air collisions which, while not fatal, were nearly as expensive of time, men and aircraft.

Meanwhile, Hughes darted about in the sky, flying the camera plane, and time and money melted away. In ponderous course his infantry of 1,700 extras fought their battle and the Zeppelin burned, but all this took weeks, months. The months became a year, and still Hughes was not satisfied. The work was not done, although the end of it seemed to be in sight.

During that year a revolution took place in Hollywood. It is the nature of revolutions not to be immediately recognized as such by those who are about to be overthrown by them. So, despite the success of the first sound picture, Al Jolson's *The Jazz Singer,* at least half of Hollywood's film makers regarded the newly invented sound track as a merely transient novelty. Howard Hughes was not so sure that it was. Sound pictures were being made, and wherever they appeared people were lining the sidewalks, waiting for admission. But for that matter, crowds were also drawn by those lavish productions that Hollywood called epics, featuring silent stars. In *Hell's Angels* Hughes had an epic, and he also had established stars.

The film, at length completed, edited, cut and fitted with titles, was given an unannounced preview at a Los Angeles neighborhood theater, with Hughes an unnoticed but excruciatingly concerned member of the audience.

The dashing British pilots gallantly pursued their beautiful lady love in utter silence. The Royal Flying Corps quietly fought its deadly duels with Baron von Richthofen's Flying Circus. Machine guns noiselessly jittered and fighting men mutely died. Smoke puffed from guns and shells burst and champagne bottles popped and Miss Nissen opened and closed her mouth and aircraft fell in flames across a splendor of clouds, and the audience made no more noise than these things did. Sitting in a stunned silence of his own, Howard Hughes completely understood that more than two million dollars had just shot itself down for want of a sound track. The catalepsy of the audience made that point terribly clear.

Hughes' aides pleaded with him. Release it anyway, they said. With luck and showmanship in advertising, they said, he might at least recover the cost. Belaboring the obvious, they told him the picture was good; that the aerial scenes were in fact great. He could use all the flight and battle scenes as they were, dubbing sound in for them, they said. That way, only the actors would be silent.

Hughes barely heard them. To him, the central fact seemed to be that he was a two-million-dollar failure at the age of twenty-two. The idea of dubbing in sound only for the battle sequences was, to his mind, ridiculous. Across the nation the theaters doing the most business were those that could truthfully advertise, "One Hundred Percent All Talking!" The word "talkie" was already a part of the common speech. But more to the point, Hughes had set out to make the greatest movie ever filmed. Now that sound films were being made, could a great movie be only half audible? Who wanted half an epic?

In the mood of a man who had lost more than he could afford but who could hope to recoup only if he placed a second, still larger bet, Hughes said work on *Hell's Angels* would begin anew. Sounds of flight and battle could be dubbed in on most of the existing exterior scenes, but all of the interior scenes and any others in which the actors were to speak would have to be filmed all over again, this time in sound.

It was a decision which an older man might not have made even if he had been as wealthy as Hughes, particularly since his corporate advisers were already worried about the rate of current expenses. Two million dollars was a frightening amount to have spent on a film in that day, and in a position similar to Hughes' many a producer might have released *Hell's Angels* as it was, realized what he could and chalked the rest off as a tax loss. But to reshoot the picture would cost perhaps another two million dollars. How many people would then have to pay their way into the theaters for the producer to break even? How many motion pictures had played to an audience of sixteen million people?

Hughes was adamant. The first task was to write a new screen play. Actors in silent films might mouth their words, but in a talking picture they would have to say something that made sense. New writers were hired, but Hughes himself wound up writing much of the dialogue. While the rewriting was in progress, the actors were given voice tests. Fortunately, Lyon and Hall passed, but Miss Nissen's Norwegian accents were hardly those of an English socialite. Hughes paid her off.

Gossip soon spread through Hollywood that Hughes was looking for an unknown actress, partly because his costs were getting out of hand and he could not afford a star, and partly because he was reluctant to direct a temperamental star in his first sound picture. Dozens of aspiring actresses paraded through his casting office, including Ann Harding, June Collyer, and a willowy blonde named Carol Peters. Miss Peters never got much work under that name, but after further dramatic lessons and additional experience she became Carole Lombard and did rather well.

Hughes eventually decided to gamble upon an ash-blonde bit player who had appeared in Laurel and Hardy comedies. Perhaps better than anyone else, he understood that the story line of his film was relatively unimportant. The girl was pretty; he signed her to a $125-a-week contract, had his hairdressers further bleach Jean

Harlow's naturally light hair, and had his public relations staff see to it that the world would not be unaware that *Hell's Angels* would feature an exciting new star, "the girl with the platinum-blonde hair."

Once again *Hell's Angels* went into painstaking production, and Hollywood wits told a story about leading man Ben Lyon. They said his Filipino houseboy asked him, "Mr. Lyon, every day you go to the studio, painting on your face for the picture. Oh, sair, you have done this now for a long time, but yes, I do not see a picture. Sair, you have much moneys and are very rich. You are a bootlegger?"

And once again the money flowed out at an incredible rate. His advisers pleaded, and this time Hughes ruthlessly chopped his expenses. He rid himself of his theater chain.

To make matters worse at the worst of times, the stock market collapsed. The effect of the 1929 market failure would not be completely felt until another year had passed, but Hughes Tool was now reporting lower earnings. And Multi-Color was proving to be an impossible drain, glittering as was the promise of the money to be made in color film if only an economical process could be discovered. Just as Hughes was looking for a way to get clear of Multi-Color, and as he felt his resources diminishing on every side, he was overwhelmed by yet another disaster. Ella Hughes went back to Texas.

She had had quite enough. Her few years in Hollywood had been a lonely nightmare for her. She had been one of the most popular, sought-after women in Texas, quite literally the belle of the ball; a young woman with invitations to gentle homes throughout the South. She was a woman with notions of propriety that Hollywood did not share. She could not say that she had a husband at her side when he was here, there, everywhere, sometimes gone for days. It was hardly consoling to be told he had been seen in night clubs; no more consoling to hear that he was dissipating his fortune on footless projects and that he had not only spent an entire year and two million dollars on one film, but that he was going to spend another two million upon it in the indefinite future.

And so, at this low point in her young husband's fortunes she gave her attorneys their instructions. Their suit charged Hughes with having "steadily neglected her," contended that he "was irritable, cross, critical, fault-finding and inconsiderate." She returned to Texas grief-stricken over the first divorce in her family's history. She received an uncontested settlement for $1,250,000, paid in four installments.

When she had gone, Hughes closed up her room just as she had left it. It was left sealed and unopened until he disposed of the house many years later. He turned his mind back to *Hell's Angels.* It was as if he had the ability to turn off, like a light, that which he chose not to think about. If so, this was an unusual trait, but then young Hughes was not altogether a usual young man. He happened to be a youth who had been married before he was twenty and divorced before he was twenty-four, who had the capacity to work forty hours at a time on half a dozen different projects, and who was the master of an empire which, if beset at every turn, was nonetheless his own to enlarge or ruin as he wished. A third million dollars went into *Hell's Angels.*

If ever making motion pictures had seemed fun to Hughes, it was apparently fun no longer. He went at it as if his very life was at stake as perhaps it was. In any event, he read nothing but evil in the news that another director, Howard Hawks, was making a film on aerial combat, *Dawn Patrol.* He suspected that Hawks was stealing ideas from *Hell's Angels,* and was rushing *Dawn Patrol* to completion so as to be first in the marketplace with essentially the same product. As Hawks later told the story, this is what happened:

Hawks said he woke early one Sunday morning with a wretched hangover and an impression that he was somehow trapped in a bell tower. Coming more fully awake, he realized it was not only his head but his doorbell that was ringing. He said he made his way downstairs in a homicidal mood, threw the door open and found himself confronting a tall, slim, dark-haired and hot-eyed man who was just as angry as he was.

"I'm Howard Hughes and I'm making an aviation picture," the

apparition in the doorway said. "You're making an aviation picture, too."

Hawks said he was about to reply, but that Hughes gave him no chance.

"I've heard that you've got a scene in your picture where a pilot gets hit by a bullet and vomits blood," Hughes said. "That's *my* scene. It's already in *my* picture. You've got to take it out of yours."

Hawks said at this point he was torn between laughter, anger and wonder at the nerve of anyone who could make such an absurd demand so early on what was rapidly turning into a vile Sunday morning.

"Mr. Hughes," Hawks said at last, "it is true. I am making an aviation picture. It is true that I have a scene in my aviation picture where a pilot in an airplane is hit by a bullet, and it is true that he spits up blood. But isn't that a normal thing for a pilot who is hit by a bullet in the throat to do—spit up blood?"

Hawks said that the argument was lost on Hughes; that when Hughes continued to protest, Hawks lost his frail grip on his patience.

"I told him, 'Look, you're a rich man. You're making movies as a hobby. I'm making them for money. My scene stays in,' " Hawks said.

With that he slammed the door and returned to a more important concern—his hangover.

But in the days that followed it seemed that spies were infiltrating the *Dawn Patrol* sets, that Hughes was trying to purchase the exclusive services of all the pilots in Hollywood.

"So the pilots rather delightedly signed with Howard Hughes exclusively, then signed with me, also exclusively," Hawks said. "They had work running out their ears."

While Hughes devoted single-minded attention to his work on *Hell's Angels,* the motion picture did not, however, command his entire attention. After all, whatever else he was, Hughes was also a tall, dark, handsome young Texan, rich and single: in short, he was the most eminently eligible bachelor in a town populated by the most beautiful women on earth, who shared with him a common if not precisely similar interest in motion pictures. It was perhaps inevitable that Hughes would encounter some of these desirable young ladies. In fact, he met at least one of them every day at the studio, although she complained at the time that he hardly seemed aware of it.

"If Howard was cross-eyed, with all that dough it wouldn't matter," Jean Harlow confided to writer Adela Rogers St. John. "But he's got a lot of charm in his own funny way. But he never mixes business with pleasure. As far as I'm concerned, I might be another airplane. He expects you to work the same way—never get tired, give your best performance at any hour of the day or night, and never think about anything else. . . . The nearest he ever came to making a pass at me was offering me a bite of a cookie."

Miss Harlow, who clearly did not wish Howard Hughes to mistake her for an airplane, would always retain a high regard for the man who put her in her first starring role but who seemed to be the only man she ever met who did not, as she put it, make a pass at her.

Perhaps it was Miss Harlow's interest in him that put Hughes off. As he once said to a friend after his divorce, "Aside from my money, who'd want to marry *me?*" In any case, his attention was captured by a woman who, meeting him at a party, expressed no interest in him at all. She was Billie Dove, a Broadway showgirl, a small woman with silky blonde hair and the complexion of a Dresden doll. When a friend urgently whispered to her that the man she had just ignored was the rich producer, Howard Hughes, Miss Dove replied that you certainly wouldn't know it from the sloppy way he dressed, and anyway, what was he producing? She said she had heard that *Hell's Angels* was already the biggest, most expensive flop of all time and that he was wasting another fortune on it.

The next day there was a telephone call. Then bouquets of white roses began to arrive; after them, jewels, gowns, more telephone calls, an incessant shower of attentions and gifts. It developed that Miss Dove could not precisely call her life her own, insofar as it was most likely that Hughes was somewhere close at hand. For instance, she went on a picnic with someone else when literally out of the blue an airplane appeared, buzzed the picnic site, turned to come up into the wind and landed. Pilot Hughes jumped out, grinning, to join the party. Miss Dove could not long withstand such expressions of interest, and Hollywood gossips were shortly afterwards able to report that Miss Dove had been flying with Howard Hughes, that Mr. Hughes was looking for a suitable screen play for his friend, that she would star in a forthcoming Hughes production.

While Hughes worked on his film, flew about with Miss Dove and signed checks, 1929 became 1930 and the country sank deeper into the Great Depression it would know until Hitler's war. *Hell's Angels,* begun at a peak of conspicuous consumption, nineteen months in the making, was finally ready for showing in May, 1930, at a time when men stood in breadlines and waited, without real hope, outside the locked gates of idle factories.

Hughes had shot three million feet of film, only to discard 99 percent of it for the final version. He had spent nearly four million dollars, a sum far beyond any heretofore spent on a two-dimensional illusion. This included $754,000 for salaries of actors and pilots; $524,000 for sets and costumes, and almost $1,000,000 for aircraft and locations. Publicity, equipment rentals, office overhead and the salaries for nineteen months of an army of clerks, staff and technicians accounted for the rest. At such a somber time of national misfortune Hughes' extravaganza struck some people as bordering on the indecent, but what Hollywood wanted to know was would he ever get his money back.

The film had its premiere showing at Grauman's Chinese Theater on Hollywood Boulevard, and a near riot ensued on opening night. A reporter who apparently suffered either from astigmatism or euphoria estimated the crowd in the street at half a million souls. Whatever its number, the crowd screamed, surged and pushed at the six hundred policemen who fought to maintain a sort of order. Women fainted in the crush. There were frenzied screams for the male stars as they paraded into the theater; but when Jean Harlow stepped from her limousine, the animal noise of the crowd became, in a word, describable. Here, in the flesh, was the object, the creation, of one of the most intensive publicity campaigns ever mounted. Her startling platinum hair hung in a casual, diffident cut; her face was pale but for a scarlet slash of lipstick; with a blaze of jewels about her throat and in a white satin gown that seemed to have been painted on, she rippled toward the theater, evoking a deep-throated howl from the mob. In the presence of the goddess it was difficult for the most knowing Hollywood gossip to recall that her salary was $125 a week.

When the lights dimmed and the select capacity audience was finally hushed, they seemed to sense themselves in the grip of a unique genius. Blazing planes twisted across the screen; the sound of war filled the darkened room. There were the screams of the dying and the snarling whine of engines at speed. At one point, in the midst of a savage dogfight and gusts of gunfire, the projectionist slipped a red filter across the lens and the black and white film turned a dramatic scarlet. The audience cheered. At the film's end there was a standing ovation. Standing alone at the rear of the theater, Hughes smiled his quiet smile.

The next morning, the telegrams began to arrive. THE ZEPPELIN SEQUENCE IS THE MOST DRAMATIC EPISODE I'VE EVER SEEN, Charles Chaplin wired. One Hollywood critic said the film contained "the most beautiful shots and thrilling action the movies have yet conceived." Another wrote, "Beside its sheer magnificence, all stage spectacles and colossal circuses become puny." Attendance records toppled at Grauman's Chinese Theater where it ran for nineteen weeks to capacity houses. *Hell's Angels* became the first picture to open simultaneously at two New York theaters. But there, in a cooler climate than Hollywood's, it was possible to entertain less passionate enthusiasms.

"One shouldn't jump to the natural conclusion that it is an extraordinarily fine picture, because it isn't," the playwright and biographer Robert Sherwood wrote. "If the lamentable truth must be known, it is pretty much of a mess. But it is one of the most exciting news stories that the cinema has ever evolved, and therein lies the secret of its terrific appeal."

The point was, Mr. Sherwood wrote, "However much we may prate of economy and thrift, there exists in the hearts of all true Americans an incurable fondness for rank extravagance. The high, wide and handsome spenders, such as Death Valley Scotty or Diamond Jim Brady, are bound to become, in their immodest ways, national heroes. So it is with young Howard Hughes. His shrewd and understanding press agents have broadcast the news that he took a fortune out of oil wells and spent it on *Hell's Angels*. As a result of this, countless numbers of solid citizens want to see the picture just to find out what he got with all that money."

And, Mr. Sherwood added, "With his four million dollars, Mr. Hughes acquired about five cents' worth of plot, approximately thirty-eight cents' worth of acting, and a huge amount of dialogue, the total value of which may be estimated by the following specimen. Boy: 'What do you think of my new uniform?' Girl: 'Oh, it's ripping!' Boy: (nervously) 'Where?' "

Concluding his dispassionate appraisal, Mr. Sherwood said, "The leading players include an obstreperously alluring young lady named Jean Harlow, of whom not much more is likely to be heard."

Almost anyone seeing the film today would be inclined to agree with Mr. Sherwood in every particular, but at the time he was practically a minority of one. *Hell's Angels* set box office records in every theater in which it played in the United States, and when it was sent to England the usually difficult-to-please theater critics there had this to say: "It has no equal on the screen," "The greatest masterpiece the screen has known," "London was thrilled as never before."

In a sense, *Hell's Angels* was another triumph of popular taste over art, and the truth of its box office success seems to lie in the fact that the preferences of the general public were exactly the preferences of Howard Hughes. The appeal was visceral, not cerebral. The ingredients were visions of speed, violence, power, wealth and sex—precisely the same ingredients of a modern advertisement for automobiles. *Hell's Angels* went on to run for twenty years in theaters throughout the world, and in the end earned, overall, some eight million dollars, just double Hughes' investment. In the begin-ning, however, no one could have foretold such good fortune; the farthest-seeing prophet might have predicted that if Hughes was lucky, he would get most of his money back.

Until all that money did return, Hughes stood on the brink of a Pyrrhic victory, rather than on the verge of an Austerlitz. In fact, his financial position was still a source of worry to his executives. He must retrench, they said; some decision must be made about Multi-Color, Inc., which seemed more like a bottomless rathole than a reasonable speculation.

Faced with these problems, Hughes' apparent reaction was to spend the next six weeks in Europe.

3

On his return from Europe, Howard Hughes rapidly produced three complete failures. Seen in retrospect there seems to be no particular reason why these films did so badly, for they were no more lugubrious than some of the profitable motion pictures of their time. The first two, *Cock of the Air* and *Sky Devils,* were attempts to follow up the fantastic success of *Hell's Angels.* They obeyed the familiar, if erroneous, Hollywood dictum that if one film is well received, then two more of the same will be twice as successful. But something had gone into *Hell's Angels* that had not gone into the sequels. Perhaps the missing ingredient was Jean Harlow. Maybe the public, having seen *Hell's Angels,* had seen all it wished to see of aerial combat. Perhaps the films would have been better if Hughes had given them the time and attention he devoted to their prototype. For whatever reasons, the two pictures were both artistic and financial disasters. The third failure, *Age for Love,* must have been even more disappointing to Hughes, for Miss Dove was its leading lady.

Hughes searched through dozens of scripts before selecting *Age for Love* as being best suited to display the charms and talents of his friend. The critics were kind enough to her, but neither they nor the public had anything good to say about the film as a whole. "Brittle comedy," the critics called it, using their conventional euphemism for something they felt to be a dithering waste of time.

Stung by three fiascos in a row, Hughes was in a dark mood when Noah Dietrich demanded that he finally face up to a fourth—the foozle that was Multi-Color, Inc.

The result was that the company was liquidated to pay off its creditors. Since Hughes Tool Company was Multi-Color's principal creditor and since Hughes owned the tool company, this meant Hughes, as he had a right to, was first paying himself back before distributing the remaining assets among the stockholders—among whom the most prominent was also Hughes. In the end, Hughes wound up with Multi-Color's building at 7000 Romaine Street, which subsequently became the command center for Hughes' various enterprises, and the stockholders recovered something on their investment.

As the year 1930 drew near its disastrous end for Hughes, so did his relationship with Billie Dove. She said he was as charming and as gallant as ever—whenever she saw him. But the trouble was she never knew when she would see him. Like Ella Rice Hughes before her, Miss Dove complained that Hughes would disappear for days, reappearing as abruptly as he had left and offering no explanation. When he was in Hollywood she could seldom reach him when it was important for her to do so. They drifted apart; three years later Miss Dove would marry another man and live more happily ever after. But she had nothing but fond memories of her unpredictable young millionaire.

"It was so long ago," she said recently. "Mr. Hughes and I were both so very young, and I imagine he's forgotten about me. I still remember him, though, but thirty years is a lifetime ago. . . ."

A procession of actresses and debutantes followed Miss Dove into Hughes' public life, including a considerable number of ladies he never met at all. Both Hughes and the ladies he did not meet were victims of Hollywood's gossip columnists, whose normal duties do not always include making some attempt to ascertain the truth of what they hear and print. It is not unusual in Hollywood for total strangers to read of their engagement to one another. Perhaps to his surprise, Hughes was reported at one time or another about to marry June Collyer; actress Lillian Bond; Will Rogers' teen-age daughter, Mary; and socialite Timmie Lansing, a New York debutante who married the cartoonist Peter Arno. Hughes was seen about town with actress Ida Lupino and was photographed in night clubs on half a dozen different occasions with as many different dinner companions.

He was also seen far more often—but not by the press—in the hangars of Southern California airports, dressed in mechanic's overalls, working on aircraft engines.

"He was just a bored, rich youngster with the money to do what he wanted to do, and that was to fly," one of his Hollywood acquaintances said.

This judgment was a serious underestimation. It is explicable only within the context of Hollywood, a community so intent upon the motion picture business that its view of a man is entirely determined by his success in films. So far as Hollywood was concerned, Hughes' career was in eclipse. The gossip was that Hughes was demoralized and that his increasing carelessness about his personal appearance was proof of it. The boy who had dressed as meticulously as that fashion plate, his father, was now seen about town needing a shave. His jackets were rumpled and his trousers unpressed, and a legend grew that he wore tennis shoes to night clubs.

But Hughes was neither bored nor demoralized. As for carelessness in appearance, Hughes was beyond the point where it was important to him to keep up appearances—an activity that almost always involves some measure of pretense. Clothing was becoming less and less an important concern to Hughes. Like Einstein, he wore what he liked and dressed with more regard for his comfort than for the expectations of other people. Nor was there anything sinister about his disappearances from Hollywood. He was simply pursuing another interest somewhere else, and if he did not choose to state his whereabouts at all times, the reason was that he did not wish to be disturbed. Some people have private telephones. Hughes found a public pay phone to be cheaper and even more private. He could call out whenever he wished to talk to someone, but no one could call him. Far from being bored, his major interest had shifted from films to aviation. He did not merely enjoy flying. Rather, he was becoming absorbed by the problems and the promise of flight. California's pilots accepted him as a fully participating member of their daring fraternity; the airport mechanics respected him as a serious student of their trade.

This shift in interest from the camera to the sky was fundamentally a shift in emphasis, because film making was still a great part of Hughes' life. His three recent movie disasters were an affront and a challenge. In 1931, he went back into the motion picture business, but in the precisely calculated way he had gone into it following the miscarriage of *Swell Hogan*. He began shopping for the best talent available. Perhaps the most surprised man in Hollywood was Hughes' rival in film making, Howard Hawks.

One Sunday morning Hawks drove to the Wilshire Country Club golf course alone. He had no game lined up, but thought he might pick up a partner in the pro shop. No sooner had he entered the building than the telephone rang for him.

"I'm coming out to the course," Hughes' voice spoke into Hawks' ear. "If you don't have a game, let's play together."

Hawks said he replied with a string of curses. Not only had he clear memories of Hughes' attempt to obtain the script of *Dawn Patrol*, but Hughes was even then suing him, claiming that Hawks had pirated away from Hughes the film rights to a British play. Hawks said he told Hughes, "You got a lawsuit against me, you bastard. I wouldn't play a game of anything with you if you were the last guy on earth."

"I'm willing to drop the suit. All I want to do this morning is play a game of golf."

"I don't believe you. Have your lawyer call me back, right here, and tell me so."

With that Hawks hung up, furious at the thought that Hughes must be having him shadowed by private detectives. How else would Hughes have known to call the pro shop? The telephone rang. It was a Hughes lawyer, who said matter-of-factly that the suit was being dropped. The telephone rang again, and it was Hughes, asking for a golf game.

By this time, Hawks was sufficiently intrigued to accept. Hughes arrived shortly thereafter, shook hands with the still disbelieving Hawks, and the two men teed off in silence.

"It was cool at first," Hawks said, "but before we played eighteen holes, we decided to work together. Also, I shot a seventy-one and beat him."

It would seem that Hughes, who had a two handicap at Wilshire, was going to extraordinary lengths to placate Hawks. But Hawks was an excellent golfer himself. More to the point, he was also one of the best directors of blood-and-thunder films, and Hughes wanted to produce a gangster picture—a matter that a brief digression may illuminate:

Criminal syndicates, equipped with fleets of trucks, automobiles and ships, were the nation's suppliers of whisky during the then-current days of Prohibition. They fought one another for territorial rights, and their armory included machine guns and hand grenades. They held pitched battles in the streets; they killed from ambush; they abducted and assassinated one another. Sporadic gunfire scattered through the American nights, and as the gunfire increased, Hollywood reacted by producing an increasing number of gangster films. No fewer than fifty pictures of gang wars were made in 1931 alone. Hollywood went so far in the way of realism as to hire several real gangsters as actors.

"There was a speed, a vigor, a sense of the contemporaneous scene, a realism of character and incident about these films that was in sharp contrast to the talky problem plays that surrounded them," said film critic Arthur Knight in his book *The Liveliest Art.* "They had action, racy dialogue, the sharply naturalistic performances of people like James Cagney, Edward G. Robinson, Joan Blondell, Lee Tracy and George Bancroft. They excited audiences in ways that the drawing room comedies, boudoir romances and static musical comedies did not. They were like a breath of fresh air sweeping through the heavily padded studio of the early sound era, blowing away some of the conventions, some of the stiffness that had crept into the medium with the advent of the microphone."

So Hughes wanted to ride the wave, just as he had made aerial combat films during Hollywood's enthusiasm for aerial combat. But this time, his contribution—apart from the money—would be almost as minimal as in the case of *Everybody's Acting*. Hawks would have a free hand as director. Ben Hecht, a prolific and successful Hollywood writer, would do the screen play. The story would be based on a moderately successful book called *Scarface*. Hughes bought the screen rights, but the title was almost the only part of the book he wanted to use. America's leading criminal of the day was one Alphonse "Scarface" Capone, and Hughes told Hecht to write "the story of the Capone family as if they were Borgias set down in Chicago."

Eleven days later, Hecht turned in the following script: A thug named Tony shoots his way to the throne of Chicago's underworld. Having done so, he runs off to Florida with another gangster's girl. Returning to Chicago, he learns that his beloved younger sister has been raped by one of the mob. Tony kills the rapist, but must hide from the police. The policemen, seeking Tony, assassinate the sister instead. Tony is subsequently cornered and shot down in the street.

What all this had to do with Renaissance Borgias in modern dress, or even with Scarface Al Capone, was somewhat unclear. But no matter—the script promised a film that rattled with gunfire, conveyed visions of illegal wealth, speed, lust and violence, and wound up with blood in the gutter. Hawks and Hughes regarded Hecht's story as quite satisfactory, and all that remained was to line up a cast. Unfortunately, most of the established stars were under contract to other studios.

"So we went out and found our own stars," Hawks said, making a virtue of necessity. "I discovered Paul Muni playing at a Jewish theater on 39th Street in New York. An unknown named George Raft looked promising to us, and we signed him for a supporting role. We hired Ann Dvorak and Karen Morley for the women's parts. Down the list of supporting characters was a young British actor named Boris Karloff."

But no sooner were production plans made than *Scarface* ran into trouble more serious than the hazard of signing little-known actors. Press and pulpit had, for some time, been denouncing both the licentious nature of some of Hollywood's films, and the licentious lives of some of Hollywood's more prominent inhabitants. Truckling to this criticism, Hollywood had established a self-censoring agency—The Motion Picture Producers and Distributors of America, with Will H. Hays, a strait-laced Presbyterian who had been chairman of the Republican Party, serving as the MPPDA's chief censor. When Hughes submitted the script of *Scarface* to the Hays Office, it was returned with a warning to make no such film. Colonel Jason Joy, one of Hays' aides, said the American public and the state boards of censorship found hoodlums repugnant. He said "gangsterism must not be mentioned in the cinema," and promised that *"Scarface* will never be released."

Inasmuch as fifty gangster films had been released in the prior year alone, this struck Hughes as a late time to lock the barn, but he was not a man to argue with anyone who told him no. Instead, he ordered shooting to begin at once. He told Hawks to let his imagination run as wildly as it could in the direction of producing realistic, grisly excitement.

When the first film rushes came in, Hughes was particularly delighted with a scene wherein a speeding automobile raced into machine-gun fire and flipped over in a spectacular smash.

"That car smash is marvelous. Do some more," Hughes said.

Although Hughes inspected the rushes every day, he otherwise stayed away from the set. In later years, Noah Dietrich acidly said, "Howard Hawks ran Hughes off the set and wouldn't let him come near it again until the picture was done," but this seems unduly belittling of Hughes' role in the creation of *Scarface*. Apart from the fact that Hughes was devoting an increasingly greater part of his time to flying many types of airplanes and tinkering with engines, it would seem that he had purposefully delegated the primary responsibility for *Scarface's* success to a man whose record of success in action-adventure films was more imposing than his own. But even so, Hughes was something more than a bystander with money. As Hawks said, "I made nineteen more car wrecks. I had to—Hughes kept egging me on."

The finished film appalled the Hays Office. The censors dictated a title change, suggesting *Shame of the Nation*. They demanded

Young Howard, at the age of fifteen, was a student at the Fessenden School in Massachusetts.

Jean Harlow and Ben Lyon in a scene from the 1930 smash-hit, *Hell's Angels,* which Hughes directed and produced. The film was famous for its flying sequences, on which Hughes lavished painstaking attention.

Wide World

ver

Hughes' love of flying has played a primary part in his life. In the early 1930's he modified this Army Air Corps Boeing pursuit plane and won his first race with it. Later he worked for American Airways as a co-pilot *(right)*—using the fictitious name of Charles Howard—to gain valuable experience.

Culver

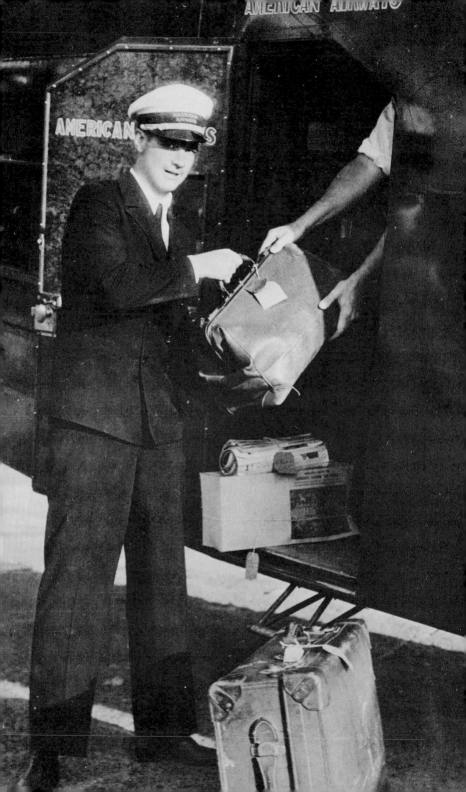

Jane Russell, 19, and Jack Beutel, 21 (shown here with director Howard Hawks), were given their first screen roles when they were signed in 1940 to star in Hughes' million-dollar production of *The Outlaw*.

Hughes on the set of *The Outlaw*.

Of the many aviation records Hughes set, perhaps the most spectacular was his round-the-world flight in 1938. He is shown here, minutes after he and his crew landed at Floyd Bennett field in New York, with Mayor Fiorello LaGuardia and official greeter Grover Whalen. The next day New York honored the fliers with a ticker-tape parade.

Wide World

Hughes in the cockpit, wearing his famous fedora, just before he took off on the first test flight of the powerful XF-11 photographic plane which he designed and built for the Army Air Forces.

Shortly after the picture below was taken, the XF-11 plummeted into Beverly Hills. Hughes barely survived the violent crash.

In a rare and dramatic public appearance, Hughes testified in 1947 before a Senate subcommittee investigating his wartime aviation contracts. Senator Owen Brewster, his prime antagonist in the hearings, is standing in the background with his hand on a microphone.

Part of the Senate investigation focused on a 200-ton wooden flying boat Hughes was building; some charged it would never even fly. Hughes said he would leave the country if it didn't. Three months later he gave dramatic proof to doubters when he lifted the giant into the air in an unannounced flight.

Jean Peters, the actress Howard Hughes married.

dozens of cuts and worst of all, an entirely new ending. They wanted Tony to be captured by the police, tried in a stern court of justice, and hanged. If a picture were to deal with crime, they said, it must clearly show the triumph of justice and so prove that crime does not pay. Tony's death in the gutter struck the censors as falling somewhat short of a glorification of the majestic triumph of an impartial law based on reason.

Hughes had a choice. He could either obey the Hays Office or not receive an MPPDA Seal of Approval. Without the seal, his film would be blacklisted in American motion picture theaters.

Amazingly enough, considering his prior history of willfulness, Hughes decided to accept the dictates of the Hays Office. Hawks was furious, but the cuts were made; the title was changed. Paul Muni, who played Tony, had meantime left Hollywood for a Broadway play. A double was found to play the added courtroom scene; instead of Muni's emotions as Tony was led to the gallows, Hawks had to settle for a sequence showing Tony's feet shuffling that last, grim distance.

"It's still a great film," Hughes said after seeing the revision. "They couldn't emasculate all of it."

The film was shipped to New York for approval by that state's board of censors. They promptly rejected it. A Hollywood rumor was that the Hays Office detested Hughes and had secretly requested that the New York board ban his film, despite the fact that it had been given an official Seal of Approval. At this point, Hughes' new-found docility vanished. He issued the following statement to the press:

It has become a serious threat to the freedom of honest expression in America when self-styled guardians of the public welfare, as personified by our film censor boards, lend their aid and their influence to the abortive efforts of selfish and vicious interests to suppress a motion picture simply because it depicts the truth about conditions in the United States which have been front page news since the advent of Prohibition.

I am convinced that the determined opposition to *Scarface* is actuated by political motives. The picture, as originally filmed eight months ago, has been enthusiastically praised by foremost authorities on crime and law enforcement and by leading screen reviewers. It seems to be the unanimous opinion of these authorities that *Scarface* is an honest and powerful indictment of gang rule in America and, as such, will be a tremendous factor in compelling our State and Federal governments to take more drastic action to rid the country of gangsterism.

Scarface was, of course, entertainment; it was no indictment of anything. Hughes' willingness to surrender to the Hays Office in the first instance was at some odds with his concern for editorial freedom. Yet his public position was that of a champion of the truth, and his statement to the press certainly created an acute desire on the part of the public to see *Scarface* at the first opportunity. It also won him support from those who believe that censorship is inherently evil. The *New York Herald Tribune* said, "Hughes is the only Hollywood producer who has had the courage to come out and fight this censorship menace in the open. We wish him a smashing victory."

Courage? Showmanship? Fit of pique? Whatever the reason, Hughes sued the New York censors. He won the right to show *Scarface* as originally filmed—with the original title, without the cuts, without anyone's seal of approval, and with the original ending. He then sued other boards of censors throughout the land, winning a majority of his battles. Like *Hell's Angels, Scarface* was an enormous financial success. Hollywood regarded it as one of the great films of all time. With *Scarface* away and running, Hughes also produced another widely acclaimed motion picture in 1932, *The Front Page*. The film made Pat O'Brien famous, earned Hughes another fortune and gave the nation a fatuously romantic view of the realities of newspaper life. Like *Scarface,* the story was largely a figment of Ben Hecht's fertile imagination.

These judgments of Hughes' pictures may seem unfair in the

sense that one probably should not judge the film techniques of the 1930s and the public taste of that time by the more sophisticated techniques and public taste of the 1960s. But Hughes' films do not stand up as works of art today, as some early films do. There is no reason why they should. On the basis of his films there is no reason to suspect that Hughes ever intended to serve the cause of art, or that of truth in the public interest. He seems always to have wanted to sell entertainment at a profit, and he certainly succeeded in doing just that.

But then, at the age of twenty-six, at what might be called the peak of his Hollywood career, with agents, writers and directors clamoring to see him, with two hit shows playing to capacity audiences, Hughes abruptly turned his back on it all.

4

In the summer of 1932, $250 a month was an excellent wage, and Charles Howard earned every penny of it. He carried the passengers' baggage through the early morning Texas heat from the Fort Worth air terminal to the waiting Fokker trimotor. He did what he could to ease the passengers' fears, assuring them that the trip to New York would be quick, comfortable and safe. Then, with the baggage aboard, he took his place in the co-pilot's seat.

At 7:25 A.M., the American Airways flight lurched into the air, and half an hour later it came down at Dallas. It is only twenty-five miles between Fort Worth and Dallas, but in 1932 it took a fifteen-passenger Fokker half an hour to negotiate the distance. The aircraft next touched down at Texarkana, Little Rock, Memphis, Nashville, Louisville, Cincinnati, Columbus, and finally reached Cleveland at 7:51 P.M., local time—ten flying hours later. At Cleveland, the Fokker's passengers boarded the 8:30 P.M. train that was due in New York at nine the next morning.

Such was the Fort Worth-to-New York flight. The fact that the Ohio-New York leg of it was made by rail may be attributed to the presence of the Appalachian mountains. The aircraft of the day were capable of flying over them, so far as the height of the mountains was concerned. But weather builds up over those hills. Thunderheads can reach altitudes higher than any the aircraft of 1932 could attain, and no one then could be sure what the weather would be at any particular hour along the route. Air mail pilots flying between the East Coast and Chicago might make as many as five landings on the way—all of them unscheduled stops in farm pastures. Aircraft instruments were primitive; meteorological re-

56

ports took the form of telephoning to the next town to see if it was raining there; pilots flew by guess and by God, and the life expectancy of pilots who regularly attempted the Appalachian route was minimal. Given these conditions, American Airways quite sensibly terminated the airborne section of its Fort Worth-New York flight at Cleveland. It was difficult enough in 1932 to adhere to a schedule in broad daylight over terrain as flat as Kansas, what with no information as to winds aloft, with no reliable instruments or navigational aids, and with the almost constant certainty that small repairs to engines would be required at airfields en route.

In those days, it was important for pilots to know how to make repairs themselves. A pilot needed to know everything there was to know about his aircraft and aerial navigation, as well as being a master of the theory of aerodynamics and an expert in his manipulation of the controls. He needed to know all this merely to get down out of the sky alive, even if his flying was limited to sailing around over an airport for an hour or so on a sunny day. In an era of simple machines it was possible for a pilot to acquire such comprehensive knowledge, just as it was possible for Benjamin Franklin to master such scientific knowledge as there was in his day.

The young co-pilot, Charles Howard, was a hangar-flyer *par excellence.* Hangar-flying is a term pilots use to describe the shop talk of their profession. Howard was interested in everything—not only in hearing how his brother pilots had surmounted difficulties and perils. He wanted to know about weights, costs, fuel loads, routes, schedules, the means of assembling weather information, the efficiency of types of instruments of all sorts and the ranges of visibility of beacons of various candlepower, lenses and colors. He was also interested in the flight characteristics of all types of aircraft, particularly those of the Fokkers he flew. Chief pilots said that Howard would one day make a first-rate airline pilot.

But Charles Howard never won his first pilot's wings. Two months after joining American Airways, he walked out on the first and only steady job he ever had. It was not until some time later that American Airways wondered who Charles Howard had really been. Someone said that he was Howard Hughes, the Hollywood

producer; at least he'd looked a lot like Hughes. Someone else produced a snapshot of Charles Howard loading bags into a Fokker
and showed it to newspapermen; and the newspapermen said if that
wasn't Hughes, it must be his twin and that Hughes didn't have a
twin.

Eventually the story reached Hollywood, where Hughes had
meanwhile reappeared. One Hollywood wit suggested that Hughes
must have been paying off a bet. Why else would a millionaire be
working as a baggage-smasher? Someone else said perhaps the
truth was that Hughes really needed the money—that despite the
successes of his most recent films, he may have lost more money
than anyone knew on his color film project and his chain of theaters. For the most part, Hollywood dismissed Hughes' career in
aviation as a joke.

For instance, Ginger Rogers sailed into a dinner party one evening with Howard Hughes in tow, and the seating arrangement
placed him between Miss Rogers and Carole Lombard. According
to Adela Rogers St. John, Hughes was silent and withdrawn; he had
nothing to say to his beautiful table companions. Miss Lombard
was fascinated. As the conversation bubbled and the laughter rose
elsewhere about the table, Hughes' black mood deepened. At last,
leaning across him, Miss Lombard spoke to Miss Rogers.

"Your boy friend ought to be in pictures," she said.

Hughes stirred uneasily.

"Not just because of his looks," Miss Lombard said, "but because he would be a strong contender in the 'ugh' school of acting.

"The best 'ugh' actor in the world is Gary Cooper," she went
brightly on. "He looks at a girl, says 'ugh', and she responds the
way Juliet did on the balcony. He walks around, says 'ugh' a couple of times, shoots people, and the movie is over."

Hughes smiled politely.

"I think," Miss Lombard continued, gesturing with her fork at
Hughes, "if you can persuade your boy friend to step before the
camera, he will be a better 'ugh' actor than Gary Cooper. He has
more natural ability in that line."

"Mr. Hughes is a pilot, not an actor," Miss Rogers replied, as if on cue.

Everyone except Hughes thought this terribly funny because no one else believed it for a minute. To be sure, Hughes flew airplanes, but as every Hollywood actress very coldly knew, Mr. Hughes was an enormously rich young man who produced motion pictures and made stars out of actresses.

What neither the ladies nor anyone else in Hollywood understood was that Hughes was really now a pilot, although he would one day make a few more motion pictures. He had no intention of producing films in the immediate future, although his Hollywood aides continued a constant talent search on his behalf. They clipped the newspapers and magazines for pictures of pretty girls, and studied the photographs that actors' agents supplied. And Hughes kept in touch with his staff. He would inspect the pictures they sent him, make a selection and order them to talk to such-and-such an actress, tell her of his interest in her and find out whether she would be willing to have dinner with him. If she said yes, as was almost always the case, Hughes would be notified and a dinner date arranged—but whether Hughes would keep the date was always a matter of chance. Frequently he did not. Many a girl would find herself all dressed up with someplace to go, but with no escort except the Hughes aide who kept looking at his watch as they sat together in a night club. If Hughes appeared, the aide would introduce the young lady to his employer and leave. If Hughes did not, she could at least console herself with the fact that she had been seen in a public place with a member of the Hughes staff and had enjoyed a free meal.

On many another occasion Hughes would appear, only to completely mystify the girl by paying no attention to her while they sat at table together. If he had brought a flyer or a mechanic with him, Hughes would spend the evening hangar-flying with his friend while the girl picked at the Lobster Newburg, wondering silently about her waistline and when the conversation would get to the point, which for her was her hopeful motion picture career. On still other

occasions Hughes would excuse himself from the table to spend the
evening telephoning in the lobby, while the maiden stared moodily at
the supper congealing on the plates. The fact that dozens of young
ladies would put up with such treatment not once, but time and
again, is evidence that their single-mindedness was as monumental
as Hughes'; they were interested in films, he was interested in airplanes and neither was much interested in the other.

In the late summer of 1932, Hughes bought himself an amphibian. Except for his first airplane ride in his school days, he knew
little about flying boats and wished to learn more. But no plane as
originally built had ever pleased Hughes. He had the craft hauled
to the Pacific Airmotive shops at Burbank to have oil coolers in-
installed and modifications made in the twin engines. The mechanic
assigned to the job was a young pilot of Hughes' age, Glen Odekirk. Odekirk had been a mechanic, then a charter pilot, flying Los
Angeles gamblers to the race track at Aguascalientes, Mexico.
When the charter business suffered in the Depression, Odekirk
signed on as a grease monkey at Pacific Airmotive, and in the
course of things found himself working side by side with a Texas
millionaire who seemed to know as much about aircraft as he did.
In fact, Odekirk found Hughes' constant presence exasperating.
Not only would Hughes watch every move he made, but during one
afternoon argued with him for three hours as to the proper place-
ment of three screws in a strip of metal.

On the other hand, Odekirk was also fascinated by Hughes. He
was particularly intrigued to hear that Hughes wanted to embark
on a coast-to-coast shakedown flight in his flying boat and was trying to find a Navy mechanic to accompany him. Odekirk tells the
following story:

"I hear you're looking for a co-pilot and mechanic," Odekirk
said one day. It was more a question than a statement, and Hughes
understood it as such.

"You're married, aren't you?" Hughes asked. "This trip will
take three months, at least. I'm going back East."

"I'd like to go with you. My wife won't care."

"Think you can handle this airplane?"

"Sure."

"I'll think about it and let you know."

Odekirk said Hughes turned and walked away. He said Hughes took perhaps ten steps across the oil-streaked hangar floor before turning and calling back, "We'll leave in the morning."

Odekirk looked after him in stunned amazement, then ran to telephone his wife.

The trip that was to take three months stretched into eighteen. It seemed that Howard Hughes not only carried no watch, but had no particular use for a calendar. Odekirk had not merely signed on for a cross-country flight; he had unwittingly embarked on what was to be a warm, if chaotic, lifetime association with Hughes; he discovered that Hughes had the exceedingly rare quality of being at once the employer and the friend of his close retainers. His first intimation of this came at the first stop, Phoenix. Odekirk suggested that Hughes go on to a hotel, while he, Odekirk, would remain at the airport to see that the aircraft was properly serviced and then find himself a cot at the airfield. But Hughes remained until the amphibian was refueled and took Odekirk with him to the best hotel in town, introducing him as "my associate"—which made the mechanic feel as if he were somehow a co-owner of the Hughes empire.

The following morning they flew to Houston, where Hughes spent five days at the Hughes Tool Company, talking with his executives and examining the corporate records. It was one of the few times that Hughes ever visited the company that is the basic source of his wealth; in the past thirty years, he has visited Houston on perhaps five occasions.

Hughes and Odekirk left Houston for New Orleans, and as they approached the city they saw a thunderstorm hanging directly over the airport. They throttled back and slanted into a wide, slow orbit to wait for the storm to move on. As they did so, one of the twin engines sputtered to a stop. They could not get it to start again. To lose power in one engine was not so much a danger as an inconvenience. The aircraft could fly safely on one, although not so rapidly, nor so powerfully, nor with the same ability to maneuver.

The blue-blackness of the storm hung across the northern sky like a curtain, shutting off a view of the city and its airfield. Below, in the strong Gulf sunshine of an early spring evening, Hughes and Odekirk could see the green, matted jungle of the delta swamps, cut by the winding silver of the Mississippi and Atchafalaya rivers. They swung through another slow orbit in the sunlight, waiting. The storm did not seem to have moved, and there was no way of knowing when it would. The question was how long should they linger in the sky in a partially disabled aircraft? Hughes nosed the plane into a long slant for the glinting Mississippi. The green jungle rose to meet them, the tufted mat of it enlarging into recognizable trees, the silver wink of the river becoming a broad, muddy flood, and then they were skimming the tops of moss-hung cottonwoods and dropping lightly as any waterfowl to a long, smooth landing on the river.

They had touched down thirty miles below the city, and a Coast Guard boat, summoned by radio, came to take them in tow. They landed in the still bright light, but it was dusk when the boat reached them at 9 P.M. The long, slow haul against the Mississippi current at flood stage did not end until seven o'clock the next morning. Newspapermen, intrigued by the fact that the Coast Guard was rescuing a flying boat, were waiting for them at the Coast Guard mooring.

"I'm Herb Jackson," Hughes told them. "This is Harold Anderson. We were on a mapping expedition for a California oil company."

It was an answer calculated to cut off further questions, inasmuch as the men who hunt for oil are well known for keeping their explorations secret. It explained the presence of a California aircraft, and that was that. But pressed as to why the Coast Guard towed them in, Hughes refused to admit there had been a crash landing; he said he just had wanted to test the craft on water. The reporters received this statement with the polite skepticism it deserved. After Hughes and Odekirk drove off, one of the reporters took down the Civil Aeronautics Administration number of the amphibian and made a telephone call. But by the time the New Orleans newspapers were able to report that a man who resembled

Hughes had arrived in an airplane belonging to Hughes, the millionaire and his mechanic were registered in a Canal Street hotel, not as Anderson and Jackson, but under still different assumed names. They remained there for the Bourbon Street revelry of the Mardi Gras season before resuming a flight that took them to New York and the opulent homes of Long Island.

Hughes dawdled for weeks among the great estates, the extra bachelor at lawn parties and yachting weekends, until one day he told Odekirk he was going away "to breathe a little." He instructed Odekirk to wait for him in New York, and that was the last the pilot-mechanic saw of his employer until late summer. Hughes reappeared as abruptly as he had left. It seemed that he had been in Europe where he had bought what he called a little boat.

"You'll see it when we get to Miami," Hughes said. "It's being delivered there."

"We're going to Miami?"

"Yes," Hughes said. "Right now."

The little boat turned out to be the yacht *Southern Cross*—320 feet overall, carrying a master and a crew of thirty. Hughes kept it a few years, seldom used it, had it sent to Los Angeles and eventually sold it to a Swede. Far more important both to Odekirk and Hughes was another purchase that Hughes had made—a Boeing P-12, an Army Air Corps single-engine pursuit plane. That, too, was waiting for them in Miami.

In retrospect it is easy to say that Hughes' random movements fit a pattern; that he was moving step by step toward an inevitable decision. A literary critic or amateur psychoanalyst might seize upon Hughes' purchase of a flying boat as meaning that Hughes was returning to a profound childhood experience, making a childish dream come true. From there the intrepid analyst could build a case: the disappearance from Hollywood to work under an alias for an airline; the reappearance in Hollywood to take pretty girls to expensive restaurants; the return to Houston and the tool company; the subsequent enjoyment of Mardi Gras under another alias; the looking-in on the graceful civilization of the East Coast and Europe; the purchase of a yacht—all these actions might seem to the analyst to be symbolic of some deeper processes of Hughes' mind. He could suggest that Hughes was very carefully touching all his prior bases in order to test them against the appeal of some new ambition that had begun to grow in him, to reassure himself as to the wisdom of a contemplated action. A simpler explanation might be that Hughes had simply got fed up with Hollywood in the way that most men in their late twenties or early thirties come to a sticking point in their lives and face the question whether to settle for their current lot, or change jobs in the hope of improving it. Those who think that life is at best a random sequence of tenuously related, if not entirely unconnected episodes might say that Hughes had just spent the greater part of two years not knowing what he was doing or where he was going. In any event, it is tempting to say that during this time, Hughes had become both consciously and unconsciously more and more committed to flight. To flight, in all meanings of the word.

5

In January, 1934, an All-American Air Meet was held in Miami, and Howard Hughes decided to enter one event—a race open to amateur pilots. He and Odekirk spent days tinkering with the Boeing. Odekirk said that some of the changes Hughes proposed were unworkable. But, he said, Hughes insisted they be made, and they were, and they did not work. Whereupon Odekirk said he suggested, more sarcastically than helpfully, "Howard, why don't you build your own plane from scratch? That's the only way you'll ever be satisfied." Hughes conceded the point. Thoughts of major revisions were put aside, and Odekirk concentrated on tuning the Boeing's radial engine to performance levels well beyond military specifications.

Hughes had never flown competitively before, but he raced away with the sportsman's cup. By way of celebrating his victory he treated the ten thousand spectators to an unscheduled display of aerobatics before coming in for his landing. He put the little biplane through slow rolls, snap rolls, spins, inverted flight. He went through the whole bag of tricks that the fighter pilots of *Hell's Angels* had taught him and landed to find himself the most sought-after guest of the Florida winter season. His aerial triumph, his fantastic yacht, his reputation as a motion picture producer, his great wealth, his tall good looks and his notoriety as the companion of a great many beautiful women put him leagues ahead of any of the East Coast's bachelors—particularly from the point of view of the mothers of society's daughters. Hughes spent several weeks accepting party invitations and gracefully avoiding domestic entanglements. While Hughes dallied in Florida's lotus land, doing noth-

ing as charmingly as it is possible to do nothing, Odekirk returned
to Los Angeles to his patient wife and to new duties.

It seemed that Hughes had taken his mechanic's sarcasm seriously. He ordered Odekirk to find and equip a shop in which to
design and build a racing plane. Odekirk rented part of a hangar at
the Glendale airport and began to assemble a stock of tools. When
Hughes subsequently flew in from the East Coast he hired an aeronautical engineer to help with the project—a young man named
Dick Palmer, fresh from the California Institute of Technology, who
already had a reputation for radical ideas in his field. Hughes next
hired additional mechanics and engineers, including a meteorologist—another bright young man from Caltech, W. C. Rockefeller.
In all, eighteen men were soon working together in the Glendale
hangar under the peculiar conditions set by Howard Hughes.

The first condition was secrecy. Their section of the hangar was
walled off from the rest. They were instructed to say nothing to the
outside world about their work. Next, they discovered that their
employer thought nothing of working straight through the night
sustained by cartons of milk, green salads and strips of bacon. Nor
was this all. Sometimes he would work days and nights on end.
There would be times when they would work alone, unable to find
Hughes no matter how urgent their need. Odekirk and Palmer had
authority from Hughes to buy whatever materials were necessary
but no one knew what name to affix to the invoices. For lack of any
other name, they began to call their operation The Hughes Aircraft
Company. Such was the informal birth of a corporation that, three
decades later, would be a half-billion-dollar enterprise, one of the
ten largest defense contractors to the United States Government
and developer of the Early Bird communications satellite. But at
that moment in 1934, The Hughes Aircraft Company was simply a
small group of men who were trying to build the fastest landplane
in the world. They called their project H-1, for Hughes One.

Rumor seeped out from behind the hangar walls, as rumor will.
"Hughes' ship is still a mystery," an aviation magazine reported at
the time. "No dope on its design, construction or performance has
been released." But the magazine added, "The wings are of com-

bined wood and metal construction. The rest of the ship is all metal. Both the landing gear and tail wheel are retractable. Wind tunnel tests are supposed to have indicated a possible speed of 365 m.p.h."

What happens to a model in a wind tunnel and what happens to a real aircraft in actual flight may be two entirely different things, although wind tunnel tests are fair predictors of probability. If the magazine's report was accurate the Hughes group at least had come up with a basic airframe design that, in theory, could be moved through the air at more than twice the speed of the airliners of the day—and sixty miles an hour faster than the swiftest racing land-plane in the world. This did not necessarily mean that the Hughes group was working on a project of striking originality. Rather, they were working well within the state of the art, but with a hard eye for detail. For example, all aeronautical engineers understood that a glass-smooth object shaped like a raindrop would offer less resistance to wind than a pitted, broken-surfaced, squarish lump. Therefore, the streamlined shape would move more rapidly through the air than the lump, given the same propulsion.

So like every other group of aircraft designers, the Hughes group paid respect to streamlining, but unlike most others they carried the point as far as they could. For instance fixed landing wheels dangling beneath an aircraft offer resistance to the wind. Most designers were content to minimize this wind resistance by streamlining the landing gear struts and enclosing the wheels in teardrop housings. Hughes, however, insisted that the H-1's landing gear should fold smoothly up into the wings once the craft was airborne. Designers were sheathing aircraft in metal skins, and Hughes reflected that protuberant screw and rivet heads would offer a measurable—if not significant—amount of wind resistance. He therefore ordered that all the H-1's screws be flatheaded and countersunk and the rivets installed flush. The essential difference between the Hughes plane and all other racing aircraft was the extent to which the Hughes group carried a passion for such detail and the extent to which they made use of the practical and theoretical knowledge of the day. Their contribution was original in Carlisle's sense of the word: that is, he is most original who adapts from the greatest number of sources. It was just here that Hughes' great wealth enabled him to make a major contribution. His money gave him time and freedom to seek out the sources.

"Howard was the greatest brain picker I ever saw," Palmer said years later. "He'd disappear for a few days and go to the National Advisory Committee for Aeronautics at Langley Field, Virginia. There, he'd drink coffee with the government's top engineers and flight designers. He'd find out what he wanted to know then fly home, tell us, and our problem would be solved."

Hughes and his men worked on their H-1 for eighteen months, sometimes taking it entirely apart and beginning again. Hughes would come to the hangar at night and stand beside his craft for hours, silently considering it and from time to time jotting a note to himself on a scrap of paper. Then, as silently, he would leave— without a word of suggestion to his men. On other occasions he would call them at their homes at whatever hour of the night he needed their help. One evening, for instance, he telephoned to Palmer and Rockefeller, insisting that he must see them at once. The two men had been working on the H-1 all that day with Hughes standing beside them, and they wondered what could possibly have occurred to Hughes in the hour or so since they had seen him last. But Hughes said the matter was too important to be discussed over the telephone.

When they reached Hughes' house, he told them what it was.

"I want you to drive me to Santa Barbara," he said. "I have a dinner date up there."

The problem was Hughes at the time had neither a driver's license nor an automobile. He had no car of his own for a somewhat unusual but perfectly good reason: he kept losing them. Once he borrowed an automobile from one of his engineers and drove it somewhere. Days later when the engineer got up his nerve to ask his millionaire employer about the car, Hughes had to admit he had no idea where it was. Nor did it ever turn up. After that Hughes would borrow company cars, preferring dingy, old, low-priced automobiles—feeling that no one seeing a jalopy wheeze past would think it contained a millionaire. At any event, when Hughes called Palmer and Rockefeller he had neither car nor license, and wanted a ride.

The two young scientists set out with Hughes for Santa Barbara, ninety miles away, and en route they struck a dog that darted into the road in front of them. Hughes told Palmer to stop. He jumped out, picked the bloody animal up in his arms, carried it into the car and said they must find help. Palmer and Rockefeller argued that it was a stray dog, dying, and that a veterinarian could not help it.

But Hughes insisted that a veterinarian be found. He was already two hours late for his dinner date, but a detour was made to an animal hospital, and Hughes watched while the veterinarian did what he could. The prognosis was that the dog might live. An hour later the journey to Santa Barbara was resumed with Hughes dressed for supper in a coat stained with dog's blood.

The girl was a California socialite. Hughes insisted that Rockefeller and Palmer join the party. The two men tried to beg off, but Hughes would not hear of it. He offered no explanation to the girl for his tardiness nor did he talk to her during dinner. Instead he divided his time between talking to his engineers about the H-1 and rushing to the telephone at random intervals to call the animal hospital to check on the dog's condition. The dog, incidentally, recovered and was kept by Palmer.

Some people might think the girl would be reluctant to renew acquaintances with Hughes, but their number would most certainly not include Katharine Hepburn. At this point in Hughes' life, Miss Hepburn had appeared on his somewhat cluttered stage. Mercurial, slender, an enormously talented actress, daughter of a proud family and possessor of a Bryn Mawr accent, Miss Hepburn also happened to have a view of the world remarkably like Hughes' own.

They golfed together in Los Angeles, stepping outside his back door to a tee of the Wilshire Country Club. They flew together, with Miss Hepburn taking the controls to learn how to spin, loop and roll. They flew across the country, leading gossip columnists a

merry chase. Late one evening in Chicago, Miss Hepburn's press
agent sought to disperse a band of reporters besieging Miss Hepburn's hotel.

"Miss Katharine Hepburn wishes to announce that she will not
marry Mr. Howard Hughes in Chicago today," he said.

This was scarcely a comprehensive answer to all the questions
the reporters had in mind, but it was the only one they could get.
Believing it to be truthful, so far as it went, one of the reporters
telephoned to a clerk in the marriage license bureau. He told the
clerk to go home. The clerk had been keeping the office open all
night just in case.

The newspapers' interest in Hughes and Miss Hepburn stemmed,
of course, from the fact that they were public figures. There was no
good way for them to tell the press to go jump in a barrel of its own
ink because the constant problem of those in public life—and particularly of those in the entertainment business—is how to preserve
a decent privacy while courting favorable publicity. But granted the
mutual interest that a motion picture actress and the press have in
one another, it is still somewhat difficult to understand why the
newspapers and society in general presume that any friendship between a man and a woman is a matter of public concern and that it
must result in matrimony. It is almost as if the world feels threatened by any such friendship that is not conducted within the marriage contract and considers matrimony as a kind of price that
must be paid—as an inevitable penalty. If all the world loves a
lover it would also seem that the world loathes or at least fearfully
envies a bachelor—particularly a wealthy one. At any rate, the
press gibbered around Miss Hepburn and Hughes like so many
marriage brokers with police powers, meanwhile speculating about
Miss Hepburn's career and about the aircraft Hughes was trying to
build in secret.

The racer was taking shape during Hughes' presences and absences, and in August, 1935, eighteen months after work had begun, it was ready for flight. Palmer wanted to hire a test pilot.
When the ship was building he had spoken to Hughes about finding
a pilot and Hughes had promised that he would. But the pilot

Hughes had in mind was himself. It was his plane, built with his money, he had put a lot of time and thought into its construction and he explained to Palmer, "I fly my own planes."

To Palmer and the H-1 associates this seemed carrying a sense of responsibility beyond the limits of prudence. No matter how sound the theories that go into its design; no matter how careful the workmanship; no matter what the wind tunnel tests indicate, no one can ever know whether an aircraft built to exceed the performance of all others will, in fact, fly—much less outfly all the rest. Only the attempt itself will prove that. The best designs of the best aeronautical engineers not infrequently fall apart in the air for reasons not imagined on the drawing boards, or calculated on the slide rules. The test pilot is paid a wage that seems unusually handsome until one reflects that it is the price he is putting on his life. It was all very well for Hughes to wish to take all the risk and responsibility for a machine of his own creation, but there were practical matters to consider. For one thing, Hughes was an expert pilot, but he was not an experienced test pilot. For another, a pragmatic argument could be made to the point that Hughes' life was more valuable than any test pilot's, for what test pilot was also the millionaire employer of hundreds of people whose fortunes are bound up in his own?

"I wish I'd made the plane safer," Palmer muttered, as if to himself, as he watched Hughes' gangling, flight-clad figure climb up into the cockpit.

Word of the test flight had got around the aeronautical community, and dozens of flyers and mechanics stood in the shade of a hangar looking at a scarlet shape of speed on the tarmac. It was a stubby-winged monoplane with a long fuselage that was slick as lacquer, and it stood like a spindly-legged insect on its widely spaced landing gear, aiming its blunt nose at the sky. Beneath the engine cowling was an air-cooled 1,000-horsepower Pratt and Whitney twin Wasp—a radial engine with two banks of cylinders. The aircraft more than a little resembled the Japanese Zero fighter of the Second World War, and it would later be said that the men who built the Zero had borrowed heavily from the H-1.

The starter whined; the propeller swung slowly; the engine coughed and blew a gust of blue-gray smoke from its exhausts. Then the engine caught and settled into a smooth thunder of explosions. Hughes released the brakes and slowly taxied to the end of the airstrip where he paused to stand on his brakes and race the engine preparatory to takeoff.

The watchers at the hangar listened carefully to the engine sound and saw the ship begin to move, hearing instants later the engine-song deepen into full power. Hughes kept the ship down for nearly the full length of the airstrip before lifting off. He climbed in a rising turn, the landing gear folded up into its housing, and the ship rapidly diminished into the yellow glare of a torrid August afternoon.

Hughes' ground crew watched all this with no little pride and apprehension. It flew. In fact, it flew very well. There was no apparent sloppiness in that climbing turn. Most important, it flew rapidly. They all followed the long, curving flight path that Hughes described around the airfield, and it was clear to them that they had built a very fast airplane. Palmer wondered what its landing speed would be. They had built what pilots call a hot ship, just as automobile mechanics speak of a car tuned for excessive speeds as a hot rod, and Palmer's theory told him that the plane would land hot. It needed to move rapidly in order to create sufficient vacuum over its shallow-cambered wing in order to be pulled up into the air. In the event of power failure the H-1 would probably have the glide angle of a brick. And when it came in for a landing Hughes would have to fly it all the way down onto the ground—he couldn't safely cut power and stall in—and the H-1 would roll a good long way before it could stop. Getting it up into the sky was one thing; getting it down again in one piece was something else. There was no question that Hughes was a competent pilot, but if all Palmer's theories were correct no pilot had ever sat at the controls of such a ship.

Fifteen minutes after liftoff Hughes touched down in a long, swift, smooth slant, and when he did the watchers did not shout and laugh and clap one another's backs. Instead, they did something far more eloquent of their pride in Hughes and in themselves and of the relief of their tensions. They burst into applause.

Hughes came taxiing back to the hangar, killed the engine and unwound his long form from the cockpit. He stood on the wing root and reached back into the cockpit for a note book. He climbed down and looking thoughtfully at Palmer he said, "I think we can do it."

Hughes' brooding features relaxed for an instant into one of his rare smiles.

"Let's try," he said.

Hughes meant that he wanted to try to break the world's speed record for landplanes, which, in 1935, was 314.32 miles per hour, set by the French pilot Raymond Delmotte in an airplane developed by the French government at a cost of more than a million dollars. The rules of the National Aeronautic Association and of the Fédération Aeronautique Internationale demanded that an existing record could be broken only on condition that the challenging aircraft surpass the old mark on each of four successive flypasts over a measured course, made on the same day and witnessed, timed and photographed by official judges. The average speed of the four flypasts would be regarded as the official top speed of the aircraft.

On September 12, 1935, Hughes brought the H-1 to Martin Field at Santa Ana, California. It was here that Dr. Albert A. Michelson had found that light rays moved through the atmosphere, at ground level, at a speed of 186,000 miles per second, and here photoelectrically operated cameras were set up 1.86 miles apart. Hughes shook hands with the three judges, all old friends of his. They were Amelia Earhart Putnam, the aviatrix; Paul Mantz, one of Hollywood's greatest stunt fliers; and Lawrence Therkelson, a representative of the National Aeronautic Association. It was late afternoon before the H-1 and the timing gear were finally tuned for trial, and there was now a question whether the flights should not wait until the following day.

But Hughes did not wait. He took off, climbed rapidly to ten thousand feet, and pushed over, firewalling the throttle. The H-1 came flashing by the cameras at 346 miles per hour, but a judge's voice, chattering in Hughes' headset, told Hughes the flypast could not be counted because when the H-1 entered the course it was still pulling out of its dive. The rules called for level flight between the cameras.

Hughes climbed, banked, dove and straightened out well away from the field. This time he came whistling along in level flight past the cameras at 352 miles per hour. Turning at the far end, he came back up the course at 339, and it was perfectly obvious to everyone that Hughes was flying a record-setting racer. But as he sped away into a long climbing turn preparatory to his next flypast the judges reluctantly told him the afternoon light was failing; that it was already too dark for the cameras to photograph his darting plane. Since he had completed only two acceptable passes the ruling was that he had failed to establish an official mark.

Hughes spent the entire night checking his airplane, tuning its engine for maximum speed. Ordinarily a man who goes a night without sleep is not in the best possible shape to fly the world's fastest airplane, for the fine edge of his perceptions may be blunted, and when one speeds over the earth at minimum altitude at three hundred miles per hour it is advisable that one's perceptions be razor sharp and one's reflexes instantaneous. But then Hughes was no ordinary man with respect to sleeping habits. He was in one of his awake periods, and, further, was buoyed by the exhilarating certainty that the world's speed record for himself and for America was within his reach. So, after a sleepless night, he climbed into his H-1 and took off.

Each of his first four passes was well in excess of the 314-miles-per-hour record. But since his second pass had been a relatively slow 337 miles per hour, he added a fifth. The judges radioed their enthusiastic congratulations. They said the average speed of his last four consecutive flypasts was 352.39 miles per hour, but Hughes was dissatisfied. He felt he should be able to squeeze still another ten miles an hour out of the H-1, and this time he climbed to twelve thousand feet before nosing down for a sixth try. He came down out of the sky in a wild powerdive to level off for a straight run past the cameras, and just as he pulled out of his dive the engine died.

Hughes' fingers flew to the switches, cutting out the main gasoline tank and switching to the auxiliary fuel supply. Nothing happened. The engine would not start. Hughes shut off both the ignition and the fuel line and began to lower his landing gear. The powerless H-1's swift glide had already carried it past the airport. The drag of the lowered landing gear slowed the ship, and the ground approached still more steeply.

Hughes had not sufficient altitude to turn and glide back to the airstrip. His best alternative was a plowed beet field. On such a surface the landing gear would dig in, tipping the plane over on its nose. Such an accident occurring at better than a hundred miles an hour would plow quite another kind of furrow among the beets. He retracted the landing gear again, used what control he had to keep the nose up and slid the racer into a belly landing in the middle of the field, bouncing and grating along in a shower of dirt until the plane skidded to a lurching halt.

The judges and the ground observers, fully aware of Hughes' difficulties and all that was implied, saw the plane disappear into a cloud of dust and dirt. They hurried to the scene fearing to see a crumpled wreck and a dead pilot. Paul Mantz reached the H-1 first to find Hughes sitting on the cowling, writing in a notebook. Hughes looked down at Mantz and grinned.

"Did I make it?" he asked.

"You not only broke the record," Mantz said, "but you are the luckiest son of a bitch I ever saw."

Hughes was unhurt, and the H-1 had suffered surprisingly little damage. A bent propeller could be replaced and the dents in the cowling and in the metal skin could be hammered out with minimum difficulty. The plane was loaded onto a flatbed truck and taken back to Glendale at night when highway traffic was light.

The next morning the name of Howard Hughes moved from the entertainment pages of the nation's newspapers to the front pages. He had flown faster than man had flown before, and in an aircraft of his own design had restored the world speed record to America. The press did not know quite how to describe the hero of the hour.

Motion picture producer? Yachtsman? Millionaire playboy? Eligible bachelor? Thrill seeker? Amateur flyer? Texas industrialist?
These aspects of Hughes seemed to prevent the press from understanding that he was also a self-taught aeronautical engineer of
considerable inventive ability, that he was a skilled and resourceful
pilot and that he was an inspired mechanic with an infinite capacity
for work.

Despite all his associations in the entertainment and business
worlds, Hughes was nowhere so much at home as he was in the
aeronautical community. He fit well into the easy camaraderie of
young men who knew, as he did, the lonely wonder of flight; who
stirred to the deep sound of aircraft engines at speed; who found
meaning and purpose in the constant challenge to build swifter,
higher-flying wings. The young men in the grease-stained coveralls
had an enormous respect for him. He might have a lot of money,
they said, but he never let you know it; he'd work right along with
anybody and harder than most. The aeronautical engineers in their
white shirts recognized Hughes as a colleague; the windburned men
in goggles and leather were the first to say that Howard, as they
called him, was a really hot pilot.

But somehow the press could not think of Hughes in these terms,
despite the fact that he had built and flown the fastest plane in the
world. They kept thinking of him as a millionaire playboy-producer
who flew for fun. Perhaps only the members of the aeronautical
trade press, unlike the representatives of the daily papers, took
Hughes seriously and understood the work and the promise that
was implied when Hughes spoke of his H-1 at a press conference.

"I think she can go three hundred sixty-five easily, maybe three
eighty-five. And four hundred miles an hour is not far off."

The daily press duly recorded this statement, but what interested
them more particularly was "What about that crash landing?" A
post-flight inspection of the H-1 brought to light a small wad of
steel wool in the main fuel line. Did Hughes suspect sabotage? No,
Hughes said matter-of-factly, he didn't. He said a mechanical dis-
order caused the crash; that "my supply of gasoline had been ex-

hausted, and when I tried to cut the other tank in, the engine refused to take it."

A somewhat withdrawn, vaguely melancholy man who seldom smiled and who wore the abstracted look of one who wished himself somewhere else did not precisely fit the reporters' preconceptions of a wealthy daredevil. Yet in a sense the press was perfectly justified whenever it called him an amateur flyer. He was spending money on flight, not making money from it. Hughes happened to be sufficiently rich to do what pleased him, but the press was grievously mistaken whenever it implied that Hughes played at whatever he did. No matter what might have impelled him to want to fly faster than anyone else, the process of putting himself in the position to do so had made Hughes a serious student of his avocation. He was wondering how to make the H-1 even faster, and when the reporters had gone he took the matter up with Palmer and Odekirk.

The consensus was that a shallower and narrower wing might be part of the answer, and Palmer estimated that this and other modifications would take at least six months of work. Meanwhile, Hughes was also interested in long-distance flight. Colonel Roscoe Turner, one of the *Hell's Angels* pilots, held the transcontinental speed record, having flown between California and New York in ten hours, two minutes and fifty-one seconds in the Bendix Air Race of September, 1932. Hughes appreciated the difference between flashing over a 1.86-mile course and flying at speed nonstop across a continent. He weighed one project against the other and decided to do both at once—to redesign the H-1 and, while this work was under way, to procure another aircraft in which to set a new transcontinental record. He called on a flying friend, Jacqueline Cochran, and leased from her a standard Northrop Gamma mail plane that she owned.

The Northrop was a sturdy, stable aircraft of no great speed. But Hughes was interested only in the airframe. At the Glendale hangar the Northrop was gutted; its fuel tanks were removed and much larger tanks installed. The weight of the additional fuel posed a problem: how to get it off the ground, high into the air, and then moved at speed. The Northrop was therefore fitted with a novel power plant.

Hughes persuaded the Army Air Corps to lend him a new Wright G Cyclone engine that had not yet been released for public use. It generated 925 horsepower on takeoff at sea level. It was equipped with a two-speed blower, or supercharger, which made it possible to use full power at low altitudes without burning up the engine, and then to shift to a ten-to-one supercharger speed in higher, cooler air. In addition Hughes obtained a Hamilton constant-speed propeller which contained a mechanism that altered the pitch of the blades in flight, so that the propeller blades could be set for a maximum bite into the air on takeoff and be gradually changed to progressively higher pitches when the aircraft gained its cruising altitude. The combination of experimental Air Corps engine and variable-pitch propeller could, in theory, get the Northrop's fully loaded ten thousand pounds off the ground after a run of only eighteen hundred feet, which was half the length of the Burbank, California, airstrip.

Modification of the Northrop began in the fall, and while the refitting of new fuel tanks and a new engine did not consume an undue amount of time, other preparations for the flight took longer to complete. Hughes was by this time an original investigator of theoretical speeds; and he worked at his subject in the machine shop, in the meteorological chart rooms, in the wind tunnels and in the design studios as well as in the cockpit. On every test flight he took meticulous notes on oil temperatures, manifold pressures, the effect of altitudes on engine performances and on the varying efficiencies of sundry fuel mixtures at different altitudes and humidities.

"Howard flies with a slide rule in one hand and the stick in the other," one of his fellow pilots said.

The point here is that Hughes was slowly making his own discoveries in the fall and winter of 1935, and in characteristic fashion he labored at his avocation without particular respect to time. So it was that late on a December night Hughes was working in the harsh glare of overhead lights in the Glendale hangar, trying to tune his new, high altitude engine to even more efficient high altitude performance.

Odekirk and the others kept looking at their watches, thinking of their wives and children. It looked very much to them as if this would prove to be still another all-night session with their eccentric employer. Finally Odekirk could stand it no longer. He took Hughes by the arm and said, "Howard, do you know what day this is?"

Hughes looked up in honest puzzlement. Odekirk could almost see Hughes' mind groping for a memory of some familiar date. Then Hughes' features brightened with sudden pleasure, as if he were delighted that someone had remembered.

"Why yes," he said. "It's my birthday!"

"Howard," Odekirk said, as steadily as he could, "it is also Christmas Eve."

part iii Around the World

6

Shortly after noon on January 13, 1936, Howard Hughes came to the Burbank airport wearing a double-breasted gray suit, a yellow poplin jacket, helmet and goggles. He regarded the weather without surprise. It was a typical January day in Los Angeles; gray, dim, with a thick overcast hanging low over the city. The millionaire shook hands matter-of-factly with his ground crew, climbed into the Northrop mail plane's cockpit, gunned his engine and taxied to the end of the airstrip to await the timer's word of readiness and the tower's permission to take off. Seconds later he was airborne and lost to view in the clouds. Nine hours, twenty-seven minutes and ten seconds after takeoff he landed at Newark, New Jersey, and ran to the Western Union office to send a telegram, SAFE AND DOWN AT NEWARK, to Katharine Hepburn in Hollywood. Whereupon, he hailed a taxi and drove to New York City to sleep out the rest of the night.

The following morning the press called at Hughes' Waldorf Astoria hotel room to ask him how he felt about having broken the transcontinental speed record. The newspapermen wanted to know the answers to a great many more personal questions, none of which Hughes had the slightest intention of discussing. What he wanted to talk about was his airplane and aviation. So he praised his aircraft, and the ground crew in California who had helped make the flight possible, and he predicted that it would not be many years before regularly scheduled airliners were making the trip between Los Angeles and New York in ten hours.

"But how does it feel to beat the record?" a reporter persisted. "Are you going out for any more records?"

Patiently, Hughes began again. It seemed that everyone had missed the point he had been trying to make.

"There isn't a record that can't be broken," he explained. "I am chiefly interested in an airplane's performance. On this flight, I was checking on altitudes. I am interested in this type of work as I hope to make some real speed some day at altitudes of thirty thousand feet or more in my racing ship—with a new engine which will be ready in a year."

"Thirty thousand feet!" a reporter said. "What will it be like, up that high?"

"I don't know," Hughes said. "But I'll find out."

The language barrier separating Hughes and the press was a construct of their different points of view. To the newspapermen Hughes was a transient novelty in their lives, and it was their job to try to present him to the public as a hero; that is, as a more colorful and somewhat larger than life-size version of the man next door. The fact that Hughes, the man, had just crossed the continent in less time than anyone in history meant something to the newspapermen. On the other hand Hughes was trying to talk about as serious a subject as a man can discuss: his life's work. For having arrived at his thirtieth year—precisely that time in life at which most men begin to make the most effective use of their full powers —Hughes had found a purpose and a direction for his considerable energies. He had decided to devote his life and fortune to the advancement of aviation. To be sure he was glad to have established new records, but like every pilot from the Wright brothers to the astronauts, Hughes was anxious for the world to know that any particular flight is merely the logical, predictable culmination of scientific preparation; that it represents the end product of the labors of a great many men other than the pilot. This to all serious pilots is the real story of flight—although when Lindbergh flew to Paris the press made more of his blond good looks than of the characteristics of his aircraft. They made it seem as if he had negotiated the distance on the basis of a ham sandwich and a chocolate bar, rather than on the basis of long hours of preliminary mathematics. Just so, Hughes was called HRH by the tabloids, punning on his initials and on those of the honorifics of a crown prince. Almost lost in a sea of print was Hughes' statement that he attributed his record time in an ordinary commercial aircraft to the fact that the United States Army Air Corps had loaned him their newly developed high altitude engine.

In all this Hughes may have been unduly modest, for while contemporary mathematics and the state of the arts of shipbuilding and navigation might have forecast Columbus' safe arrival in the New World, it nonetheless took a sailor of skill and courage to put theory to the test. And in the case of Hughes' transcontinental flight something more was involved than a new engine bolted to a conventional airframe.

For one thing Hughes' radio antenna broke away on takeoff. He discovered this when he tried to call Burbank tower for weather information as he flew blind into the overcast. He was still flying blind at fifteen thousand feet, guided only by a compass heading which—in event of a cross wind—might not indicate his actual course over the unseen earth below. Two hours out of Burbank he broke into clear sky over Santa Fe, New Mexico, on course and on schedule. For a while he flew in the strong light of the semi-arid West on a winter afternoon, but winter days are short and as the earth turned beneath him, he flew into the approaching night. As darkness closed around him he could no longer check his compass heading against the earth's similarity to his map, and so estimate his wind's direction and speed. Then near Wichita, Kansas, he flew into turbulence so severe that his compass dial jumped off its bearing point. Now without either radio or compass to give him lines of bearing or heading, Hughes took the moon for his guiding star— but the moon could only indicate in a general way which direction was east. Fortunately the night was clear and Hughes was entering an increasingly populous part of the country. He guided himself by comparing the towns and cities that appeared on his map with the wink and glow of lights scattered about the darkness below. There, according to the time and his estimated direction, must be the lights of Indianapolis. Very well; the moon is east; Columbus bears just a bit north of due east from Indianapolis. So the next loom of a large city ought to be that of Columbus, and then the course is almost due east to Newark, in which case the lights of Pittsburgh should appear off the port wing . . . Following such dead reckoning Hughes eventually raised the vast jewel of light that was the metropolitan New York City area, and let down over the welcoming beacon of Newark Airport. He was concerned about landing without permission from the tower, but he could not radio for landing instructions. He could only hope that his was the only aircraft in the sky as he made his approach, and that he would not be landing in a strong down wind or cross wind. An anxious timer who, of course, had had no news of Hughes' flight since takeoff, and who did not know whether Hughes was dead or alive and in either case, where, was delighted to check the Northrop down at Newark at eighteen minutes past midnight, Newark time. He offered Hughes his enthusiastic congratulations. For Hughes to have set a transcontinental speed record was no inconsiderable feat in itself, but for him to have found his way across the country by dead reckoning at night, and set a new record in the process, was altogether remarkable. But no mention of Hughes' difficulties appeared at length in the press, for the very good reason that Hughes did not mention them.

Hughes spent a few days in New York before flying to Miami for a winter vacation of swimming and sunning, but on his return he shattered the speed record between those cities by more than half an hour. In the light of his conversation with reporters following the transcontinental flight, it is not easy to suggest why he attempted, and broke, the Miami-New York speed record. What was proved? That a faster airplane could cover the distance in less time than a slower one? Or was it that Hughes wanted to see just what the Northrop could do on a long-distance flight, now that its instruments were again in working order? Or was there just something about a record—any record—that, like Everest, is there and so constitutes a challenge?

Hughes landed in New York's front pages once again, as he might have expected. But Hughes professed to be annoyed by public attention. He grew a beard and assumed the name Carlos Gomez. Perhaps he thought his disguise would shield him and his friends from such gossip columnists as the one who, the year before, had preposterously written that "the thirty-year-old multimillionaire oilman, aviation enthusiast, motion picture producer and playboy will marry Ruth Moffett, the fifteen-year-old daughter of James A. Moffet, vice-president of the Standard Oil Company of California and former Federal Housing Administrator. . . . Last winter, it was Ida Lupino, the English actress, who supposedly was palpitating the Hughes heart . . . now comes the report he is head-over-heels in love with little Miss Moffett and at long last is in the market for a wedding ring. She even has plans for redecorating his yacht, and he's willin'!"

But as the only six foot, three inch bearded pseudo-Mexican called Gomez who wore rumpled suits and tennis shoes into Manhattan's most fashionable night clubs and who carried his head diffidently canted to one side and spoke with a Texas drawl, Hughes was no more conspicuous than a burning barn on a dark night. The headwaiters smiled, bowed low, ushered Señor Gomez to the best available tables, and then slithered off to their telephones to earn the wages that gossip columnists paid them for reporting the presence of the famous.

Again, as in the case of his setting a Miami-New York speed record, it is not easy to explain Hughes' flimsy masquerade as Gomez. It would seem charmingly hopeful, if not utterly naïve, for a man as worldly-wise as Hughes to imagine that a crop of whiskers and an alias could constitute a disguise; but more important, how can a passion for anonymity be reconciled with a predilection for conspicuous consumption in gossip-ridden New York night clubs?

Whatever the reason for Hughes' assumption of a disguise, the effect of it was to enhance his growing public reputation as a somewhat mysterious, wealthy eccentric of improbably diversified yet unquestionable achievements. Legends grew up around him. Like all legends they were based on facts. One widely circulated story was that Hughes was once negotiating a business transaction by transcontinental telephone in the course of which he instructed a New York lawyer to obtain certain information and then call back to Hughes in Hollywood. Moments later the telephone in New

York rang again. "Call back after six and get the night rate," Hughes is supposed to have said. But while Hughes' use of the public pay telephone was a source of amusement to his friends the fact of the matter—which they seem to have forgotten—was that Hughes had no office.

True, the building at 7000 Romaine Street was the center of his manifold enterprises, but its primary function was as a switch-board. Those who wished to talk with Hughes would call the Ro-maine Street number and leave their names and a brief statement of their business. From time to time Hughes would call in from wher-ever he was to see what the day's—or the week's—messages had been. Then at whatever time it happened to be he would return such telephone calls as he chose to answer. The fact was Hughes' office was the nearest public telephone booth and his filing cabinet was his brain, in which he kept and made use of the details of his various businesses and projects. Moreover no one but Hughes could conduct his businesses for him because he would tell his employees only as much about their jobs as he thought they needed to know at any one time. For example the women secretaries who worked in the gray stucco building at 7000 Romaine Street were all carefully screened; they were not allowed to wear nail polish or perfume; each worked behind closed doors in her own office so that as one of them said, "Nobody knew what anybody else was doing"; and at the end of the day a Hughes man would drive them to their homes. They operated under the following instructions from Hughes: "You may have breakfast, one drink, no phone calls during the day, and do not talk to anyone about your job." Probably never in history has so much wealth been controlled and so many affairs attended to in such minute detail by means of long-distance calls placed by a man in a telephone booth.

While Gomez-Hughes fascinated the headwaiters and gossip col-umnists in New York, the Hughes Aircraft Company expanded in California on receipt of his telephoned instructions. It now had fifty employees, including fifteen engineers, and moved from the Glen-dale hangar to larger quarters at Burbank airport. Work on the H-1 was nearing completion under conditions of great secrecy. Hughes was ever watchful for industrial spies, and the H-1 was under heavy guard twenty-four hours a day.

In May, 1936, Hughes returned to California to see his new factory and check on the progress of the H-1. As he was about to depart for the West Coast, he wondered whether it would be possible to eat breakfast in Chicago and have dinner in California. He thought it would not only be fun to try, but that he could also drive home his point about the feasibility of rapid transcontinental airline service. When he reached Chicago, a friend had a different idea.

"I'll bet you fifty dollars you can't eat *lunch* in Chicago and dinner in Los Angeles," his friend said.

Hughes later admitted it was a foolish bet, but on May 14, after a hearty lunch at the Chicago airport, Hughes lifted his Northrop into the spring head winds. Because of the even heavier winds aloft he planned to fly half of the 1,885 miles at three thousand feet before climbing to sixteen thousand to clear the Rockies. He was not long airborne, however, before trouble came into the cockpit to keep him company.

He ran into severe turbulence east of Kansas City and was forced to climb in an attempt to find smoother air. He climbed to ten thousand feet and donned his oxygen mask. Still, the turbulence persisted. He went up to twenty thousand feet—as high as he had ever flown—and while the air at that altitude was smoother, he was now flying into strong winds and, much worse, his oxygen equipment failed.

Hughes had several choices. He could stay at twenty thousand feet, fighting the dizziness that comes with anoxia. He could descend into the rough air below and waste even more gasoline than he was expending against the winds aloft. He could land and lose his fifty-dollar bet. He chose to remain at twenty thousand feet and he flew into a thunderstorm. Groggy, dizzy, deadly cold and fighting sleep, he flew blind for hundreds of miles. Ice began to form on his wings. Nonetheless, he pushed on through and over the mountains. A hundred miles east of Los Angeles the mechanism activating his oil pump failed. He had to operate the pump manually the last hundred miles. Then, his airspeed indicator ceased to function, but by this time the lights of Los Angeles were at last in view. At 7:15 P.M. he put the storm-tossed Northrop down at Grand Central Air Terminal, eight hours and ten minutes out of Chicago. He happened to have set a speed record for an east-to-west passage between the cities, but another thought was uppermost in his mind as he hurried to the airport luncheon counter and ordered the seventy-five-cent blueplate special. While it was cooking he telephoned his friend in Chicago.

"I figure I'm $49.25 ahead," he said. "And I've learned more in the last eight hours than in my last ten years of flying."

Later Hughes admitted that the most intelligent thing he could have done would have been to have landed at Kansas City.

"I must have been goofy from the altitude with no oxygen," he said, "or I'd never have done some of the things I did."

7

On his arrival at the new Hughes Aircraft Company building at the
Burbank airport, Howard Hughes looked around and realized that
someone was missing. He wondered, and then he had it.

The missing man was a mechanic who had accompanied Hughes
on a flight to New York two years earlier. He had been instructed
to take a hotel room and remain on call until he received further
word from his employer. But Hughes had flown away alone, leaving his employee parked in the hotel much like one of the company
cars whose whereabouts Hughes had such trouble remembering.

"Where is he?" Hughes wanted to know.

"Still in New York, I guess," Glen Odekirk told him. "Waiting
for you to tell him what to do."

A hurried call was made to the New York hotel, and the mechanic answered it. He seemed pleased to get back to work again.

The work, incidentally, was by no means confined to modification of the H-1. Another project shrouded in equal secrecy was
begun. Hughes confided to Odekirk, Palmer and Rockefeller that
he intended to fly around the world. The idea of such a flight had
been at the back of Hughes' mind since the summer of 1933, when
a one-eyed former parachute jumper, Wiley Post, became the first
man to fly alone around the earth. It had taken Post seven days,
eighteen hours and forty-nine minutes to do this. While Hughes and
every other pilot applauded Post's feat, Hughes felt it would be
more to the point to wonder what a multi-engined airliner manned
by a crew could suggest with respect to world travel.

Of course no one just gets up from a breakfast table, climbs into
an airplane and flies around the world. Even in today's world of

jets one must at least pack a bag. In 1936, matters were somewhat
more complicated—one must first find or design an appropriate
airplane, discover what could be learned of climatic and meteorological conditions in remote corners of the earth, prepare oneself
with maps and procure special equipment to provide against all
sorts of desperate contingencies. So it was that a planning project
was established while Hughes looked about for an airplane. Late in
1936 he bought one of the promising new Douglas DC-1 transports
which he and his men then began to fit out with new engines, enlarged fuel tanks and a radio compass. He told his staff that they
would have to seek ways to extend the Douglas' range to fifteen
hundred miles.

Hughes made more than twenty test flights before reluctantly
concluding that the Douglas "was too damn slow." As testing continued, Hughes heard that the Sikorsky factory in Bridgeport, Connecticut, would shortly bring out a new amphibian, reputedly much
faster than the DC-1 and possessing the considerable advantage of
being able to land on water. The Sikorsky executives promised that
they could have a plane ready for him in July. This was good news,
for any world flight should be attempted during the summer when
weather conditions are best. He immediately placed an order for
the new amphibian.

Meanwhile, as the year ended work was completed on the H-1.
Practically all that was left of the original monoplane that had
crashed in the Santa Ana beet field was the basic fuselage. There
was a new fourteen-cylinder Twin Row Wasp engine up front, rated
at 1,100 horsepower; there was a new high speed wing; the original
scarlet paint had given way to blue, yellow and gray. The H-1's
equipment included a newly designed oxygen mask built to
Hughes' specifications: he intended to fly high to take advantage
of the jet stream winds, and two previous failures of the former
oxygen equipment had created problems which Hughes had no intention of having to cope with again.

Normal procedure in grooming a racing plane for its payoff performance calls for several dozen hours of flight tests, but Hughes
had heard that another pilot was readying an aircraft for an at-

tempt on Hughes' still-standing record of nine hours, twenty-seven minutes. Hughes was apparently satisfied that the revamped H-1 was ready to go as it was, and all he waited for now was a favorable weather report from meteorologist Rockefeller.

"I heard that Hughes was planning another cross-country flight in his new plane some day, but he never told us in advance," said Joe Nikrent, an official timer for the National Aeronautic Association. "We had to sense when it would be. So when the phone rang that night I wasn't too surprised. Hughes said, 'Come on out to the airport, Joe, I'm going.' "

Nikrent said he drove to the airport to find Hughes waiting impatiently.

"He said, 'Hello, Joe,' and a few minutes later he said 'Goodbye, Joe.' He was in the air fifteen minutes after I reached the field. I clocked the takeoff and he was gone."

Hughes was airborne at 2:14 A.M. on January 19, 1937, and he climbed rapidly toward the San Bernardino Pass. The following morning, the *New York Times* reported:

All landplane distance speed records were broken yesterday by Howard Hughes, millionaire sportsman pilot, who reached Newark airport 7 hours 28 minutes and 25 seconds after he took off from Los Angeles, Calif. He was then forced to stay aloft until the runway at the field was clear and landed at 1:03 P.M. His average speed was 332 miles an hour for the 2,490 miles he traveled.

The *Times* article described in some depth the familiar elements of a typical Hughes cross-country flight: the radio proved faulty; the oxygen failed again; Hughes came through on dead reckoning; there was the unannounced arrival at Newark. The *Times* said that Hughes "minimized his achievement," but its coverage suggested that, on this occasion, Hughes was not unduly reticent with reporters. Indeed, the *New York Sunday News* was able to add a footnote to the *Times'* exhaustive coverage: "Reporters who met Hughes at Newark Airport after his second transcontinental record-

smashing hop observed that he was wearing the same double-
breasted gray suit he had donned for the flight the year before," the
News said. They asked him if he regarded the raiment as a lucky
talisman.

" 'No-o,' said the flier, whose income is estimated at $2,000,-
000 a year. 'I suppose I'd better get rid of it and get a new one.'

"Hughes' indifference to dress is not an affectation, but a part of
his scheme of life to shun the conspicuous. Shy by nature, his
aloofness is enhanced by defective hearing, the result of an illness
during his childhood. His extraordinary height . . . further alien-
ates him from persons who fail to speak distinctly."

Hughes' seven-and-a-half-hour flight was banner news in the
press in 1937, as well it might have been—for the record stood
until the jet age dawned in the years following Hitler's war. No
doubt the newspapermen would have been even more astonished
had they known that Hughes had been without sleep for thirty
hours before he took off from Los Angeles, but even without this
knowledge the press began to understand that it was in the presence
of a most unusual man for whom the appellation "playboy" was
not a complete description. Nor did he seem to fit the epithet "aviation enthusiast." Gradually "Hughes, the sportsman pilot" became
"Howard Hughes, the speed pilot," and before long the press
would simply say, "Howard Hughes."

He remained in New York City through January, and with
Mayor LaGuardia he officiated at the opening of the National Aviation Show at Grand Central Palace. Then Hughes and several of
his key men slipped off to Bridgeport to act, as it were, as midwives
at the birth of the new Sikorsky amphibian.

Hughes hovered about the factory watching the aircraft come
slowly into shape. He made friends with the Russian mechanics,
and they accepted him. One of them, taking his first look at the
gangling Hughes dressed in greasy overalls and a wrinkled shirt,
looked down at his own apparel and back at Hughes again.

"I may not be a millionaire," he said, "but I can dress like one!"

Such jokes helped, but they did not speed the work. Hughes
chafed as the months began to melt away. He returned to Califor-

nia to see what could be done with the Douglas. He returned to Bridgeport. High summer arrived, and it was obvious that the flying boat would not be ready in July as promised. Disgusted, Hughes abandoned all thought of a world flight in 1937. "We'll have to wait until next year," he told Odekirk.

During all the time that flight was uppermost in Hughes' mind, and many were the hours he devoted to it, Hughes nonetheless remained in control of other ventures. Through Noah Dietrich he followed closely the progress of the Hughes Tool Company; he bought a Texas brewery, and real estate in California, Arizona, New Mexico and Florida; in Hollywood a Hughes staff kept books on the earnings of his films that were still being exhibited in foreign countries; Hughes talent scouts assiduously collected photographs of pretty girls for their employer and at his orders gave certain of them screen tests and took options on their services. Hughes fit all these activities, as well as those of his aircraft company, into the computer of his mind and gave the necessary instructions. He also remained a familiar figure on the golf course and at fashionable restaurants as the escort of Miss Hepburn.

Not until September was the Sikorsky amphibian ready for delivery to Hughes in New York City. It had been tested no more than an hour in the air, but he accepted it. He would put it through its shakedown flight himself, and his idea of a shakedown was to fly it to California, together with a crew. The first leg of the journey ended at Indianapolis, where Hughes put down for the night. Odekirk volunteered to supervise the refueling while Hughes took the rest of the air crew into the city to find them accommodations at the town's leading hotel.

When Odekirk arrived from the airport he asked the hotel clerk for the number of Hughes' room.

"Mr. Hughes?" the clerk asked distantly. He looked through the register. "We don't have a Mr. Hughes," he said.

"That's funny," Odekirk mused. "He said he was going to stay here. Are you sure you don't have a Hughes—a Mr. Howard Hughes?"

The clerk stared at Odekirk in horror.

"You mean that was Howard Hughes—*the* Howard Hughes?" The clerk's hands fluttered helplessly.

"Why, I thought he and his friends were *bums!* I sent them to a flophouse!"

Odekirk laughed and checked in. Then he sought Hughes out and asked him why he had not registered at his original choice of hotels.

"They said they were full," Hughes explained. "How the hell did *you* get in?"

Odekirk said there were other times when Hughes' unprepossessing costume and his reluctance to identify himself did not always work to the millionaire's advantage. For example, Hughes once told him of a solo cross-country flight during which he made an unscheduled landing in a Midwestern city and checked into a hotel. Then he went out into the rainy night to buy a bottle of milk and a box of crackers. The rain was driving down when he started back from the delicatessen, so Hughes took shelter under the awning of a closed garage. The headlamps of a prowl car, lancing through the rain, illuminated a wet, rumpled, unshaved man clutching a brown paper bag, standing anxiously in the doorway of a locked business establishment late at night. Not unnaturally, the policemen demanded his identification. Hughes had none. He had no wallet.

"I'm Howard Hughes," he explained.

"I'm the Grand Duke of Albania," one of the policemen said. "Get in the car, buddy."

So they took him off to the precinct house, where the prisoner with great difficulty persuaded the duty officer to telephone the regional representative of the Hughes Tool Company. The executive hurried downtown, took one fearful look at his discomfited employer and told the police to release Mr. Hughes at once.

On another occasion, Hughes was denied admission to his own aircraft company. He had no pass, and the guard—under orders to admit no one without a pass—refused to believe that the unkempt man before him could possibly be the man who owned the place and paid his wages.

Odekirk delighted in telling these stories in later years. To him the point was that though Hughes was wealthy and famous he never threw his weight around.

What Hughes did throw around, however, was money—money enough to see through to completion any project to which Hughes had committed himself. The usual expensive Hughes modifications began the moment the Sikorsky was trundled into the Burbank hangar. Work proceeded for a few weeks until Hughes learned that the Lockheed Aircraft Company's new transport, the Lodestar, was much faster.

"Hell," Hughes said, looking at the Sikorsky. "If I broke the record in this one, somebody would buy the Lockheed and go out and beat me . . ."

Wherefore Hughes ordered one of the new Lockheeds. It was the third aircraft he had purchased within a year in his search for the best possible plane to carry him around the world.

8

To make a beginning, Howard Hughes drew up a list of two hundred basic items of emergency equipment. Two rifles, for instance: one for stopping dangerous game, in the event of his being attacked by a bear in the Siberian mountains if it so happened that he crash-landed in a region of Siberia infested by bears; a lighter rifle for shooting small game for the pot. There would also have to be tins of canned turkey, concentrated foods, malt tablets, honey and canned pumpernickel. And fishing equipment, medicines and a sun still to convert salt water to fresh. Five parachutes, to each of which would be attached a pack containing iron rations and small radio transmitters. Pingpong balls. Thousands of pingpong balls, to be stuffed into every available empty space in the aircraft to insure at least temporary flotation in the event the Lockheed came down at sea. And life rafts, each with its own radio transmitter. The life raft transmitters themselves posed a problem: how to erect their antennae? Hughes provided two solutions. First he designed a kite to carry an antenna aloft, and spent days on a lake near Los Angeles flying kites. The experiment was a success, but just in case there might be no wind Hughes also included balloons in the life rafts' equipment, with small canisters of helium to inflate the balloons. Then there was the matter of fuel. The plans called for a refueling in Siberia, but Hughes could not count on Russian gasoline available at remote airstrips being the high-octane fuel that his engines required. So he added to his list a supply of tetraethyl lead, to be added to any low-octane gasoline that might be offered him, and he also included 200-mesh copper screens to strain such gasoline of any possible foreign matter.

Few things delight the heart of a man more than making out lists of camping supplies for an intended journey, but to these delights Hughes added other labors of love. The new Lockheed was stripped to its shell, and two 1,200-horsepower Wright engines were installed. Hughes devised a unique dual fuel system to draw upon the outsize fuel tanks that were built. He also found a way to make the fuel tanks self-sealing, by means of wrapping them in neoprene, a compound that had something of the quality of liquid rubber. Modifications of the Lockheed were carried out in a secrecy that would do credit to a modern missile installation.

Hughes was not interested merely in setting a speed record around the world. He wanted to test hundreds of principles of flight; to experiment with new navigational aids and new radio equipment. He wanted a crew of four. From the Army Air Corps he obtained the services of Lieutenant Thomas Thurlow, who was in charge of experiments in aircraft navigation at Wright Field. From the National Broadcasting Company he borrowed Richard Stoddart, a thirty-eight-year-old radio engineer. Another navigator and co-pilot was Harry P. McLean Connor, at thirty-nine the oldest member of the crew and a veteran flyer who had been co-pilot on Captain Erroll Boyd's flight in 1930 from Montreal to London. As mechanic Hughes wanted Glen Odekirk, but he decided that Odekirk could best contribute to the flight by serving as ground crew chief. He asked another old friend, Ed Lund, to serve as the air crew mechanic—Lund having helped on the work with the DC-1 and the Sikorsky.

While the aircraft was being modified, the crewmen—including Hughes—practiced target shooting and rowing, studied jungle survival techniques and techniques of survival at sea. In addition, Hughes was involved with obtaining the necessary licenses, permits, courtesy privileges and clearances from his own and foreign governments. Together with meteorologist Rockefeller, Hughes worked out a flight path around the world. Rockefeller enlisted the help of his foreign colleagues to arrange for a system of weather codes to be transmitted to the aircraft in flight. In addition to his other duties, Rockefeller was instructed to keep Katharine Hepburn informed of each stage of Hughes' journey. Arrangements were made to insure the availability of food and mechanical assistance at each projected stopping place en route; radio operators around the world were asked to help monitor the flight and assist in helping the navigators establish radio lines of bearing. It was discovered that for long stretches of the proposed flight path no accurate maps were available. Hughes and his staff made what educated guesses they could.

Hughes obtained the most advanced radio transceiver built to date—actually three radios in one. Four specially designed compasses were installed with a view to checking and double-checking course and position. A new Sperry automatic pilot was added—a device that could fly the plane while pilots slept. The Federal Communications Commission assigned thirty wave bands to the aircraft for its flight, varying from a long wave of 333 to a short wave of 22,000 kilocycles. Ships sailing the Atlantic were notified to assist the Lockheed in taking its bearings; the plan was for the aircraft to take a radio bearing on a ship and another on a radio station in England, with the resulting intersection of the lines establishing a positive fix.

Months went into the drawing of plans and the rebuilding of the Lockheed; months of stress analysis and of test flying; of calibrating fuel consumption at various altitudes at various speeds with various payloads; months of working with the new navigation and radio equipment. Seven months were required to ready the crew and the aircraft for the flight. Closely guarded as was the Hughes Aircraft Company's area, no project of such proportions could be kept entirely secret, and toward the end of the preparations the news leaked out.

"Is Hughes Planning World Flight?" one newspaper headline asked, and the story beneath it implied that yes, he was. "Look Out World—Here Comes Hughes!" another headline more forthrightly said. Hughes himself gave the press short shrift. He issued terse denials. He had "no comment." "We may fly to New York someday," he told reporters. Badgered further, he admitted that he was "considering" a flight from New York to Paris. The reporters added these fragments together and wrote that Hughes was not planning to fly to Paris, but around the world. Then it was announced in New York that Hughes had been persuaded to serve as aeronautical director of the forthcoming 1939 New York World's Fair; in fact, his airplane would be named *New York World's Fair, 1939;* he was, indeed, planning a world flight which, among other things, would advertise the Fair.

At this point the nation's newspapers published biographies of Hughes. The stories emphasized his wealth and dwelt on those aspects of Hughes that most suggested the daredevil, the sportsman, the playboy and the lover. They were illustrated with photographs of beautiful women reputed to have been his friends. Whether he welcomed it or not, Hughes most certainly had the attention of the press, but then, in 1938, when aviation was in its lusty adolescence, flying around the world was hardly the path to obscurity.

On July 7, all was ready; the Lockheed flew to New York for a scheduled takeoff the following day. A crowd of several hundred waited for the plane at Floyd Bennett Field, and they saw Hughes brusquely, almost rudely, brush reporters aside.

"Not now," he kept saying, as he strode across the tarmac from the airplane into a hangar office and closed the door. The Lockheed was brought into the hangar and the metal doors clanged shut. There, away from the curious and the well-wishers, Hughes, Odekirk and Lund began to give the aircraft a thorough inspection.

"The cylinders," Lund said. "Take a look."

Hughes looked. The cylinders had been badly pitted.

"Take them out and put new ones in," he said, knowing as he gave the order that there would be no takeoff on Friday, July 8, as scheduled. The repairs could not possibly be completed in a day; the *World's Fair* could not depart until Saturday morning at the earliest. Hughes and his men worked through the night. Just before dawn Hughes slipped away for a brief rest at a New York hotel. By midmorning he was back at the field where crowds were beginning to gather. By noon it was apparent that there would be no Saturday takeoff, either; at four P.M. he sent word to the reporters clamoring outside the locked hangar that he was now planning to depart on

Sunday. Still the crowds gathered, and on Saturday night they arrived with sleeping bags; they pitched tents on adjacent fields,
spread picnic lunches and slept in shifts so as not to be surprised
by any sudden takeoff.

Hughes spent that Saturday night working on the Lockheed and
at dawn he told the reporters, "It now looks like we'll get off about
three o'clock this afternoon." Whereupon the reporters groaned.
Some wondered if he would ever leave. What they did not wholly
understand was that Hughes was an exhausting perfectionist. He
had taken out heavy life insurance policies on his crew. He refused
to gamble on there being the tiniest defect in his airplane.

As Sunday wore on the crowds grew larger. Hughes and his crew
left the field at one point to take a brief rest, and this led to a rumor
that the flight had been called off. While those in the crowd asked
one another if this were true, Hughes drove to Manhattan to telephone Miss Hepburn. (The next day, gossip columnists reported
that Hughes had broken away from the airport in order to hold a
tender goodbye rendezvous with Miss Hepburn.)

In the late afternoon a new trouble developed. The starboard
motor suddenly refused to function, and Lund's diagnosis was a
faulty magneto. A new magneto was hurriedly furnished by the
Wright Aeronautical Company which, because it was Sunday, had
to locate its storeroom manager, and send him to their warehouse
and then to the airport. It was six P.M. before all was ready. Hughes
hastily scanned the latest weather map prepared by Rockefeller,
tossed it aside, summoned his crew and said "Let's go."

But he had forgotten something. Grover Whalen, the distin-
guished-looking clotheshorse who was New York's official greeter
of distinguished citizens, and who was also president of the World's
Fair, and New York City's Mayor Fiorello La Guardia, each
wished to say several thousand words. Neither shared Howard
Hughes' view of the press. On the way to the microphones Mr.
Whalen turned to Hughes and said, "Wish I could go with you."
Hughes ignored him.

"It gives me great pleasure to participate in this formal step in a
dramatic and glorious undertaking," Mr. Whalen began, when the

newsreel cameras were ready. He turned to Hughes. "In a few moments, you and your companions will be taking off on your flight to Paris. You have with you all the factors that make for success—your own skill and daring, courageous companions, equipment that is mechanically perfect, and plans that have been wisely laid and carefully put into action."

Mr. Whalen paused.

"Your flight," Mr. Whalen began again, "will remind the world of the good will and understanding that has long existed between great democratic nations. It will further cement deep rooted . . ."

Mr. Whalen and the Mayor were beaming, and the crowd was applauding; the speeches were over. But now it was Hughes' turn to say something to the multitude. He stepped forward and in a strained, high voice began to read from a paper that had been prepared for him:

"We hope that our flight may prove a contribution to the cause of friendship between nations and that through their outstanding fliers, for whom the common bond of aviation transcends national boundaries, this cause may be furthered. We are glad to bear invitations from the New York World's Fair, 1939, to these fliers, for we feel that they understand that with the development of air transportation, increased communication will further international cooperation and friendship.

"It is particularly fitting that you should have christened our ship the *New York World's Fair, 1939* inasmuch as the purpose of the Fair and this flight is to further international peace and progress."

He spoke at a time when it was obvious to a child that international peace and cooperation were wistful dreams, and that in no case could an advertising venture for a commercial fair help to make such dreams come true. So Hughes hurried through the conventional claptrap, and then put the paper aside to speak his mind:

"I want to apologize to the newspapermen and photographers if I seemed rude and impolite last night and this morning. I had received favorable weather reports and had only the thought of hopping on my mind. I did not mean to be rude or impolite, and I want to apologize right now."

With that the press broke into its only applause of the day, while Hughes turned to ask an aide whether ten pounds of freshly prepared ham, cheese and tomato sandwiches had been put aboard as he had requested. Lieutenant Thurlow embraced his pretty wife and small son, and Mrs. Connor broke through the police cordon around the airplane to stick a thick wad of chewing gum on the tail.

"For good luck!" she called to her husband. "Be sure and bring it back safe to me! You, too!"

At thirteen seconds past 7:19 P.M., the silver monoplane's twin engines began to pull it slowly—agonizingly slowly, it must have seemed to Hughes—and then more rapidly—but not rapidly enough, it seemed—down the airfield's longest runway. There was a question in everyone's mind whether it would, in fact, lift off. Hughes had tested the plane with a 24,000-pound load in California, but he was now carrying 1,600 pounds more than that, plus 10 pounds of last-minute sandwiches and a wad of chewing gum. The takeoff used the whole length of the runway, and the Lockheed's wheels clipped the tops of the red clover at the south end of the field before the *World's Fair* was airborne. The crowd watched until it disappeared, low over Jamaica Bay.

At 8:26 P.M. Boston tower reported Hughes overhead; by 9:55 Nova Scotia was sliding under the Lockheed's wings. At 10:30 P.M. the first broadcast from an aircraft in flight was heard over the nation's radio networks, and Katharine Hepburn in Connecticut was one of millions of Americans who heard Stoddart's voice enter the living room from the skies over Newfoundland.

"The flight is progressing smoothly," Stoddart said. "The weather is clear, but we cannot see anything below us because of a cloud cover. Mr. Hughes is busy right now, but he will be able to say something a little later."

What radioman Stoddart did not say was that Mr. Hughes was worrying about his fuel consumption. Perhaps because of its extra load or because of adjustments to the engines, the ship was using far more gasoline than anyone had anticipated. Hughes was also busily trying to get in touch with Odekirk, who at that moment

after three days and nights of steady work had gotten a police escort to a Manhattan hotel and was walking wearily through the
lobby on his way to bed. A Hughes aide rushed up to him and
said:

"They want you back at flight headquarters at the World's Fair.
Something terrible has happened. Mr. Hughes is trying to get you."

Odekirk's weary face went white. Police motorcycle sirens
carved a path through midtown traffic for Odekirk's car as he was
whisked back to the headquarters office where the static of radios
filled the room. Hughes' voice came to him out of the ether. Nothing serious had happened. Hughes wanted Odekirk to stay by the
radio for the duration of the flight, just in case anything did. So a
cot was brought in and the weary man at length fell asleep, perhaps
dreaming about aircraft and the sometimes exasperating men who
flew them.

Meanwhile, out over the Atlantic, Hughes drank milk and told
his crew to rest. They catnapped for half hours, stretched out on
the aircraft's metal floor, but Hughes continued to sit at the controls. At 2:30 A.M. Monday, Stoddart called the radio networks,
and America heard Hughes' voice for the first time.

"I hope we can get to Paris before we run out of gas," Hughes
said, "but I am not so sure. All I can do is hope that we will get
there. I hope that we will have enough gas to reach land. I am
throttling back the engines as fast as the reducing load permits."

On that cheerless note, he signed off.

In New York newspaper editors prepared bulletins stating that
Hughes was down at sea. These bulletins would be used on the
front pages of extra editions if the word came that Hughes was
going down. Reluctantly, the editors put their last regular morning
editions to bed, afraid that the plane would be in the ocean before
the papers hit the streets.

9

Far out over the North Atlantic the Lockheed picked up a brisk tail wind that blew it to Ireland at a great—and badly needed—saving of fuel. There were more than a hundred gallons of gasoline aboard as the island swung beneath the aircraft's port wing; enough to continue to Paris as planned. Lieutenant Thurlow gave Hughes a course heading and an estimated time of arrival at Le Bourget airfield, and Hughes happily radioed ahead for landing instructions.

Because the Lockheed flew east while the sun sped west, it was early Monday evening in Paris when the silver monoplane touched down just sixteen hours and thirty-five minutes after leaving New York. It was a new record for the New York-Paris flight; two hours better than the most recent record and roughly half Lindbergh's original time.

And because it was early evening in Paris thousands of the curious were waiting at the airfield to welcome the Texas millionaire, along with dignitaries of Paris and United States Ambassador to France William C. Bullitt. Mr. Bullitt, together with his military and air attachés, ran to greet Hughes.

"Congratulations!" Mr. Bullitt said. "Did you have a good trip?"

"We had a good flight," Hughes said. He turned to his crew. "We'll allow two hours here," he told them, as if Paris was nothing more than a filling station at which one must stop in the course of a long trip. He started to walk toward the terminal building.

But it was Lund, again, who called Hughes' attention to a problem. The mechanic pointed to ominous wrinkles in the aircraft's metal skin near the tail assembly. Hughes immediately knew what had happened. On takeoff in New York, as he had turned the plane from taxiway to runway, the tail wheel had slipped off the pavement into soft earth and the resulting jolt had buckled several of the metal structural members of the fuselage. Hughes and Lund climbed back aboard and crawled into the narrow area aft to inspect the damage. Outside the aircraft French mechanics looked at the wrinkled skin and shrugged.

"*C'est fini,*" one of them said, demonstrating a Gallic fatalism with respect to the mysteries of machinery and a serious underestimation of American make-do.

But Lund, with a United States Army sergeant from the Embassy staff, very shortly procured a quantity of angle irons from a nearby hangar and began bolting them inside the fuselage to carry the stress forward to undamaged structural members of the airframe. It was slow work. The rest of the air crew took advantage of the delay to sleep, but Hughes went to the terminal restaurant where he ate a lamb chop and a bowl of French-fried potatoes and refused continually offered glasses of champagne. He glanced through a sheaf of congratulatory telegrams and made a long-distance telephone call to Miss Hepburn, but failed to reach her.

Reporters milled about asking whether the trip would be called off. Some of them filed stories saying that the trip was a fiasco, despite Hughes' having broken the transatlantic record between New York and Paris. Hughes refused to talk to any of them. He maintained his brooding silence throughout the eight hours that elapsed while the repairs were being made. When Lund finally announced that all was ready, reporters dogged Hughes all the way to the airplane.

"When will you get to Moscow?" one of them asked.

Hughes regarded the man bleakly, and spoke for the first time.

"I don't know," he said.

He climbed into the aircraft and the door shut behind him.

As the Lockheed climbed through a thick cloud layer, Le Bourget tower had this to say: "Be most careful in landing at Moscow. Your left wheel is damaged." A check was made, and Stoddart reported, "There is nothing to worry about. It looks like a normal condition which was very much enlarged upon by someone who didn't quite understand the situation." But there was something else to worry about. The original route would have taken the plane directly over Germany into Russia. Just prior to leaving New York, however, Hughes was told that the German government had reconsidered and demanded that Hughes follow an alternate route over Scandinavia instead. The Germans, busily arming themselves for another Teutonic migration into their neighbors' territories, did not want a foreign aircraft flying over their military installations. Hughes, having lost eight hours in Paris fiddling with angle irons, was in no mood to pay the slightest attention to Hitler's notion that he should waste more time touring Scandinavia. So he steered across the German border, and there was an immediate angry chattering in his radio headset. The most frequently used and familiar word was *Verboten*.

"Ah, it's dark," Hughes muttered. "We're not going to see anything, and I don't think they'll shoot us down."

It was not only dark, but Hughes was flying blind. Shortly past midnight Hughes radioed back to New York, "As far as we can see, everything is okay.

"We have picked up speed and are now traveling at two hundred twenty miles an hour. Our altitude is thirteen thousand three hundred feet. We are traveling over solid banks of clouds that come right up to the plane. When we get into them, they cover the plane with ice, so we must try to stay above them. We have been flying entirely by instruments. In fact, we have not seen the ground since we left Paris. We were flying on instruments before we completed the turn out of the airfield."

The next news that America heard of the flight came in thick, excited accents: "Hello, hello America! This is Radio Moscow! It is 4:10 A.M. here and Hughes just went around the field and is making a landing!"

The roar of a crowd threatened to drown out the broadcaster, but he shouted above it.

"The plane is landing! What a beauty it is! The people are storming him now! They simply won't let him go! We can't get him to the microphone!"

Hughes was pushing through a sea of exuberant Muscovites that included three Russian flyers who had established a long-distance record in pioneering a transpolar flight from Moscow to the United States: Andrey Yumasheff, Georgi Baidukoff and Mikhail Gromoff. A Russian soldier saw on the tail of the aircraft the red star that was the Lockheed trademark, and was reported by the Moscow press to have said, "Look, they fly under the red star! That will bring them luck. It is fine to show Fascist vultures that we democracies fly better than they." And Hughes was reported to have said, "Please refuel as quickly as possible. We would like to leave in twenty minutes."

The Russians were just as anxious for Hughes to stay a while. They had planned a tour of Moscow for him, an elaborate feast, and a suite of rooms in the best hotel was reserved for him. They had even obtained American corn flakes for his breakfast. Inside the airport building Hughes passed up the vodka and the caviar that were offered him, accepting black bread and cheese instead. Pilot Gromoff talked briefly with Hughes about flying conditions and the repairs that had been made in Paris, and then, loudly, with a significant look at the newspaper reporters, said, "I know what long flights mean, and so none of us will bother you any more."

Gromoff took the reporters outside to look at Hughes' airplane. "What a plane!" he told them. "More than two hundred miles an hour the whole way, with five people aboard and all that load of gasoline and equipment."

It was two hours, not twenty minutes, before Hughes could decently escape the well-meant enthusiasm of the Russians and fight his way back through the crowds to his airplane. He and his crew declined a parting gift of a huge jar of caviar, but accepted instead a case of mineral water.

Airborne for Omsk, Hughes for the first time stretched out on the cabin floor to sleep. Twenty minutes later he woke up refreshed and took over the controls. An hour before the Lockheed's estimated arrival time at Omsk, thirteen hundred miles east of Moscow, they were flying in a thick night of driving rain. The ground was not visible, but by now Stoddart had obtained a bearing on the

Omsk radio station with his directional radio compass. Flying down this line, they saw red lights flickering in the murk below. It was difficult to believe the lights marked the approaches to the Omsk airfield. An hour early in all this weather? Could the instruments, the radio compass, be in error? But the only airfield for hundreds of miles around was that of Omsk, and Hughes let down toward the lights. The field proved to be little more than a cow pasture whose rainy darkness was illuminated by the headlights of a few automobiles parked around the field. Hughes anxiously put the aircraft down on a grass landing strip and came to a halt near a handful of wet but excited citizens.

Gasoline for the aircraft was stacked along the grass runway in fifty-gallon drums. Some of the drums had fallen over; their plugs had come out, and the gasoline had poured out on the ground. Hughes and his crewmen broke open their containers of tetraethyl lead and added it to the low-grade Russian gasoline in the remaining drums. By this time it was forty-two hours since departure from New York, and the first word that New York had of Hughes' presence in Omsk came when Hughes radioed to Odekirk for help. Where had they put the box containing the gasoline strainers? Odekirk told his distant employer to look among the life rafts and the pingpong balls, and the refueling proceeded by hand pump. Four hours later the flight was once more airborne, heading out through a storm at night across the steppes, bound for Yakutsk by way of Krasnoyarsk and Kansk. They reached Yakutsk just as dawn broke, and the Siberians who met them there were puzzled by the legend *New York World's Fair, 1939* painted on the fuselage.

"They thought that we were living in 1939, while they were still in 1938," Lund said. "They wondered how we had gained a year on them."

A chain of mountains lies across the route from Yakutsk to Fairbanks, Alaska, and according to the maps Hughes carried, these mountains were sixty-five hundred feet high. Hughes had planned to fly at eighty-five hundred feet to be certain of clearing them. On approaching the mountains at that altitude, however,

Hughes was astonished to see them towering above him. Either his altimeter was wrong or the map was wrong, but in any case an immediate climb was the first order of business. Hughes climbed five hundred feet higher, and still the mountain crests rose before him. Not until he reached eleven thousand feet was it certain that he would clear the range, and during the climb Hughes had time to reflect upon the hours spent at the Paris airport. Had the trip proceeded exactly on schedule, he would have been flying this leg of the trip at night instead of in broad daylight. At eighty-five hundred feet he would have flown at two hundred miles an hour into the face of a Siberian cliff. Moodily Hughes jotted notations on his map as he steered out across the Bering Sea and saw, at these latitudes, both the sun and moon appear in the same quadrant of the heavens. Twelve hours and sixteen minutes out of Yakutsk the *World's Fair, 1939* touched down at Fairbanks, where Mrs. Wiley Post, widow of the flier whose record Hughes was breaking, was one of the crowd that welcomed the now bone-weary air crew. Hughes warmly shook her hand and expressed his admiration for Post's historic feat. "I wish you Godspeed," Mrs. Post said through her tears.

Since there were no more oceans to cross, the Lockheed was stripped of its life rafts and survival equipment while mechanics refueled the tanks. A sack of pingpong balls was thrown out of the baggage compartment and broke open on striking the runway. For a moment all work stopped as Fairbanks natives scrambled after little white bouncing souvenirs. With this excitement over, reporters returned to Hughes, who, gaunt, bearded and obviously tired, kept saying, "I'm sorry, but we can't talk now. We must get back into the air."

A study of the weather maps at Fairbanks indicated storms ahead, so two cities were selected for the next refueling; if weather closed the route to one, Hughes would try the other. Accordingly, Winnipeg and St. Paul were each advised to expect Hughes. Two hours out of Fairbanks a tracking station at Hermosa Beach, California, picked up a message from Hughes saying that he would land

at Winnipeg, and the Canadian city made hasty plans for a public
reception. Crowds began to gather at the Winnipeg airport. Meanwhile Hughes had run into heavy weather and altered course for
Minneapolis while failing to advise Winnipeg of his change in plan.
When the plane was long overdue in Winnipeg, plans were made to
send out a search party. Then Minneapolis broadcast the news that
Hughes had paid an unexpected visit to their city and half an hour
later had taken off for New York.

Hailstones big as walnuts bombarded the *New York World's
Fair, 1939* as it passed over Minnesota. "For a few bad moments,
we thought the plane was going to shake itself to death," Lund
said. "We had to lower the speed to almost stalling to keep it from
falling apart." But the aircraft struggled through the cold front that
hung over the Great Lakes, and gave New York's Floyd Bennett
tower an estimated time of arrival. Half an hour from final touchdown, Hughes received a message from the field that an orderly
reception awaited him.

"You are in no danger of being mobbed," the message said.

Even as these words were spoken, more than twenty-five thousand men, women and children were trying to wedge their way into
the airport. When the silver monoplane roared low over the administration building three days, nineteen hours and eight minutes after
its original takeoff—after having halved the record flight for a trip
around the world—Hughes could look out his cockpit window and
prepare himself for the worst. The borders of the airfield were
black with people. People lined the runway he was to use, and on
the tarmac in front of the administration building was the densest
crowd of all, pushing about the central space where the hero of the
hour would no doubt be met by the usual politicians who would
thereupon proceed to drown him in flood of self-seeking oratory.

Hughes swung away on a wide circle around the field, let down
his landing gear, let down his flaps and, with a sudden dip, dived
down to earth. He landed on a runway at a far side of the field, well
away from the administration building where the throng was waiting. He killed the engines and wiped his forehead. He sat wearily in

the cockpit and listened to the fire engine sirens screaming and the bells clanging welcome and heard the crowd's deep shout and saw them running toward him across the airfield; Grover Whalen was lumbering and panting ahead of Mayor La Guardia.

10

Hughes was the first man out of the plane. One reporter said he looked like "a naughty child in his soiled shirt and rumped trousers." The *New York Times* said Hughes had "the face of a poet and the shyness of a schoolboy." The photographs show a tall, tired man wearing a four-day beard, a nondescript suit, an old brown fedora and a look of utter emptiness. It was, perhaps, the look of a man who well understood the truth of the adage, "It is better to travel than to arrive."

Grover Whalen had worked out a carefully timed program of welcome. First he, Whalen, would speak, then the Mayor. Following this, Hughes was to place a wreath of lilies on the concrete star that marked the place where Wiley Post's aircraft had stopped after Post's solo flight in 1933. Then Hughes was to step into an adjacent circus tent where a press conference would be held. But nothing went according to plan. There were eleven hundred policemen on the field, but rather than keeping order in the crowd, they seemed to want to see the hero too. So the police came crowding around, mixed in with the frantic, shoving mob of the curious. In the tumult, newspaper reporters and cameramen elbowed their way toward Hughes, shouting at him and grabbing at his coat. To Hughes their voices became one voice that beat at him from every side:

"Hey, Howard, did ya almost crash on the way to Paris?"

"Howie! . . . This way! Look over here!"

"Hey Hughes, take off your hat!"

"Naw, ya jerk, that's his lucky hat. Leave it on, Howard!"

"Hey, Howard, when you gonna see Katharine Hepburn? You gonna see her tonight, hey, Howie?"

"What did the Russians say?"

"Did you have any trouble?" Grover Whalen shouted at him.

"No," Hughes said.

Mayor La Guardia had meanwhile recovered his wind, and practiced politician that he was, he used it to quiet all others.

"Seven million New Yorkers offer congratulations for the greatest record established in the history of aviation," La Guardia declaimed. "Welcome home!"

A microphone was thrust at Hughes, and he began to speak.

"Louder, Howard!" a reporter shouted.

"Shut up!" another said. "He's trying to say something!"

"I am ever so much honored. Thank you very much," Hughes said.

"Is that all you're gonna say?" one reporter asked.

"On behalf of the World's Fair," Grover Whalen said, moving quickly to the microphone, "we are proud to honor this greatest flight. We are proud of you and so is the world of aviation. See you tomorrow to return the compliments of the Mayor—parade tomorrow!"

Police at last established a cordon to escort the exhausted Hughes and his crew to the press tent. As the crowd surged away with them, Mrs. Connor found her opportunity to reclaim her wad of chewing gum from the airplane's tail.

The press tent, it seemed, was already thickly populated by people from New Jersey, taxi drivers, crying children and excited housewives who wished to see for themselves the world flyer who was also Katharine Hepburn's boy friend. Hughes was now openly angry. He and his men were pushed and hauled about while reporters shouted questions and photographers literally climbed on people, on each other and in one case, on top of a policeman, to fire their flashbulbs. It was ninety degrees inside the tent, and sweat ran down Hughes' dirty face onto his dirty shirt. In the midst of this bedlam, Hughes answered the questions as well as he could.

"Howard, what do you feel was accomplished by this trip?"

"I don't know," he said.

"What was the highlight of your trip?"

"When some of the photographers got ahold of me back there."

"Are you hungry, Howard?"

"Not especially."

"What did you eat on the flight?"

"Oh, anything."

"What's one thing?"

"Mostly canned goods. When we were hungry we would open a can and eat. It wasn't so good, but better than nothing."

"Would you go around the world again?"

"Why?"

"Would you do it again? I mean, *fly* around the world?"

"No," Hughes said, meaning it.

Grover Whalen interrupted the questioning to suggest that before everyone collapsed from the heat, the meeting should adjourn to his Manhattan home, where reporters would be admitted on presentation of their press credentials. Obviously the members of the public who had crowded into the press tent were making it difficult for Mr. Hughes and for the gentlemen of the press. Hughes found himself propelled toward a glittering black limousine. He sank back against the thick upholstery and closed his eyes. People hammered on the sides of the car and against its windows as it nosed through the crowds. In the confusion he had been unable to place the wreath on Post's memorial. He had also failed to receive an important telephone message: Miss Hepburn had called the airport and left her number.

On arrival at Whalen's town house Hughes withdrew to take a shower while Whalen's Chinese manservant was dispatched to buy Hughes a size 15½ white dress shirt. Half an hour later, during which time Hughes telephoned Miss Hepburn to explain what was happening to him, he came downstairs to meet the press in the new white shirt. He had not yet shaved.

As the reporters asked their questions, Hughes walked back and forth between the fawn-colored living room and the French blue study. He declined a plate of Sherry's chicken salad and a bourbon highball. There were a number of women reporters present, and each of them seemed to have a question about Miss Hepburn.

"Nothing ever felt as good as this clean shirt," Hughes said.

"When are you going to see Miss Hep . . ."

"No space for a change of anything on the plane," Hughes said. "We took only our toothbrushes with us."

Hughes told the photographers to put away their cameras until after he had shaved. He sank into an overstuffed chair and said he would answer questions limited to the flight itself.

"What do you think is the greatest significance of the flight, Mr. Hughes?"

"I was not out to beat any record," Hughes replied. "But I was anxious to find out just how well the new equipment worked. Now we know. I've got forty pages of notes on everything that happened. I even drew a map of the northern coast of Siberia. The Coast Guard maps are all wrong."

"What are you happiest about right now?"

"I proved to myself that my route was the best route to this country from Moscow," Hughes said. "And it's a good thing I didn't try to fly out of Yakutsk at night. The maps we had show mountains of sixty-five hundred feet. We measured mountains at ninety-seven hundred feet, and they were covered with snow."

Someone asked about Wiley Post's flight.

Hughes sat forward and spoke clearly, with careful emphasis.

"Wiley Post's solo flight remains the most remarkable flight in history," he said. "It can never be duplicated. He did it alone. To make a trip of that kind is beyond comprehension. It's like pulling a rabbit out of a hat or sawing a woman in half."

Questioned about his aircraft, Hughes said that it had performed beautifully, that "we didn't even have to change a spark plug." But the women reporters were not interested in spark plugs. They had in mind a recently printed account of an interview that a reporter claimed to have had with Miss Hepburn, in the course of which the actress was asked what fascination Howard Hughes held for her.

"Simple," she was reported to have said. "I happen to love this man."

But what about all those other women? What would Miss Hepburn do if she caught him in a dalliance?

"I would kill him," Miss Hepburn was reported to have said.

So the women reporters at Mr. Whalen's house wanted to know what Hughes' intentions were with respect to Miss Hepburn. Hughes replied that it was time for his crew to answer questions about the flight. When the press was at last ushered out the door, Hughes looked out the window to watch them leave and saw another crowd outside.

"We'll fix that," Whalen said, leading the four crewmen down a back stairs and putting them in separate cars. Unfortunately, reporters followed the cars to the crew's quarters at Hampshire House on Central Park South. Hughes managed to slip from Whalen's house on foot when the crowd dispersed, and after walking several blocks hailed a cab and gave the driver Miss Hepburn's New York address. But there was another cluster of newsmen waiting outside the actress' town house. Hughes ducked down in the cab and told the driver to take him to the Hotel Drake, where Hughes brushed through a crowd in the lobby, curtly told the hotel's manager that he was "dead tired and going straight to bed," gave orders that no telephone calls were to be put through to his room, went upstairs, hung a "Do Not Disturb" sign on his door and telephoned Miss Hepburn.

One might suppose that a man who had just spent four grueling days flying around the world, and who had endured such an exhausting welcome home, and who had slept perhaps a total of eight hours in the entire past week might collapse on the bed and sleep the clock around. But Hughes did not unwind. Gossip columnists the next day reported that he had slipped out of the hotel and off to Long Island with Katharine Hepburn. But what Hughes actually did was eat a light supper in his hotel room, and, still awake at 2:30 A.M., he telephoned his flight manager, Al Lodwick, apologized for waking him and asked Lodwick to come to the hotel.

The two men talked until four in the morning. It seemed that Hughes was irritated by widely published reports that his flight had cost him $300,000.

"You know that ship only cost sixty thousand dollars and the gas didn't cost anything," Hughes told Lodwick. "The Standard Oil people supplied it all, and the motors are mine. The Wright people gave them to me, and I'm going to keep them. If this three-hundred-thousand-dollar figure keeps going out, nobody will try experimental flying."

Lodwick regarded his employer with amazement. Apparently Hughes had conveniently forgotten his purchase of two airplanes other than the Lockheed and the thousands upon thousands of dollars spent on equipment and supplies, to say nothing of the thousands spent on salaries of air crew, ground crew and the staff of Hughes' New York flight headquarters.

When Lodwick left Hughes made several telephone calls, including one to Floyd Bennett Field to learn whether his airplane was safe. The hotel night manager, seeing on the switchboard the evidence of Hughes' activity, called to ask whether anything was wrong. Another room, perhaps? A different bed? Well, then, was there anything Mr. Hughes wanted? Valet? Barber? Food? Everything was fine, Hughes said. He said a shave wouldn't help him sleep. At six A.M., however, he did call room service for milk and cake. As the sun rose on what was to be his day of triumph in America's imperial city, Hughes finally fell asleep.

11

New York City's Manhattan Island is a curious place in a great many respects. One of the customs of its diurnal population is to bombard a hero with trash. The number of tons of waste paper hurled at a man from high buildings is regarded as the measure of the city's respect for the fellow, and so it is that after each Manhattan parade the press anxiously consults the Sanitation Department to discover where the hero of the moment stands with respect to heroes of the past in the city's affections.

In 1938, one city official, carried away by the welcome accorded Howard Hughes, cried out, "It's bigger than Lindbergh!"

Then more cautiously, as becomes an elected politician, he said, "Or at least as big."

The official need not have been afraid. His first instinct was correct. The Sanitation Department subsequently reported that eighteen hundred tons of paper was thrown at Hughes; Lindbergh received only sixteen hundred tons.

These New York welcomes are locally called ticker-tape parades, but more kinds of paper than tapes torn from stock market reporting machines are used as confetti. Leaves torn from telephone directories are employed, as are shreds of newspaper, rolls of toilet paper and wastebaskets full of business correspondence. A certain amount of paper streamers and colored confetti is actually sold on these occasions, but for the most part the paper blizzard, as the newspapers like to call it, is composed of finely torn trash. To be sure, it is difficult to distinguish from among the celebrants those genuinely moved by an emotional sympathy for the hero and those who, having very little else to do in their New York offices, are glad of an opportunity to throw something out the window. But it must be admitted that gross tonnages of trash are indicators of a directly proportional notoriety among the publicly acclaimed. Judging therefore by the gross aspects of his reception, Howard Hughes was clearly what one New York tabloid called him: Public Hero Number One.

Having enjoyed three hours of sleep, the hero rose at nine and ordered a large breakfast. This consumed, he set about to remove his heavy beard. At eleven, he gave thought to the fact that his only suit was wrinkled and splotched with engine oil and sent a messenger to procure him another. He had no comb, so a bellboy was dispatched to buy him one. At a few minutes past noon—the parade was to have begun at noon—he was driven to Hampshire House where his crew awaited him. Hughes had insisted that if he was to be given a parade, then his entire crew and staff must share it with him, including the dozens of mechanics, meteorologists and office staff whose labors on the ground conspired to help put him in the air and send him around the world.

Yet, as the *New York Times* reported, it was Hughes and Hughes alone that the Manhattan crowds wished to see. The object of their curiosity seemed ill-at-ease. As the procession began, his expression resembled a scowl of discomfort or possibly of fright. He frequently bit at his lower lip and bowed or ducked his head. The crowds yelled and the trash fell and Grover Whalen, who enjoyed this sort of thing, climbed to sit atop the rear seat of the open touring car, beaming and waving to the multitude and beckoning Hughes to join him on his perch. Hughes allowed himself to be persuaded, and he removed the well-worn brown fedora that newspapermen called his lucky hat, but which was simply his hat. He passed it from hand to hand, as if uncertain what to do with it now that it was no longer on his head. Whalen waved and smiled to everyone while Hughes sat beside him with his hat in his hands, the picture of a man who would very much rather have been almost anywhere else instead.

But as the procession turned into Broadway and the cheering echoed in the street and the paper came swirling down, Hughes'

mood changed. He tried a tentative little wave, and people waved
joyously back. Hughes cheered up. Gradually, he seemed to understand that here in the streets and leaning from high windows were a
great many total strangers who wished to be his friends; who, if
only for a moment, wanted him to know they wished him well.
Even if their joy was nothing more than a manifestation of the
general air of jollity that surrounds a parade, nevertheless he and
they were bound up with one another, and perhaps he owed them
something. So Hughes waved and they waved and shouted back,
and at last the fedora fell unnoticed to the floor. For the first time
Hughes smiled wholeheartedly and really waved to the crowds. The
role of returned hero was, it seemed, a happy one; easy to play.
Encouraged, the crowds at many points broke through police lines
to rush to the side of the car, trying to touch him—a phenomenon
familiar to kings and Caesars—and Hughes good-naturedly
reached out to shake hands. It was an incredible gesture for anyone
with Hughes' profound dislike of mob scenes, but somehow
Hughes and the multitude were strangers to one another no longer.
Rather, they were each celebrants of a mystery, and Hughes smiled
and reached out his hand, and confetti fell in his hair and streamers
coiled around his shoulders and he actually laughed when a large
bundle of torn-up telephone directory pages came sailing out of the
sky to land in his lap.

The procession reached City Hall where, in a hot, crowded
council room, Mayor La Guardia made a speech. Jesse Jones made
a speech. Mr. Jones was, like Hughes, a Texas multimillionaire,
and he said that he had recognized Hughes' promise long ago, when
he saw Hughes as a child, banging away on a piece of scrap iron at
the back of a tool shop. It seemed as if everyone else in that hot
council room also made a speech, until the floor was waist-deep in
adjectives. At last it was Hughes' turn, and what he had to say was
intended to restore a sense of perspective.

"I haven't a great deal to say about this," he began, "because I
am afraid I might get a little nervous and not say just what I want
to. However, I haven't it all, because the newspapermen took about
half of it away from me. I will just have to do the best I can. At

least you may be assured that no one has written this for me but myself."

There was a smattering of laughter, and Hughes looked up, surprised.

"I am not very good at making speeches," he explained, "and I have consented to make this one only because there is one thing about this flight that I would like everyone to know. It was in no way a stunt. It was the carrying out of a careful plan, and it functioned because it was carefully planned."

He said that any airline or military flight crew could have done the same thing, that "all we did was to operate this equipment and plane according to the instruction book accompanying the article."

The crowd laughed delightedly.

"The most advanced and newest equipment developed by navigators and radio engineers furnished me with such accurate information as to the position of the plane at all times that I estimate for the total trip we traveled only twenty miles more than a direct course between the various points at which we stopped," he said. "The airplane was fast because it was the product of over two hundred thousand engineering hours. Young men trained mostly at the California Institute of Technology, working in a factory in California, put in two hundred thousand hours of concentrated thought to develop that machine. Flying at all times at the altitude which was most favorable to the operation of the plane with the load aboard at that particular time—the load naturally varying continually as the fuel was consumed—and using the amount of horsepower at all times which would give the greatest range, we completed this flight without at any time using more than 590 horsepower of the 625 horsepower per engine approved by the Department of Commerce for normal cruising. In other words, this was in no way a race or a straining of the machine or its engines. The airlines of this country, using those same motors, cruise frequently at 625 horsepower.

"There is one thing about the flight which pleases me more than the actual time which elapsed. That is the fact that we made no unscheduled stops; we arrived at every destination within a few minutes of the time which we set as our arrival time."

Hughes went on to say he hoped his flight would help to create international cooperation among all those concerned with aviation; that it would restore to the United States some of the prestige it had lost when aircraft of foreign nations had flown faster, higher and farther; that he hoped his flight would stimulate sale of United States aircraft to foreign airlines and so put to work "more men in the aircraft factories of this country."

Hughes stopped, folded his paper, and walked to his seat. The audience broke into warm applause, rose in tribute and began to cheer. It seemed as if Hughes' expression of his hopes was better received—or at least better understood—than "the one thing about this flight that I would like everyone to know."

It was 9 P.M. that day before Hughes could call his time his own, and the manner in which he won free from well-wishers and the press is indicative of the respect which a democracy pays to the privacy of its more conspicuous citizens. Briefly, Hughes had to escape. He was riding up Fifth Avenue in a limousine preceded by two policemen on motorcycles, when suddenly his car stopped. Hughes jumped out and ran into an office building, through the lobby and out a side door opening on East Fifty-sixth Street. He climbed into a waiting taxi which then swung around the block to go west on a one-way eastbound street in order to lose trailing newspaper reporters. The taxi drove him to Long Island where at last he met Miss Hepburn in the comparative privacy of a supper club.

Two weeks passed before Hughes was able to return to California. During this time he spoke at receptions in New York, Chicago and Houston, trying to make clear what was, to him, the meaning of his flight. Perhaps he put it best in Houston among the familiar faces and accents of his youth.

"I find it very difficult for me to be standing up here on this platform," he told a crowd gathered to welcome a native son, "for I realize that if it were not for you men and women and your diligent work, I would probably be pushing a plow."

He referred to the three thousand Hughes Tool Company workers in the audience, nearly all of whom were seeing their employer for the first time. Just then an Eastern Airlines transport droned over the field, sweeping in for a landing.

"I think it is very fitting that this plane came in now," Hughes said when the motor-sound was stilled, "for it serves to carry out something I wanted to say. The men in the cockpits of the airliners, the airplane servicemen, the radio operators, the weathermen— they are the men who are entitled to any credit you want to pay to any phase of flying. It's the everyday service that is more important than any spectacular flying. I'll wager that during the long winter months the men in the airliners combat weather far worse than I've probably ever seen in my life. They do it, not because they probably make a little more money than in other business, but because they love the industry and want to see it get ahead."

Approaching his target from another direction, Hughes said, "When you use your vacuum cleaner in the home, you don't talk about how smart you are—you talk about how smart the man was who invented it. By that same token, it is you men and women who have enabled me to have a ship like that, one that could fly around the world. I didn't do anything except fly according to instructions."

And, at a civic banquet that night, Hughes said nothing but the truth when he told the audience, "Why, I couldn't even get a job as first pilot on any airline in this country.

"Don't laugh," he said, when he could be heard over the resultant commotion, "for that's really true. I would have to serve a long apprenticeship as a second pilot before I could hold a first pilot's job."

Then, coming truly home to Texas, he told them that "coming from Texas peculiarly fits a person for flying around the world.

"There's nothing you can see anywhere that you can't see in Texas," he assured them. "And after you've flown across Texas two or three times, the distance around the world doesn't seem so great. We didn't see any mountains on our trip that were any steeper than the mountains of west Texas. We didn't see any plains broader than the plains of central Texas. And we didn't see any swamps that were any wetter than the swamps of Houston."

The Governor made Hughes an honorary Texas colonel. And the Mayor of Houston told him that three baby boys born in the Houston hospital that day were named after him. And his lawyer told the audience that "Howard Hughes has overcome one of the most deadening of handicaps, great wealth in youth, and we in Houston understand that." Whereupon the vice-president of the Houston Chamber of Commerce said, "The greatest compliment I can pay to this young man is to say he reminds me of his father."

part iv And Into the War

12

The era began lethargically enough. In fact, just before the beginning certain of Hughes' key men left him, complaining of his inactivity.

Palmer and Rockefeller were the first to go. The Hughes Aircraft Company had been chiefly idle since Hughes' round-the-world flight. Hughes seldom appeared and rarely telephoned Odekirk or Palmer. Once in a while he would arrive from somewhere at three in the morning to have an aircraft serviced, and take off. Palmer and the engineers had been working casually on preliminary sketches for a twin-engine aircraft, but for the most part the company's hundred and fifty employees had nothing to do.

Thus matters dragged along for them until late in 1938, when the Army Air Corps announced that it was in the market for a new interceptor fighter—one that could climb to twenty thousand feet in six minutes, and had a minimum top speed of 360 miles per hour. Moreover, the Air Corps wanted such an aircraft in the shortest possible time, for it was by then terribly clear that general wars in both Europe and Asia would not be long in coming. It was also plain to the Air Corps that the fighter aircraft of their most probable enemies were in many respects superior to their own.

Palmer and the designers at the Burbank factory were immediately excited by the Air Corps' announcement. They told Hughes that the design they had been working on could easily be modified to more than match Air Corps specifications. Hughes seemed more or less interested in the project; rather less than more, it seemed to Palmer. Mention was made of the Air Corps' mood of urgency. Hughes said he was interested.

Weeks passed.

Eventually Palmer left, saying that he could not get Hughes to make up his mind whether he really wanted Hughes Aircraft to compete with other manufacturers for the Air Corps contract. Next, weatherman Rockefeller resigned. Rockefeller first tried to telephone Hughes, but could not reach him. He left word. There was no answer. He wrote a letter of resignation and mailed it to Hughes. No reply. He sent a telegram, giving Hughes three weeks' notice. No acknowledgment. At the end of the third week Rockefeller took a new job. A week after that Hughes visited the Burbank plant and discovered Rockefeller was missing. He telephoned Rockefeller at his home, who later said the conversation went like this:

"Rocky," Hughes said, "you can't quit! I need you. I have all sorts of plans . . ."

"But I've already quit, Howard. I tried every possible way to let you know."

"Listen, Rocky, I'm thinking about a round-the-world airline. All those things we learned we can use now. I have a lot of plans I haven't told you about."

"But Howard, I've already quit. I'm at a new job right now."

"Do me one favor, will you, Rocky?"

"Sure, Howard."

"Go see Neil McCarthy, my lawyer."

Rockefeller accordingly went to see Mr. McCarthy, who expressed surprise. The lawyer said he had no word from Hughes concerning Rockefeller, and he was at a complete loss to know what Hughes had in mind.

When Hughes learned that his capable engineer, Dick Palmer, had also been gone for some time, he telephoned him and suggested that Palmer was too naïve to succeed in the business world—that he would be destroyed by unscrupulous men. On the other hand, he said, "Someday my chief engineer's job will be worth a hundred thousand a year."

But Hughes' importunities had no effect on Palmer, who complained there was a lack of liaison between Hughes and the management staff.

Despite Palmer's departure, work did continue on plans for the Air Corps interceptor. Hughes would appear occasionally to inspect them, spend days hovering over the drawing boards and vanish. It would seem that during this time and during the earlier time when it seemed that nothing was happening, Hughes had been quite logically following a consistently developing interest.

Perhaps the idea had been in his mind even before he called himself Charles Howard and went to work as co-pilot for an airline. Perhaps the idea was born or at least nurtured on those early cross-country racing flights. Certainly Hughes paid ample respect to the accomplishments of airline pilots in the speeches he made after his own round-the-world flight. In retrospect it would seem that the idea had been there all the time, and that Hughes had, in his own way, been developing it. Hughes was now the principal owner of the Transcontinental & Western Airline, later renamed Trans World and called TWA. He had acquired effective control of TWA the year before—in 1937, when TWA's president, Jack Frye, telephoned, saying, "I need money."

Frye said he needed the money to buy new equipment, and that the stockholders wouldn't provide it. Hughes asked him how much he needed.

"Fifteen million in cash."

There was a moment's pause before Hughes said, "Good God, Jack, don't you realize that's a small fortune?"

Frye, who told this story, added that Hughes within a week had bought out two of the principal stockholders for less than $1,000,-000, thereby acquiring majority control of TWA. Another story is that Hughes first looked around the Los Angeles banking community and discovered he could not arrange a loan for Frye; that he then went to New York bankers and bought out their 50 percent interest in TWA for $7,000,000.

Arranging the financing and making plans to extend TWA service around the world had helped to keep Hughes' interest diverted from his aircraft company. Perhaps if Hughes had disclosed the news of his purchase to Palmer and Rockefeller they might not have left him. On the other hand a business secret involving millions of dollars is not something to be casually shared among old friends. A business secret, like any other, is a secret only so long as only one person knows it.

At Burbank work continued on plans for the interceptor. When they were finished, the Air Corps studied the plans with surprise and interest. Hughes was not, after all, merely a national hero who had won the Harmon Trophy, the Collier Trophy, and a special Congressional medal for his achievements as a pilot. He was also a designer of the H-1 who had the respect of Air Corps aeronautical engineers as well as that of Air Corps pilots.

Hughes' position in aviation was unquestionable and the plans he presented seemed quite acceptable, but certain pragmatic questions were in order. Hughes' plant was very small. Could it be enlarged to handle a multimillion-dollar order, if such an order were placed? Could he hire the necessary personnel? What plans had he for the purchase of material and equipment? When could he deliver a prototype for testing? If Hughes could do the job, fine—but didn't he have a reputation for being a kind of oddball? Wasn't it true that he had refused to come to Washington to receive his Congressional medal on grounds that he didn't like crowds—that he'd had enough of crowds in New York and Houston? Still, the plans looked good; someone better send a delegation to California to inspect that plant of Hughes' and ask him some questions.

General Henry H. (Hap) Arnold went to Burbank, found Hughes absent and was denied admission to the Hughes Aircraft Company grounds. He had no company pass. The guard at the front gate turned him away. It was explained to the guard that General Arnold was the commanding general of the United States Army Air Corps and that the United States government had sent General Arnold to inspect the factory that would, if all went well, be manufacturing aircraft for the Air Corps. Sorry, the guard said, no ticket—no admittance.

"I suppose this is the only time the chief of the United States

Army Air Corps has been denied admittance to an airplane factory," Hughes said later. "Naturally, this incident was not intentional. I had simply left instructions that no one was to be admitted. I was unaware that General Arnold had any intention of paying a visit."

On another occasion a group of Air Corps engineers were refused permission to inspect a mock-up of the Hughes interceptor. What with one sort of contretemps and another, it came as no great surprise to the aviation industry to hear that Hughes did not get the contract. It went instead to Lockheed, who brought out an aircraft somewhat similar to what the Hughes staff had in mind. The twin-engine, twin-tailed Lockheed P-38, one of the more successful fighter aircraft of the Second World War, was eventually evolved from the prototype.

Not until he had been refused the contract did Hughes seem much to care whether he won it or not. When he did not, he was furious. In later years he said, "I was bitter about the treatment I had received. I decided to lock my doors and design and build an airplane which would be so outstanding that the Army could not ignore it without facing public criticism. I did not pick a fight with the Air Corps, nor did I cater to them."

So Hughes locked his factory doors and ordered work to begin on a design he called the D-2. It was to be a twin-engine medium bomber, made of wood, capable of great range and extremely high speed.

Then he turned his attention back to TWA. He and Jack Frye were dreaming together of flying palaces. They wanted a ship that could carry passengers high and fast—an aircraft that would fly in the jet stream winds of the substratosphere and cruise at three hundred miles an hour. It must have a pressurized cabin—that is, means must be found to maintain within an aircraft flying in rarefied atmosphere the ground-level atmospheric pressure and oxygen content of the air. The seats should be thickly upholstered and adjustable into reclining positions. There should be convenient rest rooms, tasteful decor and color throughout the cabin; and excellent food and drink should be served by beautiful young women. After all, why should flying be an ordeal when it could as easily be a

pleasure? Moreover, beauty and comfort aloft would give the passengers a sense of security. One reason why the airlines were then
doing no great passenger business was that the general public considered an airplane to be something in the nature of a mechanical
invitation to suicide. Hughes and Frye dreamed on: they called
their dream plane their "Buck Rogers ship," after the hero of a
contemporary science-fiction cartoon strip that envisioned rocket
ships and space flight in the year 2430.

13

"*He wore white tie and tails,* all right," said Russell Birdwell, a Hollywood press agent, "but he actually didn't wear them. They wore him. The outfit looked as if he had inherited it from his grandfather and last wore it twenty years ago. The coat was too short, the pants were too short. His wrists stuck out. He twisted his neck so nervously that his collar appeared to be choking him. I wondered who on earth he could be, but Norma Shearer said something, and I turned back to more pleasant subjects."

The occasion was a cocktail party at the Trocadero night club in Hollywood, celebrating the premiere showing of *Gone With The Wind,* a long, star-studded film that Mr. Birdwell, its publicist, referred to simply as the greatest motion picture ever made. So well had Mr. Birdwell done his work that a great many people agreed with him to a degree they might not have, had they heard nothing about the picture before seeing it. So the party was also something of an occasion in honor of Mr. Birdwell, who was plainly annoyed when the apparition in the antique evening clothes interrupted Mr. Birdwell's conversation with Miss Shearer to ask, "May I see you?"

"In a minute," Birdwell said, not meaning it.

The stranger, properly rebuffed, drifted away into the smoke and the noise of the crowd. Miss Shearer regarded Birdwell with amusement.

"Don't you know who that was?" she asked.

"No."

"You should. It's Howard Hughes."

"Excuse me," Birdwell told Miss Shearer, and dived into the

crowd in the wake of Howard Hughes. He found the millionaire brooding in a corner.

"I'm sorry I was busy," Birdwell said. "You wanted to see me?"

"I'm thinking about making a new motion picture," Hughes said. "Would you be interested?"

Birdwell, who is the authority for this and the anecdotes that follow, said he was taken completely by surprise. Hughes had not introduced himself, nor had he sought to approach his subject by means of any preliminary social circumlocutions. But most surprising was Hughes' statement itself, for this was 1939, and Hollywood's memory being brief as it is, Birdwell had trouble remembering when Hughes had last made a film or what that film was—*Hell's Angels? Scarface?*

"I might be," Birdwell said cautiously. "At least I'll be happy to talk about it."

"You may hear from me," Hughes said. Turning away without so much as a nod, he left the party.

Weeks later, Birdwell's secretary came into his office, badly puzzled.

"There's a man outside who apparently wants to see you," she said. "He must be mute. But he has a note, and he won't give it to *me*."

"Who is he? A nut?"

"He doesn't look like one. He just won't talk."

Curious, Birdwell went into his outer office. There stood a neatly dressed middle-aged man with a piece of paper in his hand. He handed it silently to Birdwell.

"Mr. Hughes wants to see you," the note said.

"Who is Mr. Hughes?" Birdwell wrote on the note.

The stranger took the note back again and wrote on the reverse side, in block capitals, "MR. HOWARD HUGHES."

Birdwell, who with the passage of weeks had honestly forgotten that conversation in the Trocadero, quickly reached for the note again and wrote, "I'll be happy to see Mr. Hughes either at my office or at any place he names."

The visitor read this, and added a final line: "Mr. Hughes will let you know."

Days passed before the mysterious messenger appeared again with another note: "Please meet Mr. Hughes at his home on North Rossmore at 1:30 A.M. on Wednesday next."

Birdwell scribbled his acceptance.

Promptly at the appointed hour, Birdwell found himself standing before a darkened, heavily vined stucco bungalow built in a style that someone has called "petit-bourgeois Hollywood Spanish." It hardly seemed the residence of a millionaire. But Birdwell pushed the bell-button and a resounding clang boomed through the night. Birdwell thought he had set off a burglar alarm by mistake and was on the point of fleeing when Hughes himself opened the door. He had not shaved in several days. His clothes looked as if he had been sleeping in them. Birdwell presumed Hughes was ill and began to excuse himself for having called at such a time. But Hughes waved his protestations aside and abruptly asked, "Do you think you can put on another *Gone With The Wind* publicity campaign?"

"I don't think so," Birdwell said, not knowing quite what to say.

"I'm thinking about doing a picture called *Billy The Kid*," Hughes said.

"Then it may be possible to put on a *Billy The Kid* campaign," Birdwell ventured.

Hughes almost smiled at that, Birdwell said, and invited him into the house—they had been conducting their conversation in the doorway. Birdwell said Hughes steered him into the dining room, suggested they have a cup of tea and went to the kitchen to prepare it himself. Over the teacups Hughes disclosed his plan.

It would be a Western—a horse opera. Westerns had always been the backbone of the motion picture business, Hughes explained. The flying hooves of the horses put motion into motion pictures. The horses outshone any beautiful woman or strong-shouldered man. *Billy The Kid* would be the greatest Western of all time. It would be the *Hell's Angels* of Westerns; it would be the *Gone With The Wind* of Westerns. Birdwell said that Hughes told him how he had discovered Jean Harlow and made a star of her. Harlow was dead, and it was time for her successor. Hughes would find an unknown girl to play the lead in *Billy The Kid* and by means of an unprecedented publicity campaign, make her even bigger than Harlow had been. An unknown male lead would be chosen, and his name would become legend, too. Brilliant character actors would support the newcomers, and Howard Hawks would direct the film. It would be the first Hawks-Hughes film since *Scarface,* and Hughes assured Birdwell that he, Hughes, would remain in the background and let Hawks work.

Birdwell said Hughes told him, "My name doesn't mean much any more. It was brought home to me the other day when I made a telephone call and the man I wanted wasn't in his office. I left my name with his secretary, and I had to repeat it three or four times before she got it right."

Birdwell sympathized. He wondered if this was the reason why Hughes suddenly wanted to re-enter the motion picture business—so that secretaries would know who he was.

"Whenever I take a job, I always request a retainer to help create the program," Birdwell suggested.

He said a look of annoyance crossed Hughes' unshaved face.

"It isn't that I object to paying any money," Hughes said, "but don't you trust me?"

"Of course, Howard," Birdwell said, looking carefully to see if Hughes took offense at Birdwell's sudden familiarity. Apparently he did not, and Birdwell continued, "If I didn't, I wouldn't represent you. But we must create for this picture a totally new blueprint. We can never use it again. It will take money."

Birdwell said Hughes found this perfectly sensible. Dawn was breaking over Los Angeles before the two men parted. It was not until Birdwell had been working for some time for Hughes that he found explanations for two things that had puzzled him. First, Hughes' doorbell reverberated like a bass temple-gong because Hughes was hard of hearing. Second, the mute messenger was actually Charles Guest, one of Hughes' most skilled and trusted "expediters." Guest was originally Hughes' golf teacher and later his bodyguard-aide-errand man. He was by no means mute. Hughes had simply told him to deliver the message to Birdwell without comment. Therefore Guest had not opened his mouth.

14

Howard Hughes would have liked to have manufactured his own dream airliner for TWA, but government regulations prohibited the owner of an airline from building the equipment the airline bought. Wherefore Hughes—although his nose was still somewhat out of joint from losing the interceptor contract—took his dreams to his good friends at Lockheed. The company had its hands full of orders for P-38s from the United States, and for Hudson bombers (descendants of Hughes' round-the-world aircraft) for Great Britain. Hughes insisted that Lockheed's designers at least look at his preliminary plans.

As it turned out, the designers were delighted. A year earlier they had developed a thirty-passenger aircraft with a 270-mile-per-hour cruising speed which they called the Model 44 and which they hoped would become the world's best-selling airliner. But only Pan American Airways had negotiated for buying the plane, and that deal had fallen through. Now perhaps Lockheed could cut its losses by using Model 44 plans, tools and jigs wherever possible in the construction of Hughes' dream ship. So they agreed to work with Hughes, who next visited his own factory at Burbank to see how his D-2 bomber was coming along.

No one was happier to see Hughes than General Manager Odekirk. Odekirk was hiring new people daily to work on the D-2. He was also conducting experimental work on machine-gun armament systems; on booster drives to accelerate rates of fire, and on metal containers, or chutes, to hold the metal-linked belts of .50-caliber machine-gun ammunition. The Burbank facilities were badly overstrained; it was obvious to Odekirk that the plant would have to move to larger quarters. He believed that Hughes would approve, if only he could find Hughes to get him to say yes. He had left messages everywhere. He had tried waiting for Hughes at places Hughes was known to frequent; he had tipped night club headwaiters to call him if Hughes entered the night clubs; he left word at lawyers' offices, movie lots. He had been about to give up when Hughes materialized, listened to his plea for more space and said, "You take care of it, Odey; call me when you find some land, and let me know how much it's going to cost me."

With that, Hughes left as suddenly as he had arrived. Odekirk feared that Hughes, engaged now in a motion picture, an airline and plans for a new airliner, had lost interest in the Hughes Aircraft Company and its D-2.

Actually, Hughes had by no means lost interest; telling Odekirk to take care of it himself was simply his way of delegating authority. As for his mysterious absences and unreachability, the simplest explanation seems to be that Hughes was, as usual, busy with half a dozen projects at once and got around to each in his own time. And while he worked at one, he did not wish to be interrupted by another. The only new factor in the situation was that the world in 1939 was slipping ever faster toward a general war, and there was a desperate sense of urgency in all the world's aircraft industries. Odekirk flew all over Southern California looking for a site for an aircraft factory. He eventually narrowed his choices down to two parcels of land: one near Van Nuys in the San Fernando Valley, and another at Culver City. Then there was again the problem of locating Howard Hughes, for Odekirk did not wish to make the choice himself. When he found Hughes, Odekirk flew him over the two sites. Over Van Nuys the air that day was turbulent and Hughes said, "Too damn hard to land planes here." Over Culver City it was calm, and Hughes said, "Buy it." When they returned to Burbank, Hughes hurried off to another appointment.

15

It seems that one day in 1939 while actress Olivia de Havilland was on location in Modesto, California, making a Western with actor Errol Flynn, Howard Hughes sent an airplane to the set to pick up his good friend Flynn and bring him back to Los Angeles for a party. Since the film company was breaking up for the weekend, Hughes' pilot asked Miss de Havilland if she wanted a ride back to Los Angeles, too. She thanked the pilot, but said no. The next week Louella Parsons, a kind of boudoir-keyhole columnist, reported that Howard Hughes had finally been captured by Olivia and they were making plans to marry.

Miss de Havilland read this and laughed. She had never met Hughes and knew little about him, even though his name was continually in the papers in connection with those of a great many actresses. But when she returned to Los Angeles upon completion of her picture, the phone rang and a male voice rather nervously asked, "Miss de Havilland?"

"This is she."

"This is Howard Hughes."

Miss de Havilland said there was a long moment of silence before the voice said, "I read in the paper that you and I are engaged and are going to be married."

Miss de Havilland said she began to giggle.

"Since we have never met, I thought we should at least look at each other before we do something so permanent," Hughes said.

Miss de Havilland said that when she stopped laughing, Hughes asked her for a date, and the actress said she would have to ask her mother. Miss de Havilland was barely twenty-one, and her mother insisted upon the right to approve or disapprove of Olivia's escorts.

She said she told her mother, "One of the world's most re-knowned wolves has asked me to go out, but he doesn't sound very dangerous to me."

Katharine Hepburn? It was, friends said, just a case of two busy people each following different careers; they had drifted apart. Before Hughes called upon Miss de Havilland, he had been seen around town with Ginger Rogers.

The courtship of Miss de Havilland began to run along familiar, charming but erratic lines. She said Hughes would never call her for a date until the evening of the night he wanted to go out. If she said she had other plans, he would demand that she change them. Then he would appear in an old car, she said, one she called "an unintentional convertible" because when it rained the water would come pouring in through holes in the canvas top. And, she said, Hughes would never have any money: "I always had to take the money to pay for our dinners."

At one point, she said, Hughes disappeared for several weeks. Then one Sunday morning a box of three dozen white orchids appeared at her door. Every Sunday until Hughes returned the white orchids were delivered. Upon his return to Los Angeles, she said, Hughes informed her that it was now time for her to learn to fly. So up they went, with Hughes turning over the controls to his apprehensive pupil and laughing at her terror when a mistake would send the plane lurching about the sky. They would land and dine at Victor Hugo's, then a restaurant popular among the Hollywood film colony.

One evening over dinner, Miss de Havilland said quietly, "There is love between us, and we have never discussed marriage."

She said Hughes looked squarely at her and replied, "I have no intention of marrying until I am fifty. There are too many things to do."

And so it would seem there were, particularly since Hughes wished to supervise each of them in minute detail. At Lockheed, for instance, he was rejecting drawings, arguing obstinately with engineers, forcing his demands on stubborn designers. Lockheed had by now given up hope of trying to sell Hughes the Model 44 substantially as was; it had become an airplane called, on the drawing boards, Excalibur A or Model 49. Hughes insisted upon what most of the designers thought was an impractical idea: three vertical tail fins instead of the conventional one or the less conventional two. He reasoned three fins would make for a smoother, more stable flight. He also demanded—as he had in every other aircraft he had purchased—more powerful engines than the designers envisioned. He specified the colors of the interior decor and the type of fabric for the seats, the carpet for the floor and the kind of equipment to be used in the galley. As work progressed the design was given a new name—Constellation—and the schedule called for the new aircraft's appearance early in 1942.

At the 7000 Romaine Street building, Hughes paid equally close attention to the search for the as-yet-undiscovered actors to play the leading roles in *Billy The Kid*. He and his associates pored over thousands of photographs culled from newspapers and magazines, both foreign and domestic; they searched through heaps of glossy photographs sent by agents and by hopeful young people who had —thanks to Russell Birdwell's preliminary publicity campaign— heard of Hughes' need. The agents included a great number of pictures of young women whose beauty resembled that of Jean Harlow; of girls who somewhat resembled Billy Dove or Katharine Hepburn. But while the agents' reasoning was simple enough to follow, it was wrong. Hughes was looking for a face and a form not seen by the camera before. He did not know what he was looking for precisely, but he would know once he saw it.

Together with pictures of girls, Hughes and his staff studied photographs of startlingly handsome young males. But Hughes was no more in the market for the conventional Hollywood cowboy than he was in the market for a competent, established actress. Then one day Gummo Marx, an agent and one of Hollywood's Marx Brothers, brought Hughes a lad who had the spare, athletic build and babyish good looks that precisely fit the public misconception of Billy the Kid. The young man's name was Jack Buetel. Hughes

signed him to a contract for $75 a week and trusted that someone
would give him acting lessons before shooting began.

There was at this time in Los Angeles a receptionist in a chirop-
odist's office who, to implement her $27.50-a-week salary, posed
for photographers. She had dark hair, a clear complexion and a
remarkable bosom. An agent, Lewis Green, saw one of her photographs and sent it on to the Hughes office. One of Hughes' aides,
winnowing the daily batch, rejected it—but the photograph inad-
vertently wound up in the pile that went to Hughes. When the producer saw it, he stopped to look again. He turned the picture over
and saw the girl's name.

"Give this Jane Russell a test," he said, and resumed looking
through the pile.

A screen test for Howard Hughes was different from most. In
other studios a girl would be taken to a hairdresser for an elegant
coiffure; cosmeticians would paint over her blemishes and remove
the dark shadows from beneath her eyes; she would be fitted into
clothing best designed to enhance her charms; she would be
coached in a few lines of simple dialogue. But Hughes had reason
to believe that a girl at her worst appeared at her best for purposes
of testing. Girls arriving for screen tests at his studio were told to
come in simple street clothes with their faces freshly washed. No
lipstick, no powder, no artificial hair styling. And no lines to recite.

So Jane Russell was sat upon a high stool and photographed
from one side, from the other, from the front, the rear, above, below. The lighting was harsh and in no way designed to compliment
the subject. The idea was that if any woman could appear beautiful
in what amounted to the kind of photograph that might be taken at
a passport photographer's studio, she must be beautiful indeed.
Anything that artifice could add would merely make her seem more
beautiful. It was the kind of screen test that not many ladies would
welcome and that even fewer could pass. But Jane Russell walked
out of the studio signed to a $75-a-week contract. Hughes was not
altogether sure he wanted her to play the female lead. He had several other actresses under consideration. But she seemed to him to

have the freshness of face and form that he was looking for, and as in the case of Jack Buetel, she could probably be taught to act.

After all, what was there to a Western? In Westerns the most difficult acting is normally performed by the horses. Besides, the problem would be Howard Hawks'. If anyone could direct an action picture Hawks could, and he had promising script to work from. It had been written by the prolific Ben Hecht and rewritten by a well-regarded writer, Jules Furthman. The supporting cast included the veteran character actors Walter Huston and Thomas Mitchell, so what could go wrong? When Hughes eventually decided upon Russell and Buetel, he told Howard Hawks, "I'm busy here in Hollywood. You take 'em out to the desert and bring back a great picture."

But it was not quite so simple as all that, for when the shooting began Hughes had a pilot fly out to the location every other day to bring back the undeveloped film. The film would be processed and hurried to a screening room, where Hughes would watch it unreel in the midwatches of the night.

With his airline, his airliner, his D-2, expansion of his aircraft company, development of armament systems, his tool company and his motion picture, the eruption of war in Europe in the fall of 1939 brought about no obvious change in Hughes' order of priorities—at least, no change obvious to his associates—but then Hughes was already as busy as he could be at everything he did.

So busy, in fact, that he seemed to have forgotten about Olivia de Havilland. But this was not really the case. He did remember her. He called her at 10:30 P.M. on New Year's Eve to ask her for a date.

"I'll be by in a few minutes," he said. "We're going to Jack Warner's house for a party."

Now it so happened that as the year drew to an end, Miss de Havilland had met another pilot, an actor named James Stewart. Mr. Stewart had also asked her to attend a New Year's Eve party with him at the home of Mr. Warner, a Hollywood producer. She had accepted Stewart's invitation, but broke the date when taken ill with bronchitis.

Hoarsely, from her sickbed, Miss de Havilland explained about her throat, about Mr. Stewart, and about it being the same party. She also added that she had not heard from Hughes for weeks, and now he was calling her up on New Year's Eve, of all times, when he might have known that had she been well, she certainly wouldn't be sitting home alone, and . . .

"As I said," Hughes said, "I'm on my way over. Happy New Year!"

Olivia de Havilland obediently rose, primped, and put on a dress cut so low that, she said, "it practically asked for pneumonia."

She was ready when Hughes arrived and she appeared at the party on Hughes' arm.

"Jimmy," she said, "came up a little put out and took the other arm. We sat down at the bar and Errol Flynn started serving me drinks. I was twenty-two, with three of the most attractive men in the world around me. I don't know how my reputation survived. But by dawn my bronchitis was gone and my temperature was back to normal."

Looking back fondly over the years, as virtually all women who have known Hughes do, Miss de Havilland remembers him as a shy, painfully bashful man who held great fascination for women.

"I remember Howard with gratitude," she said. "I'm also grateful we did not marry. Marriage would have been unfortunate."

16

At one o'clock on a morning in 1940, Howard Hughes telephoned Russell Birdwell awake and told the publicist to report at once to the gray stucco building at 7000 Romaine Street. Moments later Birdwell was on his way.

He was not surprised to find the front door locked. It always was, even during daylight hours. So, always, were the interior doors, for that matter. Birdwell rang for the night watchman and asked where Mr. Hughes was. The watchman shrugged. Birdwell said he began an office-by-office search through the building, walking quietly and rapping gently on doors, unwilling to call out for fear that he might disturb his employer. He found Hughes at last in a small room, seated at a secretary's desk.

"I want you to see some of the rushes that Hawks has sent in from location," Birdwell said Hughes told him.

The two men walked down a hall to a projection room where Hughes climbed into the booth and threaded the machine with film. Birdwell said that Hughes seemed to take pride in his ability to do this. The show began, and after a few moments Hughes stopped the machine and called from the booth down to Birdwell.

"What do you think?"

Genuinely impressed by director Hawks' craftsmanship, Birdwell replied he thought the film very good. He said Hughes grunted and started the film again, only to stop it a few seconds later.

"What do you think now?"

"Excellent!" Birdwell said.

He said Hughes ran the film all the way through and then asked

Birdwell for his overall impression. By now Birdwell sensed that Hughes was somewhat less than pleased by the rushes, and it seemed to Birdwell that it might be wise for him to temper his earlier enthusiasm. Birdwell said he excused himself, walked down the corridor ostensibly to sip at a drinking fountain but actually to gain time for thought, and upon his return said:

"I think the rushes are brilliant. Of course they are rough, since they have not been scored or edited. But the acting is fine. The scene where Walter Huston turns his back on the Kid and walks out of the barn is very dramatic."

Birdwell said he glanced anxiously at Hughes to see how these remarks were being received.

"Didn't you notice anything?" Hughes asked.

"Notice something? What do you mean?"

"No clouds."

"No clouds?" Birdwell echoed helplessly.

"Yes. No clouds. Why go all the way to Arizona to make a picture unless you get some beautiful cloud effects? The whole purpose of going on location is to get scenery you cannot achieve in a Hollywood studio. The damn screen looks naked. Naked."

Unfortunately, Birdwell was unfamiliar with the fact that Hughes had spent months in a passionate search for clouds during the filming of *Hell's Angels,* and did not remember how many critics had remarked how much the cloud effects had added to the aerial sequences. So, Birdwell said, he said the wrong thing when he replied, "The action is so strong you can't take your eyes off the actors to look for clouds. I don't think you need them in these scenes."

"Why can't we have both?" Hughes wanted to know.

"Well, you've got those people on a tight schedule. They have to shoot every day or they'll go over their budget. Maybe they haven't got time to wait for clouds. It's expensive, sitting around and doing nothing."

Birdwell said that Hughes told him to go back home. He said that Hughes remained alone in the projection booth all the rest of that night, running and rerunning the film. In the morning, he said, Hughes telephoned to director Hawks, and the conversation went like this:

"Howard, you're turning out one hell of a movie," Hughes said. "The rushes are good. In fact, the project is so promising that I want to up the budget from four hundred thousand and give you a million dollars to work with. And Howard, I would like you to get some clouds in the sky, even if you have to wait a little while."

Birdwell said that Hawks heard the message loud and clear. Hawks had an excellent memory of Hughes' delays with *Hell's Angels,* and had no desire to devote a year to looking for clouds in a desert, nor to try to turn a cowboy picture featuring two inexperienced actors into a million-dollar extravaganza.

"Look, Howard," Birdwell said Hawks replied, "I've been offered a new picture with Gary Cooper called *Sergeant York,* and I can't take it until I get *Kid* out of the way. I have an idea. You apparently don't like what I'm doing out here, so why don't you take over on this picture? Then you can do what you want, and I can do what I want."

Birdwell said that Hughes went through the motions of pleading with Hawks before at last heaving a sigh and regretfully agreeing with Hawks' suggestion. For his part—according to Birdwell— Hawks just as skillfully registered insincere anguish. Birdwell said that no sooner had this little drama been played out than Hughes called the production manager and told him to have the company back in Hollywood by morning. He said the manager protested this was impossible; it would take all night just to turn the movie company's special eight-car train around. Birdwell, still aghast at the memory years later, said Hughes had promptly said, "Then don't turn it around. Just back it into Los Angeles."

An order from Howard Hughes, Birdwell said, was an order from Howard Hughes. So the train was loaded with 250 actors and technicians and all their equipment and was backed all the way from a point 80 miles beyond Flagstaff, Arizona, to Los Angeles. Whereupon, Birdwell said, everything began all over again, under the personal direction of Hughes.

And everything went very slowly. Hughes shortly found out that he could not devote his days to the film because of his need to devote attention to his other projects. Therefore, shooting of interior scenes took place at night on a lot belonging to the Samuel Goldwyn Studios. Meanwhile, Metro-Goldwyn-Mayer rushed through a film called *Billy The Kid,* starring Robert Taylor. Hughes was outraged. He called Louis B. Mayer and expressed his opinion of Mr. Mayer, but he might as well have shouted at a stone. Reluctantly, Hughes changed the title of his own film to *The Outlaw.*

Hughes would appear on the set close to midnight, unshaved more often than not, a coat slung across his shoulders like a cape, a clipboard in his hand and definite ideas in his mind. One night he ordered the veteran actors Mitchell and Huston to replay a scene over and over again. Retakes are common enough in Hollywood, but not for men of Mitchell and Huston's reputation. They were not annoyed; they were insulted. Huston began cursing, and the newcomer, Jack Buetel, watching on the sidelines, was terrified.

"My God," Buetel muttered, "if Hughes tears *them* up, what is he going to do to me?"

At the end of the twenty-sixth retake, Mitchell threw his hat on the floor, jumped up and down on it, and then swung striding off the set shouting something about "stupid sons-of-bitches making this bastard of a film."

Hughes merely buried his nose in the shooting script. Mitchell tore off his costume and shouted at those trying to soothe him. Huston hurried over to his colleague and slapped him on the back.

"I feel just the same way, Tom," he said. "We'll both quit."

Having thus expressed themselves, the two Irishmen then began to consider the consequences of breaking their contracts. In a calmer mood, Mitchell returned to the set and approached his director.

"My God, man," he said, "you can't dissect emotion like you do an airplane. I can't break it down bit by bit. We're trying to create a mood here, and you think it's a scientific experiment. You can't attack it like an engineer."

Hughes politely thanked the actor for his opinion. Then he explained what he was seeking in the scene, praised Mitchell's considerable ability, recalled a nuance Mitchell had got into his role as the father in *Gone With The Wind,* and so mollified the actor that Mitchell was agreeable to go through another twenty-six retakes if necessary.

It was near dawn when the scene was at last done to Hughes' satisfaction, and the company presumed they would now be let go for the night. But Hughes next wanted to shoot a scene in which Buetel entered a gambling house. The young actor was panic-stricken. He jittered through the scene and waited, expecting the worst. But Hughes merely looked up, said "Fine, print that one," smiled at his leading man and dismissed the company. Veterans on the set immediately realized that Hughes was simply making Buetel feel more comfortable. Later Buetel would be subjected to the same grueling grind of retakes that everyone else experienced.

On another occasion at witches' hours, Jane Russell was asked to register distress. She was the victim of Indian torture; she was tied by her wrists between two trees. Her bonds were leather thongs soaked in water. Presumably the thongs were drying and as they did so, they were contracting, with result that Miss Russell would be literally pulled apart unless help came. Meanwhile, she writhed about, as if in torment.

Hughes looked through the camera at her. He frowned. Hughes had a quiet conference with the wardrobe mistress. Miss Russell was untied, went to her dressing room and returned to the scene of her torture. Hughes looked through the camera once more, shook his head and motioned for the wardrobe mistress. Miss Russell was taken to the dressing room again.

This curious little drama was repeated many times as the night wore on. Each time Miss Russell was strung between the trees, she seemed a slightly different woman. The idle camera crews and the technicians sat about enjoying all this with a critical appreciation.

"They're a little higher this time," one would say to another.

"No, it's not that. I think they're a little lower, actually; it's just you see more of them."

Hughes, however, was becoming exasperated. The wardrobe

mistress' best efforts were not accomplishing what he had in mind. He asked for a drawing board and a pencil.

"This is really just a very simple engineering problem," he said to no one in particular.

Drawing upon his aeronautical experience with the sources of stress, flutter and vibration, Hughes very shortly sketched a kind of brassiere that, no matter how Miss Russell twisted about between her trees, would rather pointedly fix the audience's attention upon her thorax.

The wardrobe mistress nodded her complete understanding. Toward dawn the work was done, and now when Miss Russell wriggled between her trees, the camera saw more precisely what Howard Hughes had in mind.

Occasions such as these, which served to divert the technical crew, were rare. *The Outlaw* proceeded in fits and starts. Sometimes work would stop altogether for weeks at a time while Hughes vanished into another world—the world of high finance, or of aviation design. Meantime, the cast and crew remained on salary. There was something princely in all this to them, but on occasion Hughes would worry about production costs. Once he observed a Mexican actress who, according to the script, was supposed to chew on a piece of chicken. He called the property manager to one side.

"Did you have to get a whole chicken?" he demanded.

Hughes' constant seeking after perfection was a source of wonder and delay. In one scene a sheriff was supposed to have a rifle shot out of his hands. The special effects staff barely bothered themselves with this problem. They merely rigged invisible wires to the rifle and, at the proper instant, jerked it out of the sheriff's hands.

"Wait," Hughes said. "If the stock were actually hit by a bullet, it wouldn't fly out of the sheriff's hands—it would splinter."

Whereupon Hughes—who also insisted upon personally inspecting every stage property and every detail of the costumes, including those the extras wore—had a real rifle destroyed by someone shooting at it. He then sat at his drawing board and designed an

explosive mechanism that could be concealed in a rifle stock. It was
equipped with an electric timer to set it off at precisely the instant
the bullet was supposed to strike the rifle. The device worked perfectly. The stock splintered.

The year 1940 melted into 1941; the Army camps filled with
conscripts as the United States came closer to war, and Hollywood
turned a part of its attention to providing free entertainment for the
troops. During all this time Mr. Birdwell was seeing to it that the
world did not remain ignorant of Miss Russell's charms. An extraordinary publicity campaign was well under way; photographs of
Miss Russell were appearing everywhere; news of her tastes, opinions and activities were channeled into gossip columns. She, who
had yet to appear on a screen, was already one of Hollywood's best-
known actresses. And she was scheduled for rounds of personal
appearances at Army camps. Hollywood considered it a patriotic
duty to display its beautiful women to the troops. Presumably the
morale of the soldiery would be uplifted by visions of that which
was denied them. More to the point, personal appearances were
good publicity. Miss Russell found herself paraded before the
troops by day and before the cameras by night.

It was perhaps inevitable that a gossip columnist should report
that Miss Russell was Howard Hughes' newest girl friend. Just as
inevitably, the gossip columnist was wrong. For one thing, Miss
Russell's best friend was the man she later married, a football star
named Bob Waterfield. For another, Hughes' interest in Miss Russell was purely professional. For a third, Miss Russell said of
Hughes, "He's such a shy man I can't see him making any ad-
vances to girls." Moreover, Hughes' attention had been captured
by a child with jet hair and enormous eyes so deep a blue they
seemed, in some lights, purple.

Her name was Faith Domergue; she was fifteen years old and
attending a parochial school in Los Angeles when a Warner Brothers talent scout saw her and signed her to a seven-year contract.
The studio changed her name to Faith Dorn and enrolled her in a
drama class. Under the law at that time she could work only a few
hours a day for the film company, an insufficient length of time to

permit her being cast for a leading role. But Warner Brothers had no intention of bringing her to immediate stardom anyway. Like other studios, they were stock-piling beauty and talent to develop at careful leisure.

One day the actress Susan Peters invited Faith to a yachting party at Balboa where at dockside Faith was introduced to Howard Hughes—a tall, slender man with a several days' growth of beard and a yachting costume topped off by a sea captain's visored hat. Hughes had rented a yacht, the *Sea Ellen,* which was moored offshore; he suggested that while the others in the party take one boat out to the ship, he would take Faith out with him in a sailing dinghy.

Miss Domergue said that while Hughes slowly tacked across the bay he kept looking at her intently, but said nothing. She tried to make conversation, but nothing she said drew a reply. At length she trailed her hand in the water and wondered when this dreary trip would end.

Dinner was served aboard the yacht, and all through it Hughes said nothing but continued to stare at her until she became uneasy, Miss Domergue said. Late that evening, when he drove her home, she fell asleep in the car.

A few days later Miss Domergue learned that Hughes had bought her contract from Warner Brothers. He also bought a new Lincoln from her father, Leo Domergue, manager of a Los Angeles automobile dealership. Then Hughes called, instructed her to change her name back to Faith Domergue and told her to begin attending classes at his 7000 Romaine Street office, under tutors. Not unnaturally, Miss Domergue began to entertain hopes of being starred in a forthcoming Hughes picture. As the months passed she wondered when that would be.

17

So far as his employees knew, Howard Hughes had never been near his Culver City aircraft factory since the day he and Odekirk had flown over the land on which it now stood more than a year later. During this time the Hughes Aircraft Company had grown. Hughes had received regular reports on the progress of the D-2 and the armament systems from Odekirk, as well as from minor employees in different departments of the plant. A worker never knew whether the man beside him was in touch with Hughes. The company name for such informants was "Hughes' spies," but this was somewhat of a misnomer. Hughes wanted to be informed of every detail of all the kinds of work going on everywhere throughout the various provinces of his financial empire. Having no office of his own and therefore very little use for written reports Hughes kept abreast of affairs by telephone, storing the data in his mind. The aircraft company was just one of his interests but he had kept close track of it, as Odekirk was to discover.

One day late in 1941, the telephone rang in Odekirk's office and a familiar voice said, "Odey, I've got to show a general from Washington through our plant this afternoon. I'm going to meet him at three, so I think I'll come out there about two, and you can show me around before he gets there."

Odekirk said that Hughes arrived promptly at two, and was given a hurried tour of the premises. Familiar though he was with the operations, Odekirk said he was hard put to try to explain everything to Hughes in an hour's time.

When the general appeared Odekirk was witness to an astonishing display. He said that Hughes greeted his visitor with the warmest of Texas courtesy and personally conducted the general on a tour of the plant.

"It was like Hughes had been there since the day we broke ground," Odekirk said, marveling at the memory years later. "He knew everything we were doing, what every office was for, where every door led, even our plans for expansion. You would never have known he just set foot in the place an hour before."

At this time the Army Air Corps believed that heavily armed bombers, flying high in broad daylight, could fight their way to and from targets without the protection of friendly fighter aircraft. It was something of a theory of necessity, inasmuch as no fighters had yet been developed that were capable of flying the long distances the Air Corps had in mind for its bombers. The ability of the bombers to get in and get back therefore depended to great extent upon the amount and rate of defensive machine-gun fire they could throw at attacking enemy fighters. It so happened that Odekirk and his staff were working on this problem. One part of the answer was their development for the D-2 of a stainless steel, flexible feed chute, sixty-five inches long, leading to a box containing five hundred rounds of ammunition—a decided improvement over the fifty-round belts the Air Corps had been using.

"They went out of their mind when they saw it," Odekirk said. "They wanted all we could produce."

He said the Air Corps visitors did not show the same degree of enthusiasm for the D-2, but that on the whole the inspection trip was a great success.

Hughes returned to Los Angeles to resume his interrupted work on *The Outlaw*. Before shooting had begun the script had been submitted to the Hays Office for censoring. Among the great many changes the censors demanded was an absolute insistence that one particular line of dialogue be deleted. The line occurred during a scene in which actor Huston returned home after a protracted absence to discover that Buetel, the outlaw, had married Huston's girl friend, Miss Russell. Following Huston's recriminations, Buetel was to reply, "Waal, Doc, you borrowed from me; now I borrowed yore gal."

That line, the Hays Office said, was absolutely unacceptable.

It was one Hays Office objection to which Hughes was willing to pay attention. He changed the line. Buetel was now to say, quite simply, "Tit for tat."

It took all of one night of constant retakes before young Buetel was able to say this without breaking into hysterical laughter.

Work on *The Outlaw* proceeded in fits and starts while Hughes went from one iron to another among his many fires, and 1941 drew toward its end. Hughes had been working all that Saturday night before the Sunday of Pearl Harbor, but when he heard the Sunday morning news broadcast he worked through the day as well.

Hughes himself would probably have liked to have flown for the Army Air Corps. He was only thirty-six and was one of the world's most skillful pilots. Perhaps more important, he was a Texan. During the Second World War some Texas newspapers printed the names of those who volunteered in ten-point boldface type and list in tiny agate those Texans who waited to be drafted. The newspapers' practice accurately mirrored the feelings of the tremendous majority of their subscribers, and Hughes was as much a Texan as anyone ever born under the Lone Star flag. Unfortunately, Hughes was partially deaf and so unable to pass the Air Corps physical examination. In any case, his services as a manufacturer of aircraft and munitions would be far more valuable than any service he could possibly perform as a pilot. More valuable, if not as personally satisfying.

An obvious thing to do was to increase production of the machine-gun feed chutes.

"Material was as scarce as men," Odekirk said, "so we stole spotwelders and every bit of stainless steel we could. The government was holding up airplanes before they went overseas in order to equip them with these feed chutes."

Eventually, 90 percent of all United States bombardment aircraft were equipped with them. Also under way at the aircraft company was work on an electrically operated booster drive for machine guns that speeded their rate of fire. The device was perfected and 89,512 of them were produced by Hughes. Meantime, Hughes set other projects in motion. Hughes Tool Company opened a plant in Los Angeles, and with Hughes Aircraft produced during the war 14,766 landing gear struts, 5,576 aircraft wings, 6,370 fuselages and 18,733 aircraft seats under subcontracts to other aircraft manufacturers. Hughes also built a munitions plant that ultimately turned out 939,320 artillery shells, and a factory that produced 16,958 cannon barrels. He was disappointed that the Air Corps—soon to become the United States Army Air Force—showed so little enthusiasm for the now ready-to-be-tested D-2, but an opportunity suddenly arose to try to make a long-nourished dream come true.

In 1942, German submarines were sinking merchant shipping in plain sight of East Coast beaches. One of the war's major problems was how to deal with or circumvent Hitler's underseas fleet. In Washington, D.C., the industrialist Henry J. Kaiser made what many people considered to be a madman's proposal: that mammoth aircraft be built—planes each capable of transporting hundreds of men and their equipment. Then an army could simply fly over the submarines.

Kaiser's idea was coldly received in Washington but Odekirk, in California, thought the notion was far from preposterous.

"We have two hundred engineers working on the D-2," he told Hughes, "and they're about finished. If Kaiser is as good a production man as he claims to be, why don't we design a flying boat and let him build it?"

Odekirk could have said nothing more calculated to reach Hughes' heart. During one of the speeches Hughes made in New York City on his triumphant return from his world flight, he had looked forward "to the day when you will lean out of a New York skyscraper window and see a ship, a great ship, perhaps not as large as the Queen Mary, but larger than some of the ships that are plying the Atlantic today . . . just a few feet above the surface, gliding between two rows of buoys marking one of the landing paths across New York harbor."

Hughes' first flight had been in a flying boat; he had subsequently bought and flown flying boats; he had dreamed of huge flying boats. Hughes told Odekirk to get in touch with Kaiser at once. Before the week was out the tall, slender aircraft manufacturer and the short, fat shipbuilder had met and had agreed in principle with Odekirk's suggestion. It remained to be seen whether Kaiser could pry a contract out of Washington. He had powerful friends there and a good reputation, but it was not until September, 1942, that Hughes and Kaiser each received a copy of a letter from the Defense Plant Corporation authorizing construction of three flying boats for testing purposes. The letter specified that the aircraft would be built at Hughes' Culver City plant; that neither Hughes nor Kaiser would receive fee or profit; that they should spend no more than $18,000,000 of the government's money; that the planes were to be delivered in two years.

But in advance of receipt of this authorization, Hughes began to experiment with takeoffs and landings in the Sikorsky flying boat he had purchased in 1937 for his world flight. He was to make thousands of takeoffs from the waters of Nevada's Lake Tahoe and Lake Mead before his curiosity about certain facts was satisfied; it was as if he had to rediscover for himself all the accumulated wisdom of the designers of seaplane hulls. Some days he would make more than fifty takeoffs; in all, his visits to the lakes were spread over a year.

So he devoted his days to flying and to his defense industries, and at night he would return to *The Outlaw*. The shooting had been completed. What remained was the most difficult work in the process of making a motion picture: the dreary cutting, scoring and editing. Hughes refused to let anyone else do this. For one week of nights he did nothing but cut the picture, sleeping only a handful of hours as he relentlessly pruned eighty-five miles of film down to two miles of finished product. During the filming, Hughes had ordered his actors to speak certain important lines at least six times for "wild tracks." A wild track is an extra sound track, made as a safeguard against an actor's bad reading of his lines during the filming itself. A better recording from a wild track could be substituted for a poor one on the master track—carefully spliced so that the spoken words were synchronized to the actor's lip movements. Hughes used the wild tracks to piece words together, syllable by syllable in some cases, to get the precise sounds he wanted. For example, Hughes was dissatisfied with the way the actor Mitchell pronounced the word "gentlemen." So Hughes dissected the word on the track, snipping out the *t* sound, to come up with "gen'l'men." He cut the esses off other words; the *ings* from others. When it came to scoring in the music, Hughes pored over hundreds of compositions. Finally, he even personally directed production of the short films used to advertise *The Outlaw* as a coming attraction. In the usual studio these various tasks are entrusted to the appropriate experts, but Hughes saw to them all himself. It was as if *The Outlaw* had become a nocturnal hobby to which he could turn at day's end, but use of the word brings to mind Webster's definition of hobby as something which unduly occupies one's time and attention.

It was late 1942 before all this work was done. A question arose as to when the film would be released, and by whom. 20th Century-Fox had originally been asked to distribute the film, but as time dragged on 20th Century-Fox canceled the agreement. Hughes decided to market it himself. But there remained another matter: obtaining a seal of approval from the Hays Office of the Motion Picture Producers and Distributors of America. When Hughes sent the finished film to the Hays Office, they returned it with demand that 108 cuts be made before the seal could be granted. Hughes asked for and received a date upon which he could defend his picture before the MPPDA. Russell Birdwell tells what happened next:

"I got credit for it," Birdwell said, "but it was Howard's idea."

He said that when the censors met in their hearing room in a New York City office building, they were astonished to discover a new decor. Hughes had instructed him, Birdwell said, to obtain larger-than-life-size photographs of every famous actress of the era, and hang them about the walls. There, looking upon the meeting, were pictures of Betty Grable, Rita Hayworth, Marlene Dietrich, Irene Dunne, Norma Shearer, Loretta Young, Madeleine Carroll,

Claudette Colbert and, to be sure, Jane Russell. Miss Russell's photographs showed her in virtually all of the 108 scenes in question.

"It was true," Birdwell said, still pleased by the memory, "that we had a girl named Jane Russell who was healthy in every possible way. It was also true that in that fine motion picture, *The Outlaw,* she was often seen bending over to pick up a rock or something from the ground. The role called for her to play a simple country girl, so she wore simple, peasant-type skirts and blouses. And when she desired to obtain an article of clothing from a bureau, that particular garment was usually to be found in the bottommost drawer. The whole crux of the complaints was whether too much of Jane's healthy nature was being shown."

The MPPDA censors looked at the wall-by-wall display of beauty in some puzzlement. Birdwell spoke humbly, quietly, telling them that Mr. Hughes had hoped to attend, but was kept in California by the press of business in his many, vitally important defense industries. It was far from Mr. Hughes' intention to offend public morality, Birdwell said, and Mr. Hughes wished to call attention to the fact that he had not.

Birdwell turned and beckoned to a distinguished-looking gentleman who identified himself as a mathematician, and who reached into a briefcase and produced a pair of calipers. The mathematician went to each of the famous actresses' photographs, measuring with his calipers in each case the amount of bosom displayed, and then comparing it with the percentage of Miss Russell that was on public view. Birdwell and his mathematician were able to show that there was proportionately less of Miss Russell's bosom in *The Outlaw* than there had been, let us say, of Jean Harlow's bosom in a film that had won a seal of approval. This was fair enough, as far as it went. Another point of view might have been that there was a great deal more of Miss Russell to photograph than there was of Miss Harlow, just as 10 percent of a hundred is larger than 10 percent of one, but the point seems to have escaped the censors and Birdwell certainly did not bring it up.

Birdwell said of course the whole thing was a hoax, but that the censors were completely taken in. The earlier ruling was set aside. They now found only three scenes objectionable and the remaining 105 to which they had taken exception were now, on second thought, found to be perfectly acceptable.

Birdwell raced for a telephone to tell Hughes the good news. He said Hughes listened without enthusiasm.

"It's a great victory, Howard," Birdwell pleaded.

"I don't consider it a victory at all."

"Howard, you must not have understood me. We only have to cut three scenes to get a seal, and they are not major ones. You've won, Howard!"

"I will not make a single cut. I'll release it without a seal," Hughes said.

Birdwell said he flew back to California in utter despair only to find Hughes in splendid spirits, brightly looking forward to releasing a motion picture without the industry's seal of approval. Only Hughes and the censors had seen the completed picture so far; the stars themselves had not. The original negative was in Hughes' possession, and he telephoned Glen Odekirk to stop doing whatever he was doing at the aircraft company and come to Los Angeles.

Odekirk said Hughes told him, "Odey, I've got a picture here that is moody and dark, and I'm afraid some dust particles might get on the film. I want you to come over and design a room to keep the negative in. It's got to be absolutely airtight. I don't want to tiniest speck of dust to get in."

Odekirk said he led a crew which dismantled a room at the 7000 Romaine Street building, putting it back together with lead walls. To insure its absolute cleanliness, cleaning women were admitted at intervals to inspect it, but first they had to vacuum their hair to be sure they brought no loose dandruff into the room with them.

Putting the finished film securely away did not by any means end work on *The Outlaw*. Indeed, Birdwell's work was barely begun. He said he had dozens of late-night conferences with Hughes about how best to ensure Miss Russell's emergence as a super-star. Birdwell said he had one idea that Hughes enthusiastically endorsed:

"What would you charge," Birdwell asked George Hurrell, a

leading Beverly Hills photographer, "to photograph a girl from one in the afternoon to seven at night? I will pay for all your film, your lights, the props and any other costs. I will provide the setting and the poses. This girl will sit, stand, roll around, dance, smile, sing, laugh and cry. All you will do is shoot. I am after one, perhaps two, great photographs."

"About two hundred dollars, I suppose," Hurrell said.

"Not interested."

"Is that too much? I've often charged you more."

"Perhaps you didn't understand me," Birdwell said. "This must be a master photograph. It will produce a master image, like Cadillac, like Dietrich, like Gable. This picture will automatically come to mind when you hear the name of Jane Russell. It will be one of the most famous photographs in the history of photography. I am interested in spending twenty-five hundred dollars."

The following afternoon Russell Birdwell, five bales of hay and Miss Russell in peasant blouse and skirt arrived in Hurrell's studio, where Miss Russell lay in the hay, chewing on a stalk, looking up at Hurrell's camera. A three-by-five-foot version of this photograph was dispatched to *Life* magazine in New York, where *Life*'s editors instantly realized how much such a picture would do to brighten their war-filled pages. Photographs of Miss Russell very shortly began to appear on the covers of a great many other magazines throughout the world. Meanwhile Birdwell had moved on to another idea. Hughes scouts were dispatched to find a homely, lovesick country boy in uniform. One was found in a San Diego army barracks. In those war years women everywhere were knitting sweaters for their soldier husbands and fiancés; it was Birdwell's idea to photograph the San Diego soldier looking wistfully at a huge picture of Miss Russell and knitting a little sweater for *her*. This, too, became one of the decade's most published photographs —a fact in which Birdwell took great pride.

18

The flying boat's dimensions were fantastic. It would have a wing-spread of 340 feet. It would be 220 feet long, with a tail 100 feet high—nearly ten stories. Eight 3,000-horsepower engines would lift its 400,000 pounds from the water. It would accommodate seven hundred fully-equipped soldiers and transport them across an ocean; carrying a medical staff, it could evacuate five hundred wounded men on stretchers. Since priority for sufficient steel and aluminum to build three such aircraft was impossible to obtain, Hughes and Kaiser decided to build out of wood.

Unfortunately, Hughes and Kaiser did not get along at all well together. There were quarrels over matériel, personnel and production schedules. The partnership was severed not long after it began, with Hughes saying in effect, "you go back to building your ships in Oakland. I'll produce the prototype. Then you can come in and build the production models." Each man seemed glad to be rid of the other.

The government was disturbed by news of the quarrel, but Hughes said this would have no affect on work on the flying boat. An 800-foot-long hangar was built for $1,750,000. It dwarfed the rest of Hughes' small factory, which then consisted of a main building, a processing plant, a drophammer building, an engineering laboratory and a mock-up building. With construction of the hangar completed, it would seem that work on the *Spruce Goose,* as workmen were to nickname the ship, could begin at once. But there were other problems. The first was personnel. Every skilled workman not in military service was already at work in defense industries, and the government took a dim view of one manufacturer's raiding another's payroll for talent. Hughes' staff and Hughes himself went out to find a labor force among college students, women, men physically unfit for military duty and professors of mathematics. There was one accusation, never proved, that Hughes stood outside Boeing's gates trying to lure workers away to his California factory. The story is repeated here only because it indicates the mood and the conditions of the time.

There was an equally severe problem of finding top executives for the project. Hughes hired John le Duc, formerly a Ford executive, to be his works manager. He brought in a Washington lobbyist and former vice-president of American Airlines, Edward G. Bern, to be overall manager of the flying boat project. Subsequently, both men quit. Their complaint was the same as Palmer's had been—lack of liason between themselves and Hughes. Rumors swept through the California aviation industry and reached to Washington that the *Spruce Goose* was already in serious trouble, but Hughes insisted that work was making good progress.

One project which came to a complete halt was that of the D-2. The plane had been built and was being tested. But one night lightning struck the hangar in which it was stored, and the aircraft into which more than one million dollars' worth of research and development had gone was completely destroyed. Grimly, Hughes put his designers and engineers back to work on a new, second-generation version of the D-2, which he called the DX-2.

Meantime, Hughes had come to the end of his personal research in water takeoffs and landings, and he offered the Sikorsky to the military to be used in connection with construction work in Newfoundland. The government wanted larger engines installed and certain minor modifications. When these were completed, Hughes volunteered to take the plane to Nevada for its final tests. This was work any test pilot could have done, but Hughes had personally tested every plane he ever built or modified. His insistence upon doing this was, in fact, already a source of some concern to government officials and businessmen with whom Hughes had dealings. As *Fortune* magazine was later to report, "He tinkers with his planes rather than attending to broad matters of company policy, as if his deepest satisfaction came from serving as a superconscientious test pilot and mechanic."

The final test ended in wretched disaster. Aboard the Sikorsky with Hughes were two Civil Aeronautics Administration pilots, a mechanic, and a flight engineer. Coming in for the last landing the somewhat nose-heavy aircraft slipped out of Hughes' control at the last crucial instant and dug its left wingtip into the water. The wing tore away, ripping a huge hole in the passengers' compartment as it did so. One of the CAA pilots was killed. Hughes was knocked unconscious. The others managed to climb out of the wreck and inflate a life raft. Someone pulled Hughes' limp body out of the cockpit and into the raft.

Hughes, bleeding profusely from a scalp wound, recovered consciousness in time to watch the amphibian sink. Dazed though he was, he looked about for landmarks on the shore that might serve as lines of bearing to fix the scene of his crash.

It took two hours to row the raft the seven miles to shore, where Hughes jumped out and ran to telephone for help—not for himself, but for his wounded passengers. Despite all that doctors could do, the mechanic died of his injuries. Even the most experienced pilots may crash for reasons beyond their control—a sudden flaw of wind or some totally unexpected mechanical failure just at the instant of touchdown—but Hughes could not be consoled by any such philosophical view. To him the impressive thing was that he had been at the controls when two men had died.

"Odey," he said, "I want you to bring that goddamn airplane up."

It was not a job for which Odekirk had the slightest enthusiasm. In addition to being one of America's larger lakes, Lake Mead is also one of the deepest, and Odekirk had no idea where the aircraft had sunk. But Hughes said he thought he knew where he had crashed.

Hughes and Odekirk flew over the lake in a small plane while a boat followed their course below. Hughes scanned the shoreline

for hours until he at last felt certain of his bearings. He circled,
waggling his wings, and the boat dropped anchor in two hundred
feet of water. Hughes turned to Odekirk.

"There," he said. "Okay. I found it. Now you bring it up."

Hughes landed, left Odekirk behind and flew on to Los Angeles.

Two days later Odekirk was still sweeping the general area that
Hughes had selected. He had rigged a metal detector at the end of a
special telephone cable. At the top of the cable there was an ordinary doorbell. He was about to move elsewhere to continue a
search that would seem as difficult and as unpromising of reward as
the proverbial hunt for the needle in a haystack, when the bell rang.
Divers following the cable down into the darkness two hundred feet
below located the wreck. It was subsequently raised, loaded on a
truck trailer and brought to Hughes' Culver City plant where mechanics were detached from their other duties to put the Sikorsky
back into flying condition. When their work was done, Hughes ordered the plane stored in a locked hangar. So far as is known, there
it sat, fully capable of flight but never flown again.

A dispassionate observer might see some misuse of men's talents
and abilities in the lengthy business of locating, salvaging and re-
pairing a 1937 flying boat—particularly in a time of war, and particularly when the men involved also included the general manager
of an aircraft factory and skilled workmen otherwise employed in
programs more important to the nation. But they were Hughes'
men, and it was his plane, and it was his money, and Hughes was
not dispassionate.

A more charitable view is that Hughes may have had a cold,
scientific interest in that wreck; that he wished to learn from a
study of it what had gone wrong, and that such a study would be
valuable with respect to construction of the giant flying boat. And
that, having made such a study, he had the aircraft repaired simply
because it *was* salvagable and therefore might as well be salvaged
as not. Likewise, a reason why Hughes did not fly it again may
have been that he had other planes to fly. It is almost always true
that the simplest, most obvious explanations are, in fact, correct.
But Hughes was never a man to go about explaining his actions to

others, and the incident—being unexplained—served only to add to Hughes' gathering public reputation as a man given to imperial caprice. It was a reputation which did nothing to help him win war contracts from official Washington.

For example, early in 1943 the Army Air Force sent Major General O. P. Echols to California to report on the progress Hughes' company was making with the DX-2. The Air Force was in need of something better than a stripped-down, disarmed P-38 to use for long-distance photographic reconnaissance. It seemed as if Hughes' design might provide an answer. General Echols told Hughes that the Air Force would be interested in talking contract in event the prototype lived up to everyone's expectations on flight tests. Hughes replied that he was not interested in building a prototype for testing; what he wanted was a contract calling for production of DX-2s in volume. General Echols, who was in charge of matériel, technical services, research and development for the Air Force, must have found Hughes' point of view decidedly singular. In any event, he filed the following report to Washington:

"It is the opinion of this office that the plane is a hobby of the management and that the present project now being engineered is a waste of time and that the facilities, both in engineering personnel and in equipment, are not being used to the full advantage of this emergency."

Hughes' response to this was to send a memorandum extolling the virtues of the DX-2 to his fellow Texan and fellow multimillionaire, Jesse Jones, then Secretary of Commerce and Federal Loan Administrator. Jones sent the memorandum on to President Roosevelt, who read it and wrote, "What is there in this?" and forwarded the memorandum to General Arnold. General Arnold reported to the President that the Air Force had been negotiating unsuccessfully with Hughes. Meanwhile, back in California, Hughes, busy with his affairs, had at last decided it was time to remove *The Outlaw* from its lead-lined room and disclose Miss Russell to the public.

19

None but the Spartans have ever gone about the grim business of war purely on a basis of black soup and laconic speech. The very worst of human circumstances must be lightened by some absurd *non sequitur*. As if to satisfy this need, Howard Hughes introduced *The Outlaw* into the pinched, gray world of 1943 with all the bravura that had obtained in some tinsel time of the fat and frantic 1920s.

The ancient tribal rites of Hollywood specify that none but the press and a houseful of those who ordinarily give the press something to write about shall attend a premiere. As a matter of form, the general public is given to understand that an event of extraordinary significance is about to take place—an event from which they must first be excluded, but which they will subsequently be permitted to enjoy at a second serving provided they bring with them the price of admission.

In accordance with these rites, Howard Hughes first engaged the Geary Theater in San Francisco. He chose San Francisco because of that city's deserved reputation as a city of refined intelligence; the Geary because it was a legitimate house that normally showed Broadway plays as opposed to Hollywood productions. Lest the public not be unaware, he caused San Francisco to be plastered with posters telling of "The Outlaw—The Picture That Couldn't Be Stopped." Billboards about the town showed La Russell in her hay pointing a revolver at the viewer, who was challenged by the accompanying large print: "How'd You Like To Tussle With Russell?"

Hughes himself piloted a special airline flight from Los Angeles

to San Francisco. The plane carried forty-eight Hollywood reporters and columnists and their spouses. Every one of them had
his expenses paid by Hughes—from breakfast to nightcap. These
gentry were joined at the Geary by representatives of the national
press and by a select gathering of eminent Californians, including
the redoubtable Oakland shipbuilder, Henry J. Kaiser. A widely
believed lie was that Hughes spent the afternoon before the performance wiring seats in the theater to enable him to eavesdrop on
conversations from his vantage point in the projection booth. He
merely installed an amplification system for his own seat in the
theater, to aid his defective hearing.

Of course it did no good to keep the audience waiting for more
than an hour before the lights were dimmed, but the delay was due
to certain mechanical failures. It was not intentional. When *The
Outlaw* screen titles at last appeared there was general applause for
the man who was at once the film's producer and the guests' host.
The first few scenes of the picture itself were good. There was
skilled camera work by veteran photographer Gregg Toland; there
was the capable presence of Walter Huston. From there on the
audience did not know whether to laugh, weep, or maintain an uncomfortable silence. Some few hoped that they were witnessing a
burlesque of Westerns and kept waiting for some wildly ludicrous
moment that would put all that had so far happened into comic
perspective. No such moment arrived. It became painfully clear
that this was not a burlesque. It was equally clear that the second
reel was worse than the first; that the third was worse than the
second. A restive audience grew increasingly embarrassed.

There were two scenes that left no one with anything to say. One
showed Miss Russell's peasant blouse to be a bit too large for her
as she stooped to pick up something. In the other, outlaw Buetel
was shaking from chills despite the blankets piled atop his bed.
Unbuttoning herself, Miss Russell said, "I'll get you warm," and
popped under the covers with him.

The acting of Miss Russell and Buetel left everything to be desired. Mitchell's performance was little better, and only Huston
seemed to be making a wistful attempt to preserve his considerable

reputation. When at last the happy lovers rode off into the sunset together, Russell Birdwell was too wise to ask reporters for their opinions. Instead, he ushered them into buses that would take the audience to a celebration party at the Bal Tabarin—a night club. There one reporter said, "In the forty years I have been going to the theater, this is the worst thing I have ever seen."

This sentiment seemed to find its way into most of the reviews. *The Hollywood Reporter,* a trade magazine, simply ignored the film. *Time* said, "All advance signs indicated that *The Outlaw* would be the best or the worst picture of the year. Its making cost $2.5 million. Its two young stars, fullbreasted Jane Russell and slim Jack Buetel, had been ballyhooed to magazine cover fame for two years—and yet the U.S. had never seen them on the screen.

"Howard Hughes, the eccentric designer-aviator-producer personally directed the picture and surrounded it with such provoking secrecy that not even the actors in it were allowed to see the finished product. Last fortnight *The Outlaw* had its premiere. What Hughes apparently had for his pains: a strong candidate for the flopperoo of all time."

Hughes was not unduly impressed by the reviews. His view was that he had a highly saleable product; the problem was how to market it. He conferred with Birdwell, and shortly thereafter Birdwell called the San Francisco chief of police, posing as an irate private citizen. Citizen Birdwell demanded that the picture be suppressed. It was an outrage to public morality, he said.

Nothing happened.

The picture was shown, and some people came to see it.

Birdwell and his staff began telephoning to parent-teacher associations, to ministers of the Gospel, to various leagues of women. Birdwell's secretaries, posing as housewives, called genuine housewives. Unfortunately, it was difficult to drum up a Philistine mob out of the sophisticated San Francisco electorate. Birdwell had a moment of inspiration. He wrote an article entitled, "What Time Does Reel Six Go On?" and persuaded a friend to plant it in a San Francisco newspaper. The article suggested the Geary Theater was being stormed by soldiers, sailors and Marines who desired only to see Reel Six of *The Outlaw*.

"Actually," Birdwell said with modest pride, "there was nothing in Reel Six that you couldn't have seen in Reels Five, Four or Seven."

But the article had its desired effect. The box office *was* stormed, some protests *did* come in from others than Birdwell's staff—and the police arrested the theater manager for exhibiting a lewd film. Hughes was delighted. He hired a well-known lawyer to defend the manager. Birdwell was not so delighted. He heard there was an order out for *his* arrest.

"I fled my hotel without baggage and went to the airport," Birdwell said. "As I walked in the terminal, I heard the public address system paging 'Mr. Birdwell, Mr. Russell Birdwell, please report to the TWA ticket counter.' There were two large cops waiting there for me."

Mr. Birdwell said he took the first flight out to anywhere, which happened to be Seattle, using an assumed name. He need not have fled. Hughes' lawyer, bringing a replica of the Venus de Milo into court in order to compare a three-dimensional display of one perfect bosom with a two-dimensional display of another, convinced the court that *The Outlaw* was innocuous and that it would do violence to the Constitution to deny a man the right to exhibit that which did no harm.

In the fervent hope the court was wrong about this, the public pressed into the Geary Theater in such numbers that all records for San Francisco motion picture attendance were broken in the ensuing ten weeks.

Whereupon, Hughes immediately withdrew the film from distribution and sealed it away again in the airtight, lead-lined room at 7000 Romaine Street. No one knew why, and he did not say.

While Hughes was thus diverting the war-raddled multitudes, events of concern to him were on the march in Washington. Assistant Secretary of War Robert A. Lovett, touring bases in Europe and North Africa, was appalled by United States losses of photographic reconnaissance aircraft. On his return to Washington, Mr. Lovett ordered General Arnold to recheck the performances of all existing warplanes and determine which was best suited for the function. Just at this time, President Roosevelt's son Elliott, chief of the Mediterranean Allied Photo Reconnaissance Command, was called from the fighting front to Washington and given orders to help find a new aircraft to fly the dangerous reconnaissance missions. What with Howard Hughes having nudged Jesse Jones, and Jesse Jones having nudged President Roosevelt, and President Roosevelt having nudged General Arnold, and with everyone sharing a common concern, it was perhaps inevitable that Elliott Roosevelt should go to California. He was entertained in Hollywood by Howard Hughes, who made young Roosevelt familiar with the promise of the DX-2.

A picture of Howard Hughes at this time is not without some pertinence to that which follows, and perhaps no one can provide a more intimate glimpse of Hughes than Eddie Alexander. Eddie was the proprietor of a Hollywood barbershop, and one day a Hughes aide enlisted him to wait upon Hughes himself.

"I walked into the Beverly Hills Hotel where he was staying, and there was Howard Hughes in a chair, badly in need of a shave and a haircut, talking to a couple of generals," Eddie said. "He motioned for me to start cutting his hair and kept talking all the time to the generals. It took me three hours to finish because Hughes alternated talking with the brass with talking on his amplified telephone. He's hard of hearing, you know, and his phone is rigged so that he can hear the other person's voice broadcast throughout the room. It's eerie, hearing both ends of a conversation.

"I thought I did a bad job, with all those interruptions, but apparently it was all right. Because for the next seventeen years, I was Hughes' personal barber."

Hughes ordered Eddie to close his shop, go home and wait for Hughes to call him the next time he needed a haircut. Eddie said Hughes told him that he was a busy man, and he wanted his barber to be "on the hook" as Hughes employees called being on standby duty. Sometimes, after Eddie had been waiting three or four days at home, the telephone would ring at 2 A.M. and a familiar voice would say, "Just checking, Eddie, just checking. Wanted to see if you were standing by. I'm going to need you soon. I'll call you one of these days."

Eddie said Hughes also ordered him to bathe carefully and frequently.

"He said he didn't want me bringing other customers' germs into his presence," Eddie said.

While Eddie was most frequently called into the presence at the Beverly Hills Hotel, Hughes would often be found at one or another of sundry houses in and around Los Angeles.

"In those cases," Eddie said, "the driver would take such a winding route that nobody could remember it. When we'd reach the house, we'd walk up to the front door and a voice would boom out, like over a microphone, demanding to know who was there. The guard would say 'It's Eddie, the barber,' and they'd let me progress to the front porch.

"Then the guard would kick on the door a few times, I guess because Mr. Hughes didn't hear so well, and after a minute or two, Hughes himself would open the door just a crack. He'd say, 'Hurry on in, step lively, shut the door and keep the germs out.' "

If young Roosevelt saw any of the aspects of Hughes that Eddie did, he might well have been fascinated. What he did see that certainly fascinated him as a military photo reconnaissance officer was the design for the DX-2. On his return to Washington, Elliott recommended that a contract be awarded Hughes for mass production of the aircraft. In his report Roosevelt said that Hughes promised he could have the planes ready within five months; that he would be willing for the contract to carry heavy penalty clauses if production deadlines were not met. He said Hughes wanted to build the planes of plywood, since Hughes was having success working with that material on his flying boat.

Elliott Roosevelt's report provoked a mixed reaction. Some Air Force officers seemed hostile toward Hughes on personal grounds. General Echols spoke for another group when he dimly viewed the use of plywood as a construction material. But in late August,

1943, Colonel Roosevelt was made chief of the Reconnaissance Branch's Requirements Division in Air Force Headquarters. And two weeks later Hughes was awarded a $48,000,000 contract that called for delivery of one hundred DX-2s within a year.

Meantime, in that fall of 1943, it was very nearly time for Hughes to deliver the first of the flying boats which the government had given him $18,000,000 to develop. Routinely inquiring as to a delivery date, the War Production Board was shocked to hear that the flying boat was still in skeleton form. Workmen were just beginning to build the hull. The largest aircraft in history was at least a year—and possibly more—away from completion. The works manager had quit, and no one had been appointed to take his place. At one point, twenty-one engineers had resigned en masse, protesting they had no superior and were not sure what they were doing. Perhaps if these facts had been more widely known in the Air Force in the fall of 1943, the contract for the DX-2s might not have been placed—particularly in view of the fact that the British were having great success with a twin-engine plywood photo reconnaissance aircraft capable of great speed and distance, called the Mosquito. It was then in production in Canada.

But the contracts had been let. In Washington, angry voices were raised demanding that they be canceled.

20

When a man wants something during a war he most usually wants it badly and he wants it right away, and if he cannot get it from one source he instantly tries another. As with the individual soldier, so with the nation. If it could not get photographic reconnaissance aircraft from Hughes, the nation could try to get a very similar plane from their British allies, and meanwhile make do with what aircraft they had; if no Gargantuan flying boats were forthcoming from the Hughes factory, the nation could and did use the seventy-ton Mars flying boats that the Glenn Martin Company of Baltimore was producing.

So there was a feeling in Washington that the events of war could not wait upon dilatory manufacturers who sought perfection; that the wisest thing to do was cancel Howard Hughes' contracts and spend the money and the material upon some less ideal but more immediately valuable projects.

Hughes flew to Washington to join the debate. He disclosed to the appropriate authorities and the press hitherto secret photographs of the *Spruce Goose* with its ten-story tail. He explained that this aircraft would carry seven hundred fully armed troops—seven times more than any other airplane. Work was going more slowly than anyone had anticipated, Hughes admitted, but no one had ever attempted such an enormous task before. He quoted Grover Loening's report. Loening was a War Production Board aviation expert who had seen the *Spruce Goose* under construction and who had spoken of the exciting potential of such an aircraft. As a final argument Hughes offered to put up a half-million-dollar bond as guarantee that he would deliver the aircraft by the end of 1944.

177

It was then late fall of 1943. Of course money was not the point, but in a matter which is basically emotional, specious arguments may be as effective as reasoned ones. The result of Hughes' trip to Washington was that talk of canceling his contracts subsided from a clamor to an undertone, and Hughes returned to California and his problems.

One problem was that the flying boat project had no works manager now that Bern had quit. It would not have another for more than a year, and when a man was found for the job, he quit for the same reasons Bern had. Both executives complained that the real trouble lay in Hughes himself; that he was difficult to locate when needed; that he issued orders with scant regard for recognized lines of authority or for accepted business procedures. His executives complained that if Hughes wanted something changed, he would often approach the specific welder or carpenter assigned to that particular part of the job and give the man an order without informing any foreman, manager, engineer, designer or corporate executive, much less routing orders down through a logical chain of command. They complained that Hughes insisted on personally initialing every single drawing and blueprint—of which there were literally thousands.

In sum, Hughes' executives complained that it was difficult for them to make sense of their jobs when they were at once subject to the whims, indecisions and absenteeism of their employer while also being constantly surprised to discover that he had made major alterations on the work in progress without having told them.

For example, the DX-2 photographic reconnaissance aircraft, which had now been rechristened the XF-11, was to have been made of plywood, like the flying boat. So the contracts had stated, and during a war designs once agreed upon are frozen for at least the first units of a production run, after which major engineering changes are held to a minimum. A need for drastic changes most usually implies a completely new design. The basic idea is to get into production as quickly as possible with a weapon, to make minor improvements during the production run and to discard the weapon only when a totally new design makes it obsolete. The nation's supply of raw materials and labor is allotted to production in some coherent way, once judgments have been made as to how many and what kinds of tanks, ships, guns and aircraft can be produced from a known supply of metal by a known number of workmen. But Hughes changed the XF-11's specifications to call for metal wings and a metal tail with a wooden fuselage. He did this after the project had already been under way for a year. Four months later he changed the specifications to all metal. It did no good for his executives to protest, for an order from Hughes meant more in a Hughes plant than an opinion from anyone else.

Because of Hughes' penchant for immersing himself in detail and tinkering with designs and specifications and because of his notorious lack of liaison with his staff, the government assigned his projects a Group V priority—lowest of all on the aircraft preference list. This low priority made it difficult for him to obtain the matériel necessary to complete the projects. Thus while Hughes could legitimately blame delay on low priorities, he had no one but himself to blame for the low priorities.

Nor was the work sped by the delegates from Washington who now began to arrive. The Department of Commerce, the National Advisory Council for Aeronautics, the Civil Aeronautics Board, the Army Air Force and the Navy all sent investigators to Culver City to report on the flying boat's progress. Their consensus in February, 1944, was that the contract should be canceled. War Production Board chief Donald Nelson told Secretary of Commerce Jesse Jones to cancel it. On February 16, Jones did.

Hughes, furious, flew at once to Washington. He spent five weeks there talking to Jesse Jones, to Senators, to Congressmen, to any important pair of ears who would listen. This was not only the world's largest airplane, Hughes kept saying, but it was a flying research laboratory that could supply information on the flight characteristics of large aircraft for years to come. Word of the contract cancellation reached President Roosevelt, who had long been an admirer of Hughes: the adventurer in the one seemed to call to the adventurer in the other. President Roosevelt let it unofficially be known that Hughes should be given more time. Accordingly, the contract was renewed under a letter of intent dated March 27 which also eliminated Henry J. Kaiser from participation in the project, much to Kaiser's relief. It called for delivery of only one flying boat, instead of the three the government had first thought to obtain for its $18,000,000.

This news was extremely heartening to Hughes, who meanwhile was busily creating a new motion picture company in partnership with the talented director, Preston Sturges. At the time Hughes told a reporter "I want to make one thing clear: I can't devote any time whatsoever to the motion picture business until the war is over. Sturges is the one man in whom I have complete confidence. I am happy to turn over to him the full control and direction of all my motion picture activities."

Sturges was shortly to discover that although he had "full control," this did not include the power to buy a script, hire a star, build a set or change a line of dialogue without Hughes' approval. He did have complete authority to follow Hughes' instructions to the letter. But at the moment of formation of the partnership there was nothing but good feeling, enhanced by Hughes' admiration of an old sports jacket that Sturges was wearing. The director thought for a moment that Hughes must be joking, for he was just on the point of throwing it away. But Hughes was serious. He knew the value of a comfortable coat. Not long ago he had brought a company car to the shop to be cleaned. The cleaning man, discovering a grimy, ripped, oil-stained jacket in the rear seat, threw the thing into a trash can. When Hughes reappeared to claim the car, he was horrified to discover the jacket missing. For the next few minutes everything in the world of Howard Hughes came to a complete halt while Hughes pawed through the trash can, muttering, "That was my best coat."

So when Sturges protested that the sports jacket Hughes admired had seen its day, little did he know he was addressing a connoisseur.

"That's a good coat," Hughes told him. "If you're going to throw it away, I'll take it."

Sturges was amused by the thought he had just gone into business with a man who volunteered to take the coat off his partner's back. But at that time, Sturges' problems were all ahead of him.

Turning to another project, Hughes flew to Washington once more, in April, 1944. Airlines were an important industry to the total war effort, as all other transportation industries were, and TWA was beginning to receive an allotment of the new Lockheed Constellations that Hughes had done so much to design. By way of celebrating—and at the same time publicizing their airline— Hughes and Jack Frye loaded the first TWA Constellation with Hollywood stars and flew to Washington from Los Angeles in a little over six hours. Hughes called it the Constellation's maiden flight.

In August he was back in Washington in a far less triumphant mood. The Bureau of the Budget had been looking through his Culver City factory and had suggested the XF-11 contracts be given to some other manufacturer—to one who had enough space, manpower, equipment, experience and organizational ability to build the hundred planes. Once again using time that might otherwise have been devoted to other uses, Hughes flew to Washington to plead his case for the XF-11, insisting that the nation needed his airplanes, that he was the man to build them and that he would meet his production schedules. He tried unsuccessfully to obtain higher matériel priorities. He did succeed in retaining the XF-11 contracts.

But the flying boat was not finished by the end of 1944. Nor was it near completion in the spring of 1945. Nor was the XF-11 anywhere near ready for testing in May, 1945, when the European war ended. With their major enemy defeated, the Allied Powers had only to glance at their preponderant strength to compare it with that of the Japanese. So armaments contracts were everywhere canceled as being in excess of need, and among them were Howard Hughes'. The XF-11 contract was renegotiated to call for only two experimental aircraft and a static test model, with the government making an $8,600,000 settlement with Hughes. Hughes had failed to produce either his flying boat or his reconnaissance aircraft during the war, but his case was far from unique. More than sixty other designs failed to reach the fighting fronts, including Boeing's

B-50 and XC-97; Consolidated Vultee's B-36 and XC-99; Douglas' XC-74; Lockheed's XP-58; Northrup's B-35; and Republic's
XF-12. In all, more than $824,500,000 were spent on aircraft that
never saw action; more than $6,000,000,000 worth of other
weapons had not been delivered by the time the war ended.
Hughes' two contracts, totaling $60,000,000, thus accounted for
less than one percent of the total of unfinished business, but during
the war he had provoked more controversy and had made more
enemies than all other defense contractors put together.

What had become of his promise to lock his doors and build a
fighting aircraft so excellent that there would be a public scandal if
the government refused to buy it? To certain powerful men in
Washington the scandal was that Howard Hughes had failed to
furnish a single aircraft to the war effort although the United States
had given him $60,000,000 to do so, and they wanted to know who
in the government had been so foolish as to give the public's money
to Howard Hughes.

At the war's end, Hughes seemed tired and dejected. To add to
his problems, Faith Domergue, now nineteen, demanded to know
when—if ever—she would be starred in a Howard Hughes production. One reporter said that Miss Domergue's insistence took the
form of a tantrum, upon which Hughes capitulated, saying, "All
right, you pick the story you want to do." Miss Domergue's
choice was a script called *Vendetta,* created from an antique melodrama called *Colomba,* the legend of a young Corsican noble-
woman's revenge. Hughes told Sturges to begin production. Then,
like a guest who becomes ill at a banquet, Hughes vanished from a
world that was deliriously celebrating its survival of the war. Only
a few trusted associates knew that Hughes had gone to Acapulco,
then a sleepy Mexican town sadly diminished since the days when
it had been the entrepôt for the Manila galleons. He remained there
for months, inaccessible to the captains of his businesses, slowly
recuperating from nervous exhaustion. He was forty years old.

part v The Full Life

21

"Only the other day I came upon the real explanation of why Howard Hughes did not marry Lana Turner," a Hollywood gossip columnist rather breathlessly informed her readers. She nattered on that the plans had all been made, that Hughes "seemed to understand the strength and sweetness and loyalty behind the glitter of this girl who is one of the great stars of our day." She said Lana Turner had ordered a wedding dress, "yet suddenly it ended and nobody seemed to know why."

But now, she said, she knew. She asked her readers to recall that Hughes could offer Miss Turner nothing that Miss Turner did not already have in the way of wealth and fame, and "besides, Lana hasn't a mercenary cell in her whole make-up. What Lana was looking for was the kind of love that means peace, security, companionship and the protection of a husband and a home for herself and her small adored daughter." And, the columnist said, Miss Turner thought for a while that she "had found all these in Howard Hughes, in his quietness, his power, his silent affection." But then, she said, Miss Turner would wake at night "all atremble, her throat dry, her heart pounding" at the thought that Howard Hughes was just about to test-fly his new XF-11. It was not that Miss Turner had a premonition of disaster, she said, but "way beyond that, it was an awareness of constant danger, violence, uncertainty, never-ending pain and strangeness and loneliness. . . . Lana, at twenty-five, had had enough of excitement and madness and danger and loneliness. . . ."

Two hard kernels of fact in this ball of corn are that Hughes had been seen having dinner with Lana Turner on his return to Holly-

wood from Acapulco, and that he did fly the XF-11, which was
finally ready for testing more than a year after the war ended.
Those who might think the worse of Hughes for not having completed work on the aircraft on schedule would have missed a point.
Reflection suggests that Hughes was a man who kept his own time,
worked in his own way his wonders to achieve and put much of
himself into everything he did. In the case of the XF-11, he added
money of his own to the millions the government invested in the
project. The end result was a machine that promised to satisfy the
enormous demands that Hughes made upon himself. There was
some ineffectual manuvering among Hughes' aides to persuade him
to hire a test pilot, but Hughes was determined to be first in the air
with a plane he called "my brightest dream come true." On a Sunday morning in July, 1946, all was ready and a sprinkling of Hollywood friends and curious newspapermen came to the Culver City
airstrip to see the show.

All through the morning Hughes taxied the XF-11 up and down
the runway. He brought it back to a hangar where mechanics adjusted the rudders. For the next three hours he taxied the ship
again, only to return it once more to the hangar. Newspapermen
asked if that was all there was to be to the day's test; if everything
was over.

"Not yet," Hughes said, and would say no more.

Later in the afternoon Hughes told his ground crew chief, "Let's
take her up; that's the only place I can find out if anything's wrong.
I'll be gone about thirty minutes."

Moments later the XF-11 was smoothly airborne, climbing high
out of sight of the Culver City airfield and swinging over the Pacific
at more than four hundred miles per hour. Its speed was an apparent justification of one novelty of its design. Each of the two engines spun two four-bladed propellers mounted one behind the
other. A theory was that eight propeller blades could take a more
efficient bite out of the air than the conventional three-bladed propeller. For whatever reasons, the ship was fast and climbed well.
Hughes turned east to return to the airfield and as he did so the XF-
11 pitched violently to starboard.

The airspeed fell a hundred miles an hour and continued to drop. And as the speed fell, so did the plane.

The instrument panel showed no malfunction. The engines were receiving full horsepower; instruments indicated that the landing gear was up, that the flaps were up. But the XF-11 wanted to drop its right wing and pull to the right. Hughes, fighting the controls, looked out to see if a part of the right wing had torn loose. The wing was intact. Could the right landing wheel have dropped without this having been registered on the instrument panel? Hughes lowered and raised the landing gear again and again. Each time the gear worked perfectly. Nor was the problem a lowered right wing flap. But something was exerting a pressure against the wing as if someone had tied a barn door broadside to it. There was an enormous drag and no lift. The aircraft was pitching badly, losing speed and falling, and Hughes hurriedly unbuckled his seat belt and prepared to get out before the plane tore itself apart in the air.

The XF-11 fell toward Beverly Hills. A pilot who thought only of saving himself would have taken to his parachute. Several miles ahead Hughes could see the green swatch that was the Los Angeles Country Club golf course. It was the only possible place to crash-land. Hughes grimly fought his wildly bucking ship toward the golf course.

In Beverly Hills back yards, motion picture stars and studio executives looked up from beside their swimming pools to see a stricken aircraft hurtling at them. In the cockpit of the XF-11, it must have been fearfully evident to Hughes that he was not going to reach the golf course. The only possible alternative was to try to smash into the largest available piece of open ground among the houses.

He sheared through the upper roof of one house. In a matter of seconds, the XF-11 sliced through the upstairs bedroom of a second house, rammed through a garage, clipped down a row of poplar trees and plowed into the two-story brick home of an army colonel, with one of its engines tearing loose to dig itself into the lawn of a fourth residence twenty yards away.

Barely conscious, Hughes lifted bleeding, shredded hands to pry back the plastic cockpit canopy as debris rained down around him. With strength that came from somewhere, he managed to wrench his broken body up and over the side of the cockpit. He fell to the ground. There he lay as the wreck began to burn.

A Marine sergeant, William Lloyd Durkin, was a block away when the XF-11 struck. Sergeant Durkin jumped out of his car and ran to the scene. He saw a tattered figure try to rise to crawl back into the wreck. Was someone else inside? Sergeant Durkin, holding an arm in front of his face against the flames, ran to Hughes, grabbed his shirt and managed to pull him a yard or so before the shirt ripped. The Marine took Hughes by an arm and dragged him fifteen feet through a litter of broken trees. A Beverly Hills fireman arrived and helped Sergeant Durkin carry Hughes to a nearby lawn.

"Is there anybody else in the plane?" the rescuers asked. Hughes shook his head. He tried to get to his feet.

"Was anybody hurt?" Hughes whispered, and fainted.

Sergeant Durkin and the fireman thought Hughes had died.

Someone had meanwhile called an ambulance. Someone else had called the police. Several hundred people came to the scene, among them the director Lewis Milestone.

"Who was the pilot?" Milestone asked.

"Howard Hughes," someone said.

"Did he get out?"

"Yes, he walked away."

"Then he'll be all right," Milestone said.

At the emergency room at the Good Samaritan Hospital, a doctor said, "I don't see how he can live through the night." The doctor's colleagues agreed. There was little they could do for Hughes at that moment except give him opiates against the pain.

Hughes' chest was crushed. Nine ribs were broken. His left lung was collapsed. His left shoulder was broken. His nose was broken. His skull was fractured. Internal injuries were suspected. Third-degree burns covered much of his lower body.

So they gave him morphine, set the bones, and carried him to a private room to die.

Odekirk, who had feared something had happened when Hughes

had neither radioed to base nor returned from the flight that was to take thirty minutes, heard the news on the police radio frequency. He sped to the hospital and took the room next to Hughes. The doctors told Odekirk there was no hope. During the night, Odekirk broke a hospital rule. He tiptoed into Hughes' room to look down at the broken, dying man with whom he had flown and worked for nearly fifteen years. He stood there for more than an hour, silently weeping.

Downstairs, reporters had taken over the hospital lounge and lobby, asking every passing nurse and attendant for any possible scrap of information as to Hughes' condition. A doctor at last appeared to tell the press that Hughes had less than a fifty-fifty chance for life. The reporters thereupon kept a deathwatch through the night while newspaper editors prepared Hughes' obituary, leaving the first paragraph open.

The following dawn Hughes regained consciousness and asked to sit up and see his business associates. TWA President Jack Frye had spent the night in the hallway outside Hughes' door and Hughes wanted to see him. Lana Turner and Linda Darnell were both downstairs and Hughes wanted to see them, too. Odekirk ignored the protests of the nurse and entered Hughes' room.

"I want to see . . ." Hughes began, but Odekirk said, "Not now, Howard."

By afternoon the man who had not been expected to survive the night and for whom the doctors still entertained little hope was demanding to be propped up and given writing material. The nurses refused and complained to doctors that they could not make Hughes rest. Something could be done, however, to prevent Hughes from spending his strength in talking with those who wished to see him and whom he wished to see. Odekirk called two guards from the aircraft company to bar Hughes' door to all visitors.

By the end of the second day Hughes had given Odekirk a full report on the XF-11's performance and his opinion of what had caused the crash. He suspected that something had gone wrong with the right propellers and told Odekirk to investigate this suspicion secretly.

On the third day Hughes told Odekirk, "This pain is killing me." His hips and legs were so badly burned that it was excruciatingly painful to shift his body even slightly. Odekirk said that Hughes told him he had an idea.

"I want you to make me a bed, a special bed that will let me move around without all this pain," Hughes said.

"Here was Howard Hughes on what we all thought was his deathbed, instructing me to make a new hospital bed that he was still mentally sharp enough to design," Odekirk said. "He came up with the idea that if the bed could change pressure instead of the patient having to move, the pain would be less.

"He had thought the whole thing out, and he spelled out just what he wanted. He told me to build a bed composed of little three-inch squares of foam rubber covered by a soft cloth. These squares were each to be mounted on a three-inch square platform, and under each platform was to be a screw jack hooked up to a tiny motor. There would be about eighty of these rubber squares and eighty little motors. Each square could turn in any direction—up, down or sideways.

"I rushed out of the hospital and called Jack Sherman at the plant. He began a crash program and his crew worked twenty-four hours a day for four days to build this bed. They even created a large console with switches to move each square. But the really inventive part of the bed was a large hole in the middle that would move out, accommodating a bedpan that slid in and out. The patient thus didn't have to be shifted around by a nurse."

When the bed was finished, the men started to load it into a truck. One of them called, "Wait!" He ran to get a little decal that bore the legend *Hughes Sportster,* and slapped it onto the bed frame. The decals were otherwise used to decorate the seven-foot boats that Hughes Aircraft Company workmen had been making out of scrap plywood left over from construction of the monstrous flying boat.

At two A.M. the bed was taken up in the freight elevator to Hughes' hospital room. Odekirk eased the door ajar to see if Hughes was awake. He was.

"We made your damn bed, Howard," Odekirk said, pushing the door open, "and now you'll have to lie in it."

Odekirk said Hughes brightened as he watched the men bring the bed into the room. He said Hughes listened carefully as they explained how to work the console, but when he saw the *Hughes Sportster* label on the bedframe, he grumbled, "Who the hell did that?" Odekirk said that Hughes' feigned displeasure deceived no one; that Hughes was deeply touched by this expression of the loyal camaraderie that had always characterized the relationship Hughes enjoyed with his workmen.

A package came from Washington. It contained the special medal that Congress had voted to Hughes in commemoration of his round-the-world flight, but which Hughes had chosen not to go to Washington to receive. President Truman had found it in a desk drawer in the White House and sent it to Hughes with the message: "I'm sure you'll win this fight. I am watching eagerly all the reports concerning you. With every good wish, Harry S Truman."

And Hollywood came. Ginger Rogers arrived. So did Errol Flynn, William Powell, Joan Crawford, Harold Lloyd, Gene Tierney, Danny Kaye, David O. Selznick, James Cagney, Walter Pidgeon, Olivia de Havilland, Spyros Skouras, and Cary Grant. And so did Captain Eddie Rickenbacker, America's leading fighter pilot of the First World War and now chief of Eastern Airlines. And attracted by this procession of the famous and the notorious, autograph collectors gathered thickly around the hospital, asking of every visitor that pathetic question of the autograph collector, "Are you somebody?"

After a week of what appeared to be miraculous progress, Hughes suffered a relapse. His condition again was critical. The press mounted another deathwatch in the hospital and were told by Hughes' personal physician, Dr. Verne Mason, "Mr. Hughes' left lung has failed to respond and is still functionless. He is surviving through the restricted use of his right lung to the extent permitted by his crushed chest. He is breathing pure oxygen twenty-four hours a day."

Dr. Mason held up a hand to silence reporters' questions.

"I also have a statement from Mr. Hughes which I think will interest you," he said. "He asked me to read it to you."

There was an absolute stillness.

" 'I want you to give this message to the army,' " Dr. Mason read from Hughes' statement. " 'The accident was caused by the rear half of the right propeller. The rear four blades of this propeller suddenly changed into reverse position. This change occurred in the air and without any warning to me. . . .

" 'I had no reason to think it was a broken propeller because the engine continued to run normally and produce its full horsepower. The four front blades of the propeller were trying to pull the airplane ahead while the rear four blades were trying equally as hard to push it backward. To make things worse, these eight large propeller blades fighting one another created a dead drag on the right-hand side of the plane equal to that of a steel disc, seventeen feet in diameter, turned broadside to the wind at several hundred miles an hour.

" 'This disc destroyed the flow of air over the right wing and created a tremendous loss of lift. It felt as if some giant had the right wing in his hand and was pushing it back and down. I have thought about this carefully. Nothing small or light could have pushed the plane back with such a tremendous force. I am absolutely certain it was the propeller. Tell the army to look in the wreckage, find the rear half of the right propeller and find out what went wrong with it.' "

Dr. Mason stopped, folded the paper and said, "That's it."

And away went the reporters to write that Howard Hughes, apparently dying, had rallied long enough to deduce the cause of his crash.

22

Howard Hughes had begun the year recuperating from nervous exhaustion. Nine months later, seemingly twenty years older, he was recuperating from the multiple wounds and injuries that had brought him near death.

"I think he went home in an ambulance, but I wouldn't be surprised if he flew home in that damn bed," one hospital physician told another.

The doctors, reluctant to see him leave the hospital after a five-week stay, told him he should remain in bed at least six months. The Howard Hughes that the reporters met looked to be a very different man from the Hughes they had known before. He was rail thin; his neck seemed lost in its shirt collar. He had grown a mustache to cover scars left from wounds to his upper lip. He still wore his ancient brown fedora, but when he smiled faintly for the photographers it was the sad thin smile of a tired old man. He was carrying a quart of milk, a box of soda crackers and a paper sack containing a change of clothes.

"I have nothing to say, gentlemen," he told the press. "It looks like a nice morning, so I thought I'd go somewhere and rest for a while, then go back to work."

He had something more to say to night club columnist Earl Wilson, however, when Wilson congratulated him on a miraculous escape. Wilson's column reported the conversation:

"Miraculous?" echoed Hughes. "I guess it was, but I consider that I was very unlucky to have had that accident in the first place. It was caused by a freak mechanical failure that never should have occurred. It has never happened before, and the chances are that it will never happen again. I feel all right . . . I lost 35 pounds and haven't gained it back. But I hope to, soon. I burned my left hand pretty badly tearing the lucite canopy of the plane getting out. I'll never be able to straighten two of my fingers. That'll be my only permanent injury."

Wilson wanted to know if Hughes had any other close calls with death in his flying career. Hughes did not mention his *Hell's Angels* crash, nor his forced landing in the Mississippi, nor his Santa Ana crash in the H-1, nor the disaster at Lake Mead. Instead, he told of an incident in Siberia.

"I was in my seat, ready to take off, when I saw a little group of Russians wanting to say goodbye. I got out and thanked them. When I got back in, a cloudburst descended. I took off blind, absolutely blind. When I caught a glimpse of a boundary light going past under the wing, I knew I was at the end of the runway. I couldn't see past the nose of the plane for the rain. I just hauled back on the wheel and hoped for the best. Somehow we got up. I should have crashed out there in the tundra. After that I said, 'From here on out, whatever happens to me, I'll still be ahead because I don't have a right to be alive anyway.' Ever since that day, I've been living on borrowed time."

It now seemed as if Hughes wished to make up for the borrowed time he had lost while in hospital. Rather than follow the doctors' advice to spend half a year in convalescence, he resumed command of his financial empire, wherein events had marched with mixed success during his absence.

One project that had succeeded rather wildly was *The Outlaw*. Hughes had released it for national distribution in the spring, and now, by late summer, it had broken box office records everywhere —no doubt because it had run into censorship problems nearly everywhere it was shown. A Baltimore judge had helped matters considerably by upholding Maryland censorship, in the course of which he remarked that, "Miss Russell's breasts hung over the picture like a summer thunderstorm spread out over a landscape. They were everywhere. They were there when she first came into the picture. They were there when she went out."

Hughes said he figured the judge had added a million dollars to the gross. *The Outlaw* earned more money in Atlanta than the previous record holder, *Gone With The Wind*. Hughes warmly congratulated publicist Birdwell who had been hired to ensure this happy result. The picture broke Chicago attendance records, taking in $78,449 in one week; it reopened in San Francisco and doubled its earlier earnings there. One million persons paid to see it in Los Angeles. In all, *The Outlaw* earned $5,000,000—double its cost —before Hughes once again withdrew it from distribution and locked the film in the lead-lined room at 7000 Romaine Street. For all its notoriety, *The Outlaw* was not a dirty motion picture. Its commercial success may be attributed to a publicity campaign that made it virtually impossible for anyone to see the film without imagining that more had met the eye than actually did. Its only significance lies in the fact that its producer had both the resources and the courage—or gall—to stand up to censors, as he had done before in the case of *Scarface*. Hughes broke the way for other producers to bring out forthright films dealing with important themes that never would have received seals of approval under the Hays Office regulations with which Hughes had to contend. Hughes had defied the regulations. The climate in Hollywood improved.

A far more important project was the transformation of Transcontinental & Western Airlines into Trans World Airlines. Hughes returned from the hospital to find that TWA stock had slipped from a January high of $71 a share down to $2. The trouble had begun early in the year, when TWA began expanding its overseas routes over the bitter protests of Pan American Airways. A TWA Constellation crashed in Ireland, and the Civil Aeronautics Administration grounded all Constellations until the cause of the crash had been determined. Next, TWA pilots struck for twenty-five days. Overseas expansion meanwhile added thousands of personnel to the company's payroll. Flights from the United States to and from Europe were often half-filled. What with one thing and another, TWA faced a $16,000,000 loss in 1946—the greatest loss in any year since its birth. Worse, it also owed $40,000,000 to the Equitable Life Assurance Society. Refinancing was in order, and

TWA President Jack Frye urgently suggested that the company issue two million more shares of stock.

Even with Hughes in the hospital, the staff was reluctant to give orders of their own. For example, Preston Sturges learned the penalty of independent action. The director began shooting *Vendetta* and Hollywood gossips said he was seizing the opportunity to work at a time when Hughes could not look over his shoulder at every detail of costume, scenery and action. "Preston fiddles while Hughes burns," a sick wit said. Sturges drove the cast night and day, with Max Oefuls directing. Faith Domergue found herself being directed not only by Sturges and Oefuls, but also guided through the scenes by George Dolenz, her leading man.

"I marched for days and nights through an ammonia fog," she said. "It was supposed to be mist, rising from the swamps."

"No, that was a real fog, arising from the script," someone suggested.

In six weeks Sturges spent nearly $1,000,000 on *Vendetta*. When Hughes was able to leave the hospital, he sat down one midnight in a projection booth and studied the film until eight the following morning. Then he took Sturges to task. Sturges in turn suggested that much of the fault was Oefuls'—at which point the director resigned and returned to his native Europe. A new director was hired and quit; then another. By this time so many cooks had been stirring the broth—the ingredients of which had never been too promising—that it was a complete and unsalvageable mess. So most of what had been filmed was junked, and once again Hughes decided to take over the direction of a motion picture himself. Miss Domergue's career, which had begun to edge forward, would once again halt until Hughes could find the time to fit *Vendetta* into his schedule. His affairs now included not only TWA, his tool company and his brewery, but also his aircraft company which was still under contract to the government to produce the flying boat and a test model of the XF-11.

There followed days, then weeks of inactivity for *Vendetta*'s cast, but not for Hughes. Still a gaunt shadow of the man he had been before his crash, Hughes was every bit as busy as ever. He flew to New York as the year ended, sitting at the controls of a Douglas bomber he had converted to a private plane. There he dealt with matters of high finance, then returned to California to deal with minute affairs as well. On New Year's Eve, for example, he had a business meeting with Jane Russell who was later quoted by Earl Wilson as saying that she saw him about once a year, "when he sends his strange black car for me about three A.M. . . . it's very mysterious when you meet him."

On this particular New Year's Eve, Wilson reported, Miss Russell was blindfolded and driven through hills and forests to the door of a large house, where she was presented to a haggard-seeming, heavily bearded Hughes.

"He says, 'Do you want to sign a new contract?' "

"I say, 'I'd love to, dear,' " Wilson quoted Miss Russell as saying. "So we agree, and then I'm wafted back home with a blindfold on so I don't know where his hideout is."

The columnist said he asked Miss Russell what kind of boss Hughes was, and that she replied he was the most thorough man she had ever met, "but he's not a buddy, he's a boss."

As the old year ended and the new began and as he hurried from one thing to another quite as if his recent injuries had taken no toll of his strength, Howard Hughes managed, as usual, to give Hollywood gossip columnists something to write about. He was seen with Linda Darnell, Yvonne De Carlo, Ida Lupino, Jean Peters and Ava Gardner. Of these young actresses, Jean Peters was unique. She was an Ohio college girl who had won a beauty contest and a trip to Hollywood. She wore no makeup and $10 dresses. She often wore her hair in pigtails and she wore bluejeans. She was neither sultry nor bosomy nor dazzlingly beautiful. She was simply a fresh, good-looking young girl who would possibly have been much happier had she refused a Hollywood contract and become a schoolteacher in Ohio, as she had originally intended. Following his recuperation from the XF-11 crash, Hughes had dated Miss Peters but

then seemed to prefer the company of Miss Gardner, who bore
very little resemblance to a pigtailed ingenue. Miss Gardner had
hurried through three marriages before being seen about town with
Hughes. Hollywood gossips said she liked him well enough, but
that she did not like having to stay home waiting for him to call her,
nor did she appreciate being followed about by Hughes' guards.
Lana Turner was quoted as saying she loved Hughes, "but I know
absolutely nothing about him."

Far more typical of the reactions of the women Hughes met casually was the remark attributed to one young motion picture aspir-
ant he dated.

"Mainly," she said, "I guess I'm just sorry for him."

There are indications that Hughes at this time may have been
feeling sorry for himself. Writer Dwight Whitney said that Hughes
admitted his relationships with other people left a great deal to be
desired. Those who may have wondered at or possibly envied
Hughes' passing friendships with so many of Hollywood's most
beautiful women might consider a statement Whitney ascribes to
Hughes:

"My father was plenty tough. He never suggested that I do something; he just told me. He shoved things down my throat, and I had
to like it. But he had a hail-fellow-well-met quality that I never
had. . . . He was a terrifically loved man. I am not. I don't have
the ability to win people the way he did. . . . I suppose I'm not
like other men. Most of them like to study people. I'm not nearly as
interested in people as I should be, I guess. What I am tremen-
dously interested in is science, nature in its various manifestations,
the earth and the minerals that come out of it."

"He was a kind, quiet, shy man," a former motion picture star-
let, Sarilee Conlon, told writer James R. Phelan. She said she was
eighteen when she met Hughes and that she saw him every day for
six months—always with her parents present.

"He's really quite sensitive," she said. "Once he routed us all out
at three in the morning and flew us over the Grand Canyon to show
us the sunrise. He made us all look the other way until just the right

moment, when the sun burst over the canyon wall. Then he flew us deep down into the canyon to show us a little hidden green valley he had discovered. He said he was pretty sure no one else knew about it, and he seemed proud of this."

23

In 1947, the Republican Party's desire to capture the White House in the next election was not merely keen, it was excruciating. The party's problem, of course, was to discover some reason why the electorate might prefer to elect a Republican instead of a Democrat. What was needed was an issue, and both the Republicans and the Democrats reached for any sticks with which to beat dead horses, as is normally the case in election campaigns. Ordinarily the spectacle of American politics affords the disinterested observer a source of innocent merriment, providing that the observer has a stomach for balderdash and brummagem. But to the politicians it is all deadly serious. The consequences of the politicians' antics can be quite painful to the governed, so private citizen Howard Hughes learned to his sorrow in the summer of 1947, when he found himself selected to play dead horse to the cane of Senator Owen Brewster, Republican, of Maine. For his part, Senator Brewster learned a thing or two about the dangers of tampering with a private citizen from Texas, and the entire uproar was to assume the appearance of a mad circus and the mood of a knife fight on the docks.

Senator Brewster, who might have seen no reason why he should not become the next Vice-President of the United States, was out to build what politicians call a record. His general argument was that of his party: Democratic misrule. His task was to find a glittering example of such misrule. The stick he wielded was his power as Chairman of the Senate's Investigating Committee, which had appointed a subcommittee to look into wartime defense contracts. It occurred to him that the Hollywood playboy, Howard Hughes, had been granted $60,000,000 worth of warplane contracts, but had built no planes. Moreover, one of the contracts had been urged upon the government by President Roosevelt's son. If there should prove to have been any cloud about these contract negotiations, Senator Brewster was quite willing to magnify it into a storm. If this could be done, then he had an issue, and he also would have a national reputation as an honest politician. Moreover, he would also be doing his friend Juan Trippe a favor.

Trippe was head of Pan American Airways. Pan American was backing a bill in Congress that would merge the nation's two trans-oceanic airlines into one that would function as a chosen instrument of the United States, just as Air France and Lufthansa are the chosen instruments of their governments. It just happened that the other one of the United States' two transoceanic airlines was Trans World Airlines, whose principal stockholder was Howard Hughes, and it also happened that Hughes was vehemently opposed to the bill that Trippe wanted passed. He wanted no merger of any kind with Pan American, nor did he want to have anything to do with Trippe.

In the normal course of events Senate investigators armed with Congressional subpoenas showed up at Hughes' aircraft plant in California. They returned to Washington with certain documents found there, including the remarkably detailed expense account of one John W. Meyer, press agent and aide-de-camp to Howard Hughes. When Senator Brewster read this expense account, the expression on his face must have resembled that of Joshua watching the walls of Jericho come tumbling down.

The Senate subcommittee hearings, chaired by Republican Homer Ferguson of Michigan, began on a sweltering July day to the vast boredom of the press. To most reporters there would be no story unless Hughes should turn up: he was always news. But Hughes was grumbling on the West Coast about political hatchet men of questionable purpose, and said he did not plan to waste his time by attending. The hearings might have gone on in comparative obscurity had not someone leaked the word to a Hearst society reporter that the stars of the show would be women—pretty women; beautiful women; women whose names were in lights on theaters; other women who, although simple riveters in defense plants, were quite attractive. All of these ladies had worked for Hughes, the Hearst reporter said, and their duty had been to be friendly to lonely men who had had the power to award defense contracts to Hughes.

"That was enough for the summer becalmed tabloids," *Time* reported. "They sailed into the story with shrieks of joy and thankful indignation. They were sure they saw squads of scantily clad models, actresses and whatnots running in and out of New York and Hollywood bars, house parties, nightclubs, swimming pools, hotels —hotly pursued by grinning generals and government administrators. Was this any way for generals to behave?"

What the press actually saw on the Senate witness stand was a most uncomfortable Johnny Meyer. Meyer's career was this: He had briefly worked for the Columbia Broadcasting System and the Cleveland Wheat Exchange, then joined Warner Brothers as an aide to actor Errol Flynn. His official title was press agent, but his duties included helping Flynn to meet young ladies. He subsequently went to work for Hughes, acting as a public relations man and talent scout empowered to add beautiful young women to the Hughes payroll against the day they might be called to act in films.

Pasty and pallid, mopping his sweating, balding forehead with a handkerchief, Meyer told the Senate that his function was "to pick up the check" for Hughes. He said that he had spent more than $160,000 of Hughes' money during the wartime period of 1942 to 1945. He testified that exactly $5,083.79 of this sum had been spent on Elliott Roosevelt's entertainment. It hardly seemed necessary for the committee to point out to the press that Roosevelt was the son of the late President, and that he had personally recommended Hughes be given a contract to produce photo reconnaissance aircraft although Air Force officers superior to the then Colonel Roosevelt had previously recommended against this.

Slowly, methodically, the Senate investigators led Meyer through his testimony. He said he had bought $1,000 worth of race track tickets, liquor and hotel accommodations for Colonel Roosevelt and his date, the actress Faye Emerson; he obtained $132 worth of hard-to-get-in-wartime nylon stockings for Miss Emerson; and he had given Colonel Roosevelt a $1,000 loan just before his marriage to Miss Emerson. There was also a $106 dinner at Club 21 in New York for Colonel Roosevelt; a $576.83 hotel bill at the Beverly Hills Hotel in Los Angeles as a wedding gift; and an $850 wedding party. He said $220 worth of champagne had been drunk at the party. All of these items had been faithfully recorded on his expense account, Meyer said.

By this point the Senate investigation most certainly had the attention of the press. Reporters crowded into the hearing room, happily watching Meyer's discomfort increase as he told how he had paid train fare for Elliott, Miss Emerson and others to travel to Hyde Park simply in order that he, Meyer, could get to go along, too, and so meet Mrs. Eleanor Roosevelt. Everyone laughed when Meyer, asked to comment on a large telephone bill run up at his Waldorf-Astoria hotel room and marked in his expense account as "calls made by military officers," explained that he did not know what it had to do with Howard Hughes' airplanes, but he guessed the reason for the bill was that "it must have been be-nice-to-soldiers week."

Absolutely unamused was Elliott Roosevelt, who promptly sped to Washington and stalked into the hearing room to make the following statement: "The past records of Chairman Owen Brewster and Subcommittee Chairman Ferguson show they spent a good portion of their time since my father died trying to smear him. I think they do so in the hope of building themselves politically."

Whereupon, Elliott Roosevelt took the witness stand, and thumping his fist, he cried, "I deny with all my heart and soul that Johnny Meyer ever got me a girl!"

Then, getting down to cases, Roosevelt said that Meyer's expense accounts were "very largely inaccurate"; that he had not even been in the United States upon sundry occasions when Meyer's accounting said he had. Roosevelt called attention to his excellent, unchallengeable war record and denied that anyone had ever done him a favor which he had repaid with political influence. He then challenged the Senators, "If it is true that for the price of

entertainment, I made recommendations which would have in any
way endangered the lives of the men under me, that fact should be
made known to the public."

No one had suggested any such thing. More to the point, the
committee had no such facts. What they did have before them was
a man who had served his country well overseas, and who apparently had somewhat unwisely accepted certain favors from the public relations agent of a defense contractor at a time when he, Roosevelt, was in a position to have repaid those favors. Roosevelt's
testimony had called into question the veracity of the account
Johnny Meyer had presented to Howard Hughes for payment. But
at this stage of the proceedings it looked to the press very much as
if Senators Brewster and Ferguson had found themselves a campaign issue that was good as gold.

On the West Coast, Howard Hughes took a very different view
of the matter.

"They're lying about me," he said, kicking a zebra-skin chair
across Cary Grant's living room, "and they're not going to get
away with it."

Whereupon Hughes, whom a *Time* reporter once characterized
as being about as communicative as the Sphinx, and whose detestation of personal publicity was legendary, astonished reporters by
seeking them out. Against the advice of his lawyers and public relations counsel, he personally wrote the following statement for the
press:

> Everybody in the aviation industry recognizes that Brew-
> ster is lying. The people in the industry are only too familiar
> with Senator Brewster's relations with Pan American. And the
> people in the industry know that if Brewster were pushing the
> investigation of my war contracts for really legitimate rea-
> sons, and if Senator Brewster really believed me guilty of ob-
> taining war contracts by improper means, he would not be
> romancing me on the side, inviting me to lunch, and making
> appointments over the telephone to see me in California.

I charge specifically that at a lunch in the Mayflower Hotel in Washington, D.C., last February, Senator Brewster in so many words told me that the hearings need not go on if I agreed to merge the TWA airline with Pan American Airways and go along with the bill for a single overseas airline.

With that, Hughes took an armful of manila envelopes, a cardboard box of sandwiches and his brown fedora to the Culver City airstrip, where he climbed into his Douglas bomber and took off for Washington, flying into the camp of his enemies. One of the Senators had called him "the Tommy Manville of the West Coast"; another called Hughes "a mad genius, an insane perfectionist." And Senator Brewster called him a liar.

Howard Hughes walked into the one-ring circus that was the Senate committee's hearing room looking—*Fortune* magazine said —like "an enormously rich Huckleberry Finn, tieless and hatless, in a soiled shirt, and a rumpled sports jacket borrowed from his butler-valet, his long, thin wrists protruding from sleeves that were inches too short." Floodlights and a dozen motion picture cameras trained on him as he followed a wedge of aides who elbowed through the crowd, which included the fashionably dressed wives of government officials. The wives, in fact, had organized parties to attend the hearings and had bought new dresses just in case the newsreel cameras should flicker over them. The ladies jumped up and down to see over one another's heads as Hughes entered the room; newspaper photographers climbed atop tables; the noise level rose and drowned out Senator Ferguson's frantic pounding with a gavel. The one man in the room who paid absolutely no attention to the pandemonium was Hughes.

"State your full name and address," Ferguson said when order had been restored.

"Which address? Business or residential?" Hughes said.

Hughes gave his Los Angeles and Houston business addresses, and identified himself as Howard R. Hughes, largest stockholder of the Hughes Tool Company.

"Is that a closed corporation?" Ferguson asked.

"What is a closed corporation?" Hughes asked.

"A closed corporation is one in which the stock is tightly held by a small group," Ferguson explained.

"Oh. I own all the stock," Hughes explained.

The exchange was not the stuff of which great dialogue is made, but the tone of question and response was very plain. The mutual hatred was almost palpable. The translation of Ferguson's routine inquiries was, "We are going to fix your wagon, Buster," and the translation of Hughes' replies was, "If you want a fat lip, Sonny, you go ahead and try."

The New England accents of Senator Brewster interrupted the questioning.

"I hope no undue delicacy will delay our taking up another matter," he said. "I understand Mr. Hughes is prepared to take up this other matter now."

"I will be very happy," Hughes said, meaning it.

"A challenge to the good faith of the committee has been made which the subcommittee has decided to explore," Ferguson needlessly explained to the audience. "The committee hopes to dispose of it expeditiously. Mr. Hughes, do you understand what we have in mind?"

"I think I do," Hughes said evenly.

The audience laughed.

"I have made certain accusations to the press," Hughes said. "I stand on them. Senator Brewster, I understand, has said he would like to hear me repeat them under oath. I think Senator Brewster should take the stand. Allow me to cross-examine him and bring in witnesses."

"The subcommittee won't let Senator Brewster cross-examine you or let you cross-examine him," Ferguson angrily replied. "You and the Senator may each submit questions to this committee. The subcommittee feels that Senator Brewster should have only the same privilege that you have."

"And I want only the same privileges as the committee," Hughes retorted. "Any questions of me by the committee is itself in the nature of cross-examination. If it is unfriendly, I think I should have the same privilege as Senator Brewster. Will I have the right to call other witnesses?"

"We will rule on that when you request witnesses."

"I don't want to launch into this matter and then find my hands tied."

"It is no desire of this committee to have your hands tied."

Hughes' lawyer tried to capture his client's attention, but Hughes shrugged him off.

"Very well," he said, "my charges have been made pretty clear in the press. I charge specifically that during luncheon at the Mayflower Hotel in Washington in the week beginning February 10, 1947, in the suite of Senator Brewster, that the Senator told me in so many words that if I would agree to merge TWA with Pan Am and go along with this community airline bill, there would be no further hearing in the matter."

There was a silence. Hughes shuffled through a sheaf of papers. Brewster fidgeted at his end of the subcommittee table. Reporters looked back and forth at the two men as if they were watching a pingpong match.

"Proceed," Ferguson said.

"I have made my statement. I told you what took place."

"Is there anything else you wish to discuss?"

"No. I thought Senator Brewster would want to talk after that."

Hughes looked at Brewster from the witness stand with much the expression of the hero of a Hollywood Western who has just challenged the villain to crawfish or go for his gun. Brewster asked his clerks to find him certain papers. When Brewster took the stand, he spoke with the fervor of a William Jennings Bryan at a Sunday camp meeting.

"First," he cried, "it would be inconceivable to anyone that a man so long in the public eye as I have been—in the Maine legislature, governor of Maine, member of the United States House of Representatives and now a United States Senator—could have made so bald a proposition as he describes. It sounds a little more like Hollywood than Washington. No one of any competence or experience could make such a proposition, and I never did."

"Never did what? Made a proposition so bald?" one reporter asked another.

But Brewster, going on, said that it was Hughes, not himself, who had first brought up the possibility of a merger with Pan American. Hughes, whose distaste for Pan American and its president was well-known, looked up in angry amazement.

"At the Mayflower Hotel luncheon was anything said about calling off this investigation?" Ferguson asked.

"Not a word," Brewster said, and that was that—one of the two men had lied to the Senate under oath.

"Was anything said on which such a conclusion could have been drawn?"

"Not in the slightest," Brewster replied. "I have searched my memory and all the material bearing on the matter, and I find no indication at any time that I took any steps to retard or accelerate the investigation, and I think the committee and the staff can bear that out."

Hughes looked at Brewster and smiled broadly. The Senator fairly shouted, "It reveals pretty clearly that they were seeking to lay a trap for me. If chairmen of committees are to be intimidated, then Senate investigations may as well cease. I promptly appointed a subcommittee headed by Senator Ferguson to handle this matter and let the chips fall where they may. I cannot and will not yield to a campaign of this character."

Ferguson looked at Hughes. He asked him if he had any questions to submit to the committee.

"Between two hundred and five hundred questions, just about," Hughes drawled.

Ferguson and Brewster stared at him.

"I repeat, do you have any questions?" Ferguson snapped.

"Between two hundred and five hundred questions," Hughes said.

Ferguson declared the meeting adjourned. Hughes rose, gathered up his papers, and walked out amid a scattering of applause. It seemed to the press that the round had gone to Hughes, whose demeanor had been cold, controlled and disdainful, while that of Brewster had been loudly frantic.

Hughes spent the entire night writing out questions to put to Brewster. At sunrise he ordered black coffee and orange juice, dressed in a gray suit that had been ordered for him in lieu of the borrowed sports jacket he had worn earlier and was waiting alone in the Senate hearing room when the Senators arrived to begin the morning's session.

Taking the witness stand, Hughes said it was "obvious" that either he or Brewster had been lying; he called Brewster "one of the greatest trick-shot artists in Washington" and said, "As for me, I have been called capricious, a playboy, eccentric, but I don't believe I have the reputation of a liar. I think my reputation in that respect meets what most Texans consider important."

"What you are doing here," Ferguson cut in, "clearly indicates that you are trying to discredit this committee so that it cannot properly perform its function. The integrity of the United States Senate is at stake. I speak for the Senate. If you believe that because of your great wealth and access to certain publicity channels you can intimidate any member of this subcommittee, you are mistaken and that's final. While you may want to discredit one member, you apparently are trying to keep your contracts from being brought before the public."

"I deny that."

"Then what *was* your motive?"

"Very simple," Hughes said. "I felt a great injustice had been done to me, and I thought I should be allowed to tell my side of it. Remember that I did not speak to the press until this investigation had been in blazing headlines for four or five days."

Hughes complained that he was not getting equal treatment; that the conduct of the hearing favored Brewster.

"You *are* getting equal treatment!" Ferguson nearly shouted. "This committee is not going to have you say all the time that you are not."

In due course, Brewster took the stand to answer questions that
Hughes had written out. As writer Stephen White remarked, "his
air of confidence began to dissipate, and he became visibly harried.
His own testimony revealed closer links to Pan American than he
had earlier cared to admit; his counter-accusations were dented or
punctured. At each point upon which he clearly had a tale to tell
that differed substantially from that told by Hughes, he was called
a liar, bluntly or euphemistically, but without rancor. Hughes, vi-
ciously cold, maintained the detached air of a biologist examining
an interesting specimen."

"I have other questions," Hughes at length told Ferguson, "but
there's no use submitting them in this manner. Brewster's answers
have been evasive and in many cases not direct answers at all. I
can't submit any further questions this way. . . . Senator Brewster's story is a pack of lies, and I can tear it apart if given the
opportunity."

At this point, the audience burst into applause and cheers, for
despite the fact that Hughes' wealth made him one of the most
powerful men in America, he nonetheless conveyed the image of a
lonely man, armed only with moral right, single-handedly defending himself against all the power of the Spanish Inquisition. Perhaps
more important, he also was the image of Texas chivalry, ready to
take on—in whatever numbers—anybody who would dare to call
him a liar.

Of course none of this was moving the subcommittee investiga-
tion one inch toward its ostensible purpose: discovery of whether
Hughes had obtained his wartime contracts by improper means.
The following day saw Noah Dietrich called to the stand. While
Dietrich routinely answered questions relating to expense accounts
turned in to the company by Johnny Meyer and Russell Birdwell,
Ferguson looked around the room in puzzlement and then asked,
"Where *is* Johnny Meyer?"

The audience searched the section reserved for Hughes' staff,
and their eyes could not find him, either.

"I don't know where he is," Hughes murmured.

"He's not in this room, and the staff can't find him at his hotel," Ferguson complained, almost in the tones of a little boy pouting.

Hughes laughed. So did the audience.

"It isn't funny," Ferguson said.

"Somebody laughed behind me," Hughes said.

"Is he your personal assistant?"

"I understand he is so listed."

"Is he, or is he not? You're the president."

"He is. He handles public relations."

"Why did you send Meyer off?"

Hughes said casually that Meyer had gone to Europe.

"He is your employee," Ferguson said. "You knew we hadn't finished with him."

In fact, Meyer's subpoena had expired the day before, but Hughes replied, "I have twenty-eight thousand employees, and I can't know where all of them are all of the time."

"Do you know where Meyer is?"

"No."

"Will you see that he is here at two P.M.?"

"I don't know that I will," Hughes said. He leaned back in his chair and regarded Ferguson thoughtfully.

"Just to put him up here on the stand beside me and make a publicity show," Hughes added. "My company has been inconvenienced just about enough. I brought Meyer here twice. You had time for unlimited questioning."

"The chair feels that as president of the company, you should know where Meyer is. I must warn you of possible contempt. Give me your answer to the preceding question."

"I don't remember."

"I've just asked what your answer was."

"I don't remember—get it off the record."

Ferguson slammed his hand on the desk so hard that he must have hurt himself.

"Will you bring Mr. Meyer in here at two P.M.?" he said. It was not a question, but an order.

"No," Hughes said. A breathless audience heard him add, "No, I don't think I will."

This exchange did not advance the course of the hearing, either, nor did the following day's session. In fact, the hearing was by this time totally out of control; it had degenerated into nothing more than a display of anger on the part of Senators Brewster and Ferguson, and of arrogant disdain on the part of Howard Hughes. Nor was all the shouting confined to the Senate hearing room. Each side took its case to the press as well. Hughes complained that wiretaps had been found in his hotel room, and that a Washington police detective had put them there, acting as an agent of Brewster and Pan American Airways. Brewster told the press that he had evidence from one TWA stewardess that she feared to fly on the same plane with Hughes. The girl denied she had said any such thing. Brewster made the mistake of saying that Hughes' "flying lumber-yard"—the mammoth flying boat—would never get into the air. This was the most unkind cut of all, for Hughes was as defensive of his tremendous seaplane as a mother is of a hurt child. He could not see the slightest humor in the epithet *Spruce Goose,* and no one dared to use it near him.

In a statement to the press he said, "I had to sweat five weeks in Washington [during the war] to prevent cancellation of the contract because of the activities of its critics. This project was put behind from the start because a lot of people in the government didn't like it. We got pushed around everywhere. I had to build up a staff of engineers from scratch because the Government had issued orders not to hire anybody away from other producers. We made up a staff out of math professors, college boys, 4-Fs, old men and whoever else I could get.

"I can only tell you that I designed every nut and bolt that went into this airplane. I designed this ship to a greater degree than any one man has ever designed any of the recent large airplanes, down to one half the size. I can say this. I worked for eighteen to twenty hours a day for six months to a year on this plane. And with my other work on the XF-11 and other war work, my health was so broken down that I was sent away for a rest of seven months after the war ended. If I made any mistake, it was not delegating more of this work, and it might have resulted in a better job. I tried to do too much myself with my own hands.

"If the flying boat fails to fly, I will probably exile myself from this country. I have put the sweat of my life into this thing, and $7,200,000 of my own money. My reputation is wrapped up in it. I have stated that if it fails to fly, I will leave this country. And I mean it."

This statement had nothing to do with the purpose of the hearings, either. But it put an end to them. The question now had become not how the contracts had been obtained, but whether the airplane would fly. Hughes' fervent promise was made at the end of a Friday session, and Senator Ferguson ordered the hearing adjourned, telling reporters "Monday's session will be the most interesting yet," but Monday never came. Ferguson subsequently announced that the hearing would be adjourned until November, to give the committee time to find Johnny Meyer—a statement as self-serving as any so far made by either Hughes or Brewster.

From a lake in Maine, Brewster said he had come home "full of poisoned arrows that have been shot at me" but that he was confident "my moral code will compare favorably with that of this young man who found time while others were fighting the war to produce *The Outlaw.*"

Maine's voters thought otherwise. Brewster sought renomination and lost in the Republican primary election.

From Washington, where he held the field after the battle, Hughes said, "I thought this investigation would drag my reputation through the mud, but instead, due to the fact that the American public believes in fair play and because they supported me, I have more friends now than I ever had in my life."

By and large, the public agreed. More than an hundred Hughes-for-President clubs were formed throughout the nation—the first of them opened in Brooklyn.

"As long as we have the fair-minded American public and a free press watching over us, I guess we're all right," Hughes concluded.

Whereupon he returned to California to take up his interrupted career and his somewhat special way of life, the most striking aspect of which was a passion for anonymity. Despite his respect for the free press that watches over us, Hughes happened to be one man who paid public relations firms to keep his name *out* of, not in, the papers.

24

"At first look," said an Associated Press reporter, "you feel like the fellow who saw a giraffe for the first time—there just ain't no such animal. I thought I was looking at the biggest wing I had ever seen. Then I discovered that I was only looking at the aileron, the movable control portion that hinges along the rear edge of the wing. I remember how well the plywood was fitted, as neatly as a mandolin."

The reporter was looking at an airplane that had wings longer than a football field; wings so thick that a mechanic could stroll about inside them to inspect the eight engines. The hull was 220 feet long; the machine weighed 425,000 pounds and was designed to fly nonstop from Honolulu to Tokyo carrying two battalions of armed soldiers. Its hull loading port could permit a sixty-ton tank to be driven aboard. The hull below the cargo deck was divided into eighteen watertight compartments, and if two-thirds of them were flooded, the ship could still remain afloat. Millions of board feet of lumber had gone into the construction, and eight tons of nails had been hammered in to keep the wooden parts in place until the glue dried. Then they had been removed. The flight deck was twenty feet above the waterline, but the only crew needed to fly this machine—if fly it ever did—would consist of a pilot, co-pilot, navigator and two flight engineers. This was no larger a crew than the one Hughes carried around the world in the comparatively tiny Lockheed Lodestar.

It had taken two days and two nights to bring the aircraft's wing, hull, tail and motors down by sections twenty-five miles to the sea. Utility crews from twenty-three companies moved ahead, taking down power lines and telephone poles; reinforcing three bridges; chopping down hundreds of trees. It seemed afterwards as if a tornado had cut a small swath from Culver City to Long Beach. The moving cost alone was $55,000.

The airplane was formally named *Hercules*. It had originally been designated the HK-1, but after Henry Kaiser had ceased to be a participant in the government contract, Hughes sponsored a naming contest among his employees in order to remove from the project any reminder that Kaiser had once been any part of it.

Following the July Senate hearings, Hughes ordered work to proceed twenty-four hours a day, and one shrewd columnist guessed the reason for this was that Hughes desperately wanted to get the *Hercules* into the air before the Senate hearings were resumed in November. In midsummer Senator Harry P. Cain of Washington asked Hughes if he could inspect the flying boat. Senator Cain was a Republican teammate of Senators Brewster and Ferguson, and although he had not been as antagonistic as they toward Hughes at the hearings, it was with some apprehension that Hughes welcomed Senator Cain to the *Hercules'* hangar.

Senator Cain took one look—as much of a look, that is, as the eye could see of the vast shape from any one angle—and stood stock still.

"This looks," he said slowly, "like something Flash Gordon created. . . ."

Then, to Hughes, he said, "If you had finished it in time for the war, the Germans would have been scared into surrendering."

"If the Senator's investigating committee had gone to work on the Germans," Hughes said dryly, "you boys could have scared them to death."

Cain ignored the remark and climbed up into the fuselage. Hughes grimaced. Cain's shoes were the first to tread the satin-smooth finish; the workmen wore felt socks, like those window-dressers use, as they labored on this vastest of a perfectionist's creations.

The Senator walked through the hull, moving in the silent wonder of a tourist on his first visit to Westminster Abbey. He sat down in the pilot's seat and it was easy to see from the look on his face that the Senator, like a ten-year-old boy, was imagining himself at the controls, steering the largest flying machine in the world through stormy skies.

A courteous host, Hughes explained how the aircraft had been conceived, how this part had been built, the problems that had been posed by that part. . . .

They were inside for more than an hour and when the Senator came back to earth from the lofty hull a radio news reporter thrust a microphone at him and asked, "Senator Cain, you've emerged from this inspection tour, I imagine, rather amazed by the size alone of the physical characteristics of this flying boat?"

"I've just come out of the entrails of something much larger than I ever imagined Jonah's whale to be," Senator Cain said. Groping, he went on, "This is the largest thing that is an aircraft that one could possibly . . .

"Well," he said, trying to put it into English, "I just can't describe it. I'm sorry to have started."

"Let me put the acid test in the way of a question, Senator," the reporter said. "Would you like to ride in it on its first flight?"

"I will answer that question," Cain said quickly. "I've been thinking about it during the several hours I have been here. This has nothing to do with the United States Senate, nothing to do with the investigation, nothing to do with public life, but I can assure you, as an American who enjoys the sort of adventure that made this country possible and is going to make its future even greater, if I were given the opportunity to go on a test flight I don't know of anything that could keep me away."

Was this an "official" verdict from the Senator, the reporter wanted to know. Cain frowned and said his trip was entirely "unofficial." Well, what did he think? What was his overall impression?

"It's very difficult in words to define what I've actually seen," Cain said. "I think the greatest impression I have and one which will stay with me for a very long time is that I have been looking at the world in which we are determined and bound to live tomorrow.

This aircraft attempts to bridge the great gap between things which we understand to be practical and reasonable and normal and usual, into the realm of the fantastic and the impossible. But if this aircraft flies, and I'm not the one who says it will not fly and I hope it does, it will have achieved the impossible in our lifetime."

The reporters turned to Hughes.

"I can only say that I believe from what Senator Cain has told us, he has a little different conception of this airplane than the one which he brought here from Washington," Hughes said. "I believe he feels a little differently about this airplane. I think he understands the problems we have faced, and I'm glad he has taken the trouble to look at it."

Cain left Long Beach a staunch ally of Howard Hughes, to the discomfiture of his colleagues in the Senate, Brewster and Ferguson. In another interview, Cain said, "Once in the Puget Sound country where I live there was a bridge which fell down. It was a great tragedy, but it taught a great lesson from which future bridges will benefit. Maybe the flying boat won't fly. Maybe Hughes has ventured the impossible and, if it turns out that way, future designers will know the point beyond which they cannot go. This lesson, however negative, would constitute a mighty contribution to the potential of tomorrow. . . . Failure might destroy Hughes' reputation as a competent craftsman. But America and its aircraft industry are certain to win.

"If this be true—and surely it is—can't we all afford to hope that success, rather than failure, comes to Howard Hughes? I would wager a modest sum that Howard Hughes stands as good a chance as any mortal to show the rest of us what the next century is to be like."

In so saying, Cain drove home precisely the point that Hughes had been trying to make all along. To be sure, the war had provided both the opportunity and a sense of urgency for the creation of this flying boat, but surely to the engineer in Hughes it was not so much the war but the engineering problems that were important. Surely to the poet and the dreamer in Hughes, it was the concept that was important—not the contract. The real purpose of this tremendous creation was not actually the transportation of armies overseas so much as it was discovery. Could the thing be done? In the event of success or failure, lessons could be learned; lessons that would, as Cain said, usher in the future.

If Hughes had seen to every detail of the flying boat's creation, prosaic souls might well accuse him of undue meddling; they might well say this was no way to run an aircraft factory in wartime. But they might have missed the point that Hughes was a genius—and not necessarily the mad genius that one Senator had called him— who was almost entirely personally responsible for imagining and building what no man had imagined and built before. It is difficult to set time limits to a contract that calls for personal services; it is impossible to predict when solutions will be found to problems that have yet to be discovered. It was remarkable enough that work on the *Hercules* got as far as it did during the war in view of the fact that Hughes had the lowest of priorities on matériel and a make- shift labor force. But it is altogether astounding to consider that he dreamed this particular dream and made so much of it appear in reality, when he was at the same time directing several businesses, building munitions factories, producing a motion picture, creating another airplane and running an airline, meanwhile having to de- vote weeks in Washington to defending himself against his critics and reassuring his friends.

While Senator Cain went about the land zealous as a convert, word was heard in Washington that Senator Brewster's committee had turned up new, sensational evidence. Hughes' reply to this ru- mor was to schedule the flying boat's flight tests for early Novem- ber. He publicly invited all the members of Brewster's committee to come and watch or, if they wished, to come aboard and ride with him.

"There will only be taxiing up and down the harbor," Hughes said. "We won't attempt to fly it yet."

None of the Senators accepted—even Cain found something to keep him away. Brewster sent a sharp note saying his committee would be busy on that date conducting the first of the new hearings, and that Hughes would be hearing from the committee. So Hughes advanced the date for the tests and sent invitations to the nation's important newspapers and magazines. Thirty-seven East Coast correspondents accepted, but as many more declined when their editors took the position that it was not proper to accept hospitality from a man who offered it with a private end in view—and whose hospitality to Air Force procurement officers was the subject of a Senate investigation.

For those who did attend there were suites in a Santa Monica hotel, steak and lobster dinners and gallons of fine whisky. There were speedboat rides about the harbor and public relations men to act as *cicerones*. All expenses were, of course, paid by Hughes.

On the morning of the test date, November first, the *Hercules* was launched, but brisk winds were blowing up a choppy sea and further tests were postponed for twenty-four hours. The following dawn Odekirk collected Hughes at Cary Grant's house. He said Hughes' first question was, "How's the weather at Long Beach?"

"It's not good, but it's better," Odekirk said.

He said they drove the rest of the way in silence.

Odekirk uneasily suspected that Hughes intended to fly the plane, not just taxi it. All attempts to suggest to Hughes that he should hire a test pilot had been choked off when Hughes abruptly said, "I do my own flying." Although Hughes had told Odekirk that there would be no attempt at flight this day, neither Odekirk nor anyone knew what was in Hughes' mind. Hughes ushered reporters aboard for the *Hercules'* first water tests, and tugs pulled the monster aircraft away from her mooring and out into the harbor channel.

"We're going to make a brief three-mile test, gentlemen," he told reporters. "We'll reach speeds of only about forty miles per hour. The water is too choppy to try anything else."

Photographers who had hired an airship from which to take overhead views of the flying boat watched disconsolately from the shore. At the last moment the pilot of the airship had refused to cast off on grounds that the winds aloft were too strong for his lighter-than-air craft. But as Hughes had promised, the first test was unspectacular. He trundled the aircraft down the bay at his announced speed, turned, and brought the reporters back again. When they had disembarked, Hughes made a second run down the bay, this time bringing the aircraft up to ninety miles per hour, perilously close to takeoff speed. Odekirk, watching from the shore, feared Hughes was trying to lift off.

Before the third test run began, a helicopter appeared and hovered over the *Hercules'* wing.

"Who the hell is that?" Odekirk demanded.

"I don't know," a crewman said. "Is it one of ours?"

Hughes shook his fist at the hovering helicopter. He spoke into his radio, "This is a test area. Get out of here. You are in danger."

But the helicopter, with a *Life* magazine reporter and photographer aboard, hovered where they were.

Hughes opened the throttles and the eight engines pulled the *Hercules* away for its third run. He opened the throttles wider and the *Hercules* moved down the choppy bay faster; to sixty miles per hour, then eighty, ninety, and finally to a hundred—and the giant aircraft lifted itself from the water and climbed on a long, slow line into the air.

Hughes held it in the air for more than a mile at an altitude of some seventy feet before gently lowering it back onto the surface of the sea. As the plane touched down, the hundreds of watchers who had held their breaths throughout the momentary flight burst into cheers. Hughes taxied slowly back to the mooring, and supervised the *Hercules'* berthing. He came ashore wearing a faint smile for the press.

"It just felt so bouyant and good," he said, "I just pulled it up."

No, he said, he had not flown the ship with any thought of impressing the Senate investigating committee.

"As I said before," he told his questioners, "I don't think the committee is interested in the merit of this plane. Except for Senator Pepper (a Florida Democrat) and Senator Cain, it doesn't care whether the plane flies or sinks. As for myself, I am thoroughly satisfied with the performance of this plane on its trial run."

Naturally, there were banner headlines. *Time* magazine put it simply: "IT FLIES!"—knowing that everyone would know to what the headline referred. A thoughtful Washington photographer took a picture of Senator Brewster glumly reading a newspaper account of the flight.

25

There was a brief sequel to Hughes' adventure with the Senate committee. He strode into the hearing room something of a public hero to confront a Senator Brewster who was shortly to disappear from office. The questioning returned to the employment of Johnny Meyer as a public relations director and why his duties included entertaining military officers.

"All the aircraft companies were doing the same thing," Hughes said. "I believe Meyer patterned his work after what he saw in other companies. I don't know whether it's a good system or not. But the system did obtain. And it certainly did not seem fair for all of my competitors to entertain while I sat back and ignored the government and its officials. . . . You, Senator, are a lawmaker, and if you can pass a law that no one can entertain Army officers and you can enforce it, I'll be glad to abide by it. I never wanted to bother with it. If you can get others to do business that way, I'll be glad to do so, too."

But then the questioning turned away from Johnny Meyer, and the Senators introduced a new name into the proceedings—that of Major General Bennett Meyers.

General Meyers, it seemed, had been given a disability discharge from the Air Force on grounds he suffered from a nervous condition. General Meyers had, during his service, signed the contracts for Hughes' two aircraft—the XF-11 and the *Hercules*—over the objections of certain of his associates. He lived in a manner and style unknown to most officers of his rank. Senator Ferguson demanded that Hughes describe in detail whatever relationship he had with General Meyers.

"It is with great reluctance that I tell you this," Hughes said. "I thought originally that Meyers was one of the charter members of the Hate Howard Hughes Club at Wright Field. . . . Then he came out to California to see my D-2 experimental airplane. Hughes said that Meyers told him, "Howard, I am simply amazed. I have always thought of your airplane as a kind of myth. . . . around Wright Field the general feeling has been that it was just a balloon, nothing to it. But I have looked at it, and I am simply appalled, because this is really a fine airplane."

After this, Hughes said, he and Meyers became good friends. Months later, in general conversation, Hughes mentioned that he was looking around for a new general manager for his aircraft company.

"Benny Meyers looked at me with that little smile of his and took the cigar out of his mouth and said, 'You know, Howard, I might like to have that job myself,' " Hughes told the Senate.

Then, worse, he said, Meyers asked Hughes to lend him $200,-000 so that he, Meyers, could buy stock on margin and turn a $1,000,000 profit.

"I turned the loan down," Hughes said, "and when I did, it resulted in a complete breach of friendship between General Benny Meyers and me."

At this point, Hughes' participation in the hearing was over, for the committee went baying off on the somewhat rank scent of General Meyers. It seemed that Meyers had for many years taken advantage of his position as Air Force procurement officer. Knowing that a corporation was about to receive a government contract—for it was part of his duty to approve these contracts—he would buy stock in the corporation before the contract was let, while the price of the stock was low. In so doing he had attracted the interest of the Treasury and of the Federal Bureau of Investigation, and when the FBI brought the matter to the attention of the Air Force, Meyers had been told it was time to retire.

Hughes slipped gratefully and finally out of the circus tent that was the Senate committee's hearing room, while the Senators turned their full attention to Benny Meyers. They had started on safari to shoot a lion, only to hit a rabbit instead, but the hide of Benny Meyers was at least better than nothing.

Before Hughes could return to California, however, he was invited to a party. The Washington press corps had watched with considerable admiration as Hughes had given Ferguson and Brewster as good or better than he had received in a battle of *non sequiturs,* and they wanted to express their appreciation. So the reporters rented a suite in a small hotel across the street from the Senate Office Building. A question was, would Hughes show up?

To everyone's pleasant surprise, he did—and seemed genuinely touched by the invitation. He drank happily (but sparingly, for Hughes is a light drinker) of their liquor and he ate their sandwiches and told them flying stories. He laughed loudest when they presented him with a framed enlargement of the photograph showing Senator Brewster reading about the flight of the *Hercules.*

"This is the best present I've ever received," Hughes said. "It's going up on my office wall!"

They clapped and cheered. What they did not know—and what Hughes was too polite to tell them—was that he had no office, but directed his manifold affairs by telephone from whatever room he happened to be in or from whatever public telephone booth was at hand.

26

There would be a cast call for 8 A.M. and when everyone assembled
no one would know what to do, for the excellent reason that Howard Hughes did not appear to tell them. So Faith Domergue, her
leading man, George Dolenz, and the cast of *Vendetta* would sit
around the studio for eight hours and then go home. The Los Angeles winters can be far less comfortable than the Chamber of
Commerce will admit. On one occasion Hughes wandered onto the
set at the Goldwyn studio, saw that everyone was shivering, and
disappeared. He shortly returned with overcoats over his arm
and distributed these to the cast, telling them to put the coats on
and keep warm. With that he disappeared again.

Dolenz did not know what to make of all this. Shooting had begun in 1946 and it was now 1948, and in all that time. Dolenz had
never met Hughes. He had seen Hughes, but had never spoken with
him. He said this was ridiculous, that he was in despair, but that his
contract prevented his resigning from the film. What Dolenz may
not have realized was that the *Vendetta* cast was on the hook, just
as Eddie the barber was; just as were the executives of Trans
World Airlines; just as were the secretaries at 7000 Romaine
Street. But one evening Dolenz found his opportunity in the men's
room of a Hollywood night club, the other occupant of the room
being Howard Hughes.

"Mr. Hughes, I wanted to meet you and thank you for my job,
but something has to be done," Dolenz said.

"Who? What?"

Dolenz said that Hughes seemed startled and puzzled.

"I am George Dolenz, your leading man," the actor explained.
"Who?"

"I am Orso," Dolenz said desperately, giving the name of the character he played in *Vendetta*.

"Oh," Hughes said. "I know you now."

Dolenz said that Hughes thereupon became charm itself, gracious, delighted to meet his performer. He said they talked for twenty minutes in that men's room, discussing the picture, its problems and Dolenz' acting. He said Hughes told him, "I know we've had problems, but I'm getting a new director and we're going to start over again. Believe in me. Believe in the picture. Believe in our company. We must have cooperation if we're going to turn out a good picture."

Dolenz was appalled by the notion that things would begin all over again—would this mean two more years? Of course he would be glad to cooperate, but . . .

But Hughes had smiled a pleasant goodbye and walked away.

It would seem that Hughes had other things on his mind than Dolenz and Miss Domergue's careers as the new year began. He came riding into 1948 on a quite respectable comber of success; he had done his Senatorial critics in the eye and had flown his *Hercules;* the brewery was enjoying increased sales; the Hughes Tool Company's net worth had increased to $200,000,000; the Air Force had accepted a new version of the XF-11. Unfortunately, Trans World Airlines had lost $8,000,000 in 1947, and the $40,-000,000 loan was coming due at Equitable. Unless TWA could find $1,000,000 with which to pay the interest, the note would be due and TWA would go out of business or be taken over by the insurance company.

But Hughes persuaded the Civil Aeronautics Board to increase TWA's foreign mail subsidy by 110 percent and the interest payment was made. He also managed to obtain a $10,000,000 loan from the Reconstruction Finance Corporation with which to buy twelve new Lockheed Constellations for TWA's use. Hughes' airline competitors scratched their heads and wondered how he had done this. With the new aircraft, TWA added new routes and new customers.

So with all these affairs marching well enough, Hughes looked about for something to do. His friend Floyd Odlum, the gentleman rancher, financier and husband of the aviatrix Jacqueline Cochran, had control of a holding company called the Atlas Corporation, whose resources included, among many other things, 929,000 shares of Radio-Keith-Orpheum stock. RKO was a motion picture studio that, apart from its production facilities, also had an interest in 124 motion picture theaters.

RKO was a sick company, but in the curious world of high finance a very sick company may be more valuable to a purchaser than an extremely healthy one. Its losses may be declared a tax exemption to be set against the purchaser's profits in other enterprises, with result that the sum of these losses plus the tax the purchaser now pays on his reduced overall profit may be less than the purchaser would have paid out in taxes on his profitable businesses had he not bought the sick company. But the sickness at RKO was more pervasive than a simple failure to make money. Production was at a virtual standstill and the studio had been unable to develop stars; it had degenerated into a kind of rental lot hired out to independent producers. RKO's original reputation had been as a company that produced inexpensive, action-filled pictures. In an attempt to reverse its field, RKO had hired Dore Schary, an up-and-coming young director who brought in new ideas and a determination to make major films with established stars. But in 1947, RKO nevertheless lost nearly $2,000,000, and Odlum was quite willing to sell his controlling interest in the studio to Hughes.

There followed a series of furtive meetings between the two men, held at dead of night in parked cars, in hotel rooms and in the cockpits of airplanes. If such locales seem somewhat bizarre, the simple explanation is that Hughes already had sufficient experience with tapped telephones and concealed microphones placed in his Washington hotel room at the time of the Senate hearing. Industrial espionage had, by 1948, become a well-developed way of corporate life. If the times chosen seemed peculiar, it must be remembered that Hughes' love of eerie hours had characterized him from early youth. Had not a friend of Big Howard's remarked that sixteen-year-old Sonny was "a nocturnal varmint type"? Some people do their best work by night; others by day. Hughes was a night person.

The meetings eventually culminated in Hughes' agreement to pay Odlum $8,825,690 for his RKO stock, at which point Hughes called Noah Dietrich in from Houston. Dietrich said, in effect, "It's a good idea, Howard. Go ahead and buy RKO."

On paper, the RKO purchase did seem good. Hughes would spend nearly $9,000,000, but what with tax carrybacks and deductions, the price would be about $5,000,000 out-of-pocket. For that money Hughes would acquire a valuable piece of Los Angeles real estate, a complete motion picture-making facility, a pool of cash reserve that could be tapped if necessary, a fair amount of good will, and the services of some 2,000 skilled studio employees, plus distribution outlets in 124 theaters. A $10,000,000 loan was negotiated with the Mellon Bank, and when the deal was consummated, Hughes sent Senator Brewster a telegram: I HEREBY OFFER YOU A JOB AS A MOTION PICTURE ACTOR AT A SALARY OF $300 A WEEK. THIS IS TWICE THE USUAL STARTING SALARY, BUT YOU ARE NO AMATEUR.

It has been said that Hughes then went to the RKO lot at dead of night, drove around the property and out of it, and gave one order: "Paint it." A variation of the story had Hughes fly over the property, look down and say, "Paint it." Both stories are false; the much more incredible truth is that Hughes never did go to the RKO studio. Instead, when he was making films he used a room in the Samuel Goldwyn studio as a part-time office. Once an entire set was dismantled at the RKO lot and rebuilt on the Goldwyn lot so that Hughes could see it. Then it was torn down and moved back to RKO, rebuilt, and the interrupted filming was resumed.

Almost as soon as he bought RKO, Hughes collided with Dore Schary. Schary was a sensitive intellectual who would defend the quality of Hollywood's films against outsiders' criticisms, but who

within the industry championed the idea that the viewing public
was a good deal more intelligent than most Hollywood producers
thought it was. He regarded Hughes' purchase of RKO as nothing
but bad news. The two men met, and *Fortune* magazine said this
conversation followed:

"I hear you don't like me," Hughes said.

"Well, I hear you don't like me, either. We can either talk in
terms of gossip or talk business."

"You can run the studio. I haven't got any time."

So Schary bought a story called *Battleground.* Hughes found
time enough to call Schary, saying he did not think war films would
do well at the box office and to stop production plans. Schary
planned a film called *Bed of Roses* which would star a brilliant
young actress, Barbara Bel Geddes. Hughes found a moment to
call Schary at midnight to say he did not care for Miss Bel Geddes,
and to halt production on *Bed of Roses.* Schary had shot another
film, *The Boy With The Green Hair,* and word came down that
Hughes did not like it because it had a message in it. Apparently,
films were not to have "messages."

So Schary quit.

And, *Fortune* said, Hughes remarked that "saved me paying him
two weeks' salary."

Schary went to MGM Studios where he made *Battleground,*
which was a great success at the boxoffice; and Miss Bel Geddes
became a leading actress on the legitimate stage.

Next to resign was RKO's president, Peter Rathvon. When
Hollywood reporters wondered who would take his place, Hughes
said "It will be someone you least suspect, a shocker." But the
shock was something less than galvanizing. The new president was
Noah Dietrich, the money man, and Hughes elected himself Man-
aging Director of Production. Twenty-eight films had been produced by RKO in the year before Hughes took command, but only
one was begun in 1948 when Hughes was at the helm. It was a
comedy, *It's Only Money*—a title Hollywood wits found morbidly
humorous—and it starred Groucho Marx, Frank Sinatra and Jane

Russell. It was begun, but not finished. But then Hughes was busy with other affairs. One of them was *Vendetta,* undergoing a complete overhaul on the Goldwyn lot, and another was a completely different venture—the creation of an electronics industry.

27

To Noah Dietrich the Hughes Aircraft Company, a minor division of the Hughes Tool Company, was a harmless whim of its owner, Howard Hughes. It was a kind of basement workshop in a suburban businessman's house. To Glen Odekirk the company was life itself. The fact that Hughes Aircraft was doing nothing much in particular did not unduly depress Dietrich in Houston, although it certainly did depress Odekirk in California. About a thousand employees were on the payroll of the Culver City plant, but there were no new projects, nothing to stimulate the imaginations of the first-rate engineers Hughes had hired. A work force still carefully tended the *Hercules,* which had been put back in its hangar after its one-mile flight. There was still some continuing work on military aircraft weapons systems. Mechanics were converting a few war-surplus bombers into private aircraft for business executives. The company had lapsed into the same doldrums it had known immediately following Hughes' round-the-world flight. It was not making money. The engineers began to drift away. Four general managers quit. They had suggested new projects but Hughes had given them no answers. For that matter, Hughes was difficult enough to locate, much less being difficult to persuade. Odekirk had led a group of company executives in an urgent request that Hughes allow the company to develop an electronics department, pleading that electronics was a certain path to the future. An indifferent listener, Hughes said neither yea nor nay.

A short time later, however, one of the very few letters Howard Hughes is known to have written went winging its registered way to Lima, Peru. Its recipient was a ruddy, crew-cut, blue-eyed, cigar-

232

chewing retired Air Force general, Harold L. George, who had been chief of the wartime Air Transport Command, and who now was having some difficulty trying to put together an airline in Peru.

It seemed that Hughes had used the time between his conversation with Odekirk and his writing to George to discover an experienced executive to run what Hughes had decided would be "the best electronics business in the world." Hearing of the legalistic and financial problems with which George was struggling, Hughes had wondered if George might not prefer a job in Los Angeles to one in Lima. It would also seem that Odekirk had touched a responsive nerve in Hughes, just as he had in the case of the flying boat. Hughes' interest in electricity went all the way back to the childhood days when he had converted a bicycle into an electric motorcycle and had built and operated a ham radio set. It is quite possible that Hughes' thoughts had been paralleling those of Odekirk, and that his old friend's suggestion had crystallized them. It is possible that Hughes' indifference to the suggestion at the time it was made had been feigned, much as a good poker player, dealt four aces, will look at them with no more enthusiasm than he would display upon being dealt five ill-assorted cards. Perhaps Hughes had just been too busy with other projects to make decisions then and there with respect to his aircraft company. But the decision when it came was a delightful surprise to Odekirk, although not to George.

George read the letter and tossed it aside. He had met Hughes now and again in the years since Hughes had come to Kelly Field in Texas to search for warplanes for *Hell's Angels*. On one occasion, in the Copacabanca night club in New York City, a waiter had brought a bottle of choice whisky and a note to George's table. The note said, "Hope you enjoy this. Howard."

"Who is Howard?" George had asked the waiter.

"Mr. Howard Hughes, over there," the waiter said, nodding.

George had sent the bottle back. His impression of the Texas millionaire at that time had been that Hughes was a rich playboy who dabbled about in aviation when he was not pursuing actresses.

Since then George's opinion of Hughes had been revised in the

light of Hughes' accomplishments, but he had no desire to work for
a company that had run afoul of such heavy weather with its XF-
11 and its flying boat during the war. Still the letter demanded an
answer, and George dictated a polite refusal.

Next, George said, the long distance telephone rang.

"At least come up to Los Angeles and talk about it," Hughes
said.

"I'd like to, Howard," George said he replied, "but I've got a
business down here, and a wife and children."

"You'd probably like a vacation. Bring the whole family up at
my expense. It's really urgent that we talk."

Eventually George agreed and flew to Los Angeles where he
checked into the Beverly Wilshire Hotel as instructed. And there he
sat. And waited. He tried to telephone to Hughes but could not
reach him. Days passed. George left word at 7000 Romaine Street
that he was going back to Peru. He received instructions not to
leave the hotel. It must have been maddening to the general to find
himself a victim, at this point in his career, of what enlisted men
from the time of Xenophon have known as "hurry up and wait."

Then late one night Hughes materialized, alone behind the wheel
of an ancient Chevrolet. George said that Hughes drove aimlessly
about Los Angeles for at least an hour before pulling to the curb on
a darkened street. He said Hughes looked carefully around to be
sure no cars had followed him and that no one was sitting in the
cars parked nearby. The general said there were half a dozen such
meetings between himself and Hughes, all at night and all in the
front seat of the Chevrolet. George said his consistent answer was
no; that he told Hughes point blank that he, George, was well
aware of Hughes' reputation for capriciousness, inaccessibility and
meddling in his executives' decisions.

George said that Hughes took all this affably, smiling, laughing
aloud at some of the accusations, turning George's objections aside
to concentrate upon a dream. The dream was this: George would
be general manager of a revolutionary new company, more modern
than tomorrow, more vital and stimulating than any heretofore

conceived. It would be first of all a company of great minds. The world's best scientists would be given every facility to engage in pure research in an almost academic environment. The company's products would be new ideas to which Odekirk's skilled workmen would give actual shape. George would preside over all this at a salary of $50,000 a year.

To a military man long inured to pinch-penny wages, the salary seemed as exciting as the concept of such a company. But George said he told Hughes, in effect, "Look, Howard, I know you make good promises, but I also know your reputation. You're a busy man. You get involved in so many other projects that, unknown to you, your promises don't get carried out. I want this spelled out in writing. I want a five-year plan for my position with you."

He said Hughes smiled and said, "I won't interfere. I promise. I'll keep an eye on it, of course, but it's your show."

"All right," George said, still with some reluctance. "We'll give it a try."

With George in camp, Hughes set about building a staff. He persuaded Charles B. Thornton, a former Ford Motor Company executive, to become assistant general manager; and he chose Air Force Lieutenant General Ira Eaker to be liaison man between the tool company and its aircraft division. He was extremely fortunate in hiring Dr. Simon Ramo, a graduate of the California Institute of Technology, to conduct research, and Dr. Ramo in turn hired Dr. Dean Wooldridge away from the Bell Telephone Company's research department. Ramo and Wooldridge were young men of brilliant reputations, and when they sent word out into the academic community that here was a dream come true—an intellectual oasis where working conditions were unparalleled and salaries were more than handsome—more than a hundred first-rate young scientists joined them. The atmosphere of Hughes Aircraft, once the atmosphere of a garage where a handful of unschooled but mechanically gifted young men tinkered with an engine, became that of an institute for post-doctoral study.

Unfortunately from the standpoint of some humanitarians but

perhaps fortunately enough from the standpoint of our still-uncertain future, the post-doctoral studies at Hughes Aircraft were largely directed to the task of discovering new weapons.

Impressed by the management team and the scientific talent Hughes had assembled, the government awarded two research contracts to the infant company. One asked that a means be devised whereby a fighter pilot could fire at an enemy bomber without actually seeing his target. The other called for development of a ground-to-air anti-aircraft missile. While this work was going forward, the scientists at Hughes Aircraft, almost *en passant* as it were, considered ideas having to do with electronic guidance systems for air-to-air missiles and with the perfection of airborne search radar.

To be sure, establishment of this company, obtaining the contracts, and the work on the projects did not occur overnight. They took place during 1948, while Hughes put together his purchase of RKO and mended TWA's financial fences and gave what attention he could to *Vendetta*. But the company's growth was immediate and rapid. As the year drew near its end, the government asked General Electric to expand that company's research into the field of radar. But, George said, "GE just wasn't interested. People wanted to buy radios and television sets and air conditioners, and GE wanted to make them. We found this out and put in our bid. We fought like hell for the contract. To our surprise, we got it."

More scientists joined the Hughes organization. The Air Force gave Hughes Aircraft an $8,000,000 contract to build two hundred fire-control units for its Lockheed F-94 fighters. The company that had little to do as the year began could certainly not complain of inactivity as the year ended. It seemed, however, that the electronics department was becoming a tail that would wag the dog. And it was also apparent to George that his job was not precisely all that Hughes had promised it would be.

A cloud no bigger than Noah Dietrich's hand appeared on George's horizon. Everything that Hughes Aircraft owned, literally down to the rubber bands, was leased from Hughes Tool Company. George found out that he could not commit his division for more than $5,000 without express approval from either Hughes or Dietrich. More often than not, George was unable to reach Hughes who was busy elsewhere in his empire. And Dietrich, controlling the purse strings of the tool company and hence its subsidiary, Hughes Aircraft, took a dim view of what he regarded as his employer's expensive hobby.

At this early time, however, the central problem was not the presence of Dietrich. Rather it was that Hughes was at once too much involved in the company's affairs and too seldom seen. Specifically, the contracts that George had won demanded fulfillment. The scientists were excited and happy with the work, but there was not sufficient space for major production. Meantime, additional contracts came their way; the Air Force had commissioned them to develop electronic fire and navigational control systems for its new F-102 supersonic interceptor. The scientists asked George to find them more laboratory space as well as more production space, and George said he would take it up with Hughes. But who could find Hughes? George failed. So did Eaker, who as liaison man between the aircraft division and the tool company theoretically had access to the throne. It seemed that Hughes was living in a place that reporters had christened San Limbo, from which he sent occasional orders to the outside world.

Eventually, word came down from Hughes' answering service at Romaine Street that Father, as Hughes' employees had begun to call him, would grant George and his staff an audience at the Beverly Hills Hotel at the unexpectedly reasonable hour of 8 P.M.

On the night certain, Ramo, Wooldridge and George knocked on the door of the $100-a-day bungalow that Hughes maintains there against a possible need. Wooldridge was most curious to meet the man for whom he had now worked for the past two years, but whom he had never seen.

Hughes appeared clean-shaven, clothed in freshly pressed trousers and a coat that fit him, wearing a new shirt with a black tie properly knotted. He played the perfect host, ordered food and drink and complimented the men on their excellent work. He said he was sorry he had not been more often to the aircraft company plant, but that he was busy with RKO—"a damned nuisance, it represents 15 percent of my business and takes 85 percent of my time"—and with refinancing TWA and with the purchase of property near Las Vegas. He said he had just swapped several thousand acres of relatively worthless land in northern Nevada for thirty thousand acres of choice land that heretofore had belonged to the Federal government and lay just north of the booming gambling town. Now what was on their minds?

Ramo explained the need for increased laboratory facilities. Wooldridge said they needed to double the staff. Wooldridge said he explained to Hughes that they had worked out a minute-by-minute timetable that had to be relentlessly followed, else the government contracts would not be met. He said he found himself almost yelling because Hughes could not hear well. Wooldridge said that plans for a new laboratory had been drawn and if Hughes would only give his approval work would begin in the morning.

Hughes excused himself and retired to another room to make a telephone call. After what seemed an age to his visitors, he returned and said he was all for a new laboratory; that if they needed one, they would get it. He said he thought new men should be hired, too. They must be the best. And that he would build the laboratory in Las Vegas.

This pronouncement was met by an appalled silence.

Scientists working in the carnival atmosphere of a gambling town? Half their team in Nevada, half in Culver City; the rest of the industry laughing at their attempts to pull things together?

Wooldridge and Ramo argued there was no time to build a laboratory in Las Vegas; that it had to be built now, in Culver City, where the findings of the laboratory could be transmitted instantly to the production facilities.

The idea of Las Vegas was completely ridiculous, the scientists said. Ramo added that the schedule was too rigid to allow research and production to be conducted 350 miles apart. But Hughes was adamant. He suggested they consider his plan.

"We must have a new laboratory and we must have it here in Culver City and we must have it now," Ramo and Wooldridge wrote the next day. They threatened to quit within a week if they could not have their way.

So the days passed and nothing happened and no one heard from Hughes. Just as Ramo and Wooldridge were thinking of leaving to take jobs with the Air Force, Hughes agreed to build a $3,700,000 laboratory in Culver City and to staff it with a thousand men. Recruiters went out upon the nation and rival companies began to complain to Washington. One corporate executive cried, "A man from Hughes stood outside my laboratory door and stole half the staff. They went to work for Hughes the next week at 25 percent more than I was paying."

Hughes himself rarely visited his growing company. Sometimes he would fly in at night, first telephoning ahead for George to meet him. On one such occasion George was waiting with a car beside the runway, and as they drove toward the administration building, Hughes told him to stop.

"I've got to make a phone call," he said.

George said he stopped beside a row of telephone booths, and that Hughes turned to him and said, "Lend me a dime, will you?"

Amused, George lent his multimillionaire employer a dime. He said Hughes walked to the phone booth, glanced around to see if anyone was near and entered the glass door. But before dialing he suddenly came back to the car.

"I don't have to call from a booth," he said. "I can call free from the guard booth."

"You certainly can," George said. "But in that case, where's my dime?"

He said Hughes reached into his pocket, fished up the solitary dime and handed it reluctantly back to George. George said that Hughes looked through his sprawling electronics factory, made a few notes, stuffed them in his pocket, returned to his airplane and flew off alone into the night. The incident reminded the general of a similar experience with Hughes in Beverly Wilshire Hotel when Hughes asked George for a nickel to make a call from the downstairs pay phone, because he feared someone might listen in on the room telephone line. George said he gave Hughes a nickel and that several minutes later Hughes returned, scowling.

"Damn," he said. "Phone calls have gone up to a dime. Lend me another nickel, will you, Harold?"

Shortly thereafter the memoranda began to arrive from San Limbo. It seemed that Hughes insisted on seeing every drawing and approving every detail of the new laboratory. The plans would be sent to 7000 Romaine Street, then sent to wherever it was that Hughes was living—George did not know, but Romaine Street did. There would be weeks upon weeks of utter silence from Hughes— precious weeks from the standpoint of the company. Suddenly the plans would come back to George with personal instructions from Hughes to change this corridor, shorten that passage, add a door here, use this color in this room, that color in that room. Also, "He wanted the buildings lined up in an aesthetically pleasing row," George said.

On one occasion when Ramo and Wooldridge were anxiously awaiting the return of a particularly crucial set of plans, they received from Hughes instead a demand for a complete financial accounting for the past four years on all vending machines in the Hughes Aircraft factory. Hughes wanted to know precisely how much he was earning from the sale of candy bars, soft drinks, milk and cigarettes.

This was bad enough, but silence was worse. "I had to telephone that damn answering service at 7000 Romaine Street and tell some $40-a-week kid that I, the general manager of the aircraft division, would like to talk to Mr. Hughes," George said. "The damn kid would tell me he'd try to pass my message along if Mr. Hughes ever called in. Was that any way to run a business?"

Despite the disappearances, vagaries and caprices of its owner, the aircraft division nevertheless burgeoned at a fantastic rate. Whatever else may be said, it was Hughes who had assembled management and staff; it was he who wanted to create the best electronics industry in the world; it was he who put up the money to hire the people and build the plant. If the Hughes Aircraft Company made aircraft no longer, it was manufacturing electronic devices absolutely vital to national defense. By the end of 1951, the company sales totaled an astonishing $67,000,000. A year and a half later, sales stood at an incredible $200,000,000 a year. Here was nothing that could be called 20 percent Hughes' gambling blood and 80 percent Noah Dietrich's genius. It could be called the fulfillment of an accurate appraisal; and whether Odekirk had suggested it first or not, the appraisal had nonetheless been made by Hughes and the initial decision had been his.

But George seems also to have been quite right in attributing much of the credit to Ramo and Wooldridge.

"The people in this country with electronic know-how respected and trusted these two scientists," he said. "Within our plant at the time there were no barriers to communication. This was a situation I believe to be unparalleled in American business. We had a major corporation in which everyone worked in perfect harmony. An original idea was a treasure. The only trouble we had was with ownership, and we acted as a buffer between Hughes and the rest of the plant. We didn't let his bothers disturb the good work going on elsewhere."

28

He had given up golf. He said he no longer had time for it, as well he might not, what with having to attend to the company vending machines and purchasing twenty-five new Lockheed Super Constellations at $1,250,000 apiece for Trans World Airlines. He made sure that each of these aircraft had thick green carpeting, murals by famous artists, wide seats, adjustable reading lamps, sleeping berths, and that the hostesses were the most attractive and stylishly uniformed of all airline stewardesses. He had also to supervise TWA's struggle toward solvency, slashing its payrolls, spending huge sums on advertising to win customers enough to justify the expenditures and seeing to it that TWA began to repay its debts to Equitable, the RFC and himself.

"He had a phone by his side with three or four buttons on it," said Eddie the barber. "He'd talk to one guy, put him on Hold, then start talking to another. It was normal for a Hughes haircut to take perhaps five hours.

"Once I was being very careful with the tender skin under his chin. He took the clippers away from me—he wouldn't let me use electric clippers, by the way—and said, 'Here, Eddie, do it this way. I'm an engineer and this angle is best.' I told him the clippers wouldn't work that way; they would cut him. But he insisted so I tried it his way. Sure enough, I took a big hunk out of his neck. He hollered and said from here out he would leave my business alone."

Eddie was fortunate to have come to a working agreement so easily, for elsewhere throughout the burgeoning empire of Howard Hughes, the satraps, captains and secretaries fared less well. For example, when Hughes appeared at the 7000 Romaine Street headquarters to dictate business correspondence, two secretaries were required to type the same letter. First Hughes would adjust the margins on their typewriters for them. Then he would slowly and carefully speak, stopping to make sure that each had typed exactly what he had said. He would not let them use shorthand; he did not trust shorthand, they said.

"One night he spoke the same two sentences over and over and over again from midnight to 7 A.M.," one secretary said. "I must have typed it two hundred times." The secretaries, like Eddie, were on call around the clock. When they came to Romaine Street, they were not only refused permission to wear perfume and nail polish, but ordered to wear surgical gloves when typing. If a mistake was made on a page, the page was put into a container which was then picked up by a male attendant, carried to the roof and its contents burned. There was in all this a certain emphasis on sterile cleanliness that led the secretaries to call the stucco building with its locked doors "a second-class maternity ward," and in this ward the staff found their diet supervised by Hughes. For example, no one was allowed to go out for lunch; food was always sent in. These were all standing orders to be obeyed whether Hughes was in the building or not—and he was most usually not. Elsewhere in the world of Howard Hughes, others stood by at their respective outposts, obeying their orders. A chef assigned exclusively to Hughes was on twenty-four-hour-duty call at the Beverly Hills Hotel in the event that Hughes might arrive at any hour of day or night requiring anything from a cup of black coffee to a seven-course banquet. A Hughes aide stationed at the hotel had the duty of receiving the food from the chef in the kitchen and carrying it to Hughes, who would not permit waiters or bellboys to serve him.

The building at Romaine Street, the resort town of Palm Springs, the Beverly Hills and the neon clutter of Las Vegas, were all to be found in the extensive province of San Limbo, which someone described as being a state of mind. Within San Limbo, in various rented houses and hotel rooms at various times and moments, Hughes was at once omnipresent and elusive. Working for Hughes was "not a job," as one employee said, "but a way of life." In the early 1950s, the capital city of San Limbo was Las Vegas, which had a way of life peculiarly its own, but which perfectly accommodated the developing needs and desires of Howard Hughes. There he might be as inconspicuous as an arctic fox on a snowfield.

The point to be made about Las Vegas is that no one lives there. No one keeps time. Las Vegas is an impossible dream without beginning or end in which an eternally hopeful population forever moves like so many automatons toward a mathematically ordained disappointment. So far as Hughes was concerned, the twenty-four-hour-a-day town suited him down to the ground. The restaurants were always open at any hour of day or night, and there is probably no better place than a gambling hall for a man who wishes to be unnoticed and undisturbed. Who, with eyes fixed as in a catatonic trance watching the cards and the dice turn inevitably against him, would notice a tall, shabbily dressed, melancholy-looking figure moving like a wraith past the gaming tables? What croupier, what shill, what dice girl would pay attention to a man who never gambled? If Hughes wanted privacy, he could find it almost thrust upon him by the single-minded throng that drifts forever through the garish nightmare of Las Vegas. But further to insure his privacy, Hughes surrounded himself with a kind of Praetorian guard of Mormons.

For the most part they were young men from Brigham Young University, whose duties were to do whatever they were told. One was detailed to buy a copy of every magazine that appeared on the newsstands. Others, as the writer Stephen White said, were given such diverse instructions as to have an airplane ready at the airport in Eugene, Oregon; to gather figures on air traffic between Dallas and Tulsa; deliver flowers to a sick friend; reach by telephone someone who had not been heard from since 1936; see that some young lady had the best table at the liveliest night club and sit with her to keep the wolves away. Hughes chose Mormons to serve him because the devout Mormon does not drink, smoke or gamble, attends strictly to his job and presumably subscribes (in these latter days of Mormon monogamy) to a Puritanical sexual morality. In short, they tend to be wowsers. Hughes seems to have depended upon them as much as Cromwell on his Ironsides, trusting that they of all men would be most likely to be immune to the temptations of Las Vegas. They were certainly an improbable addition to the peculiar population of America's least substantial city. Together with Hughes, they were something of a puzzle to Abe Schiller, an executive of Las Vegas' Flamingo Hotel.

"He was a generous man and a courteous one," Schiller said of Hughes, "but he certainly gave us no gambling business. I don't think he ever did anything except drop an occasional nickel in the slot machine."

On the other hand, Hughes rented an entire wing of the Flamingo. Whereupon, he promptly refused maid service. Towels and linens, when called for by a young Mormon, were left outside Hughes' room. The rooms to either side of Hughes' room were kept vacant. One day, Schiller said, "Howard called me and said, 'Abe, I like these pink blankets on my bed. Can you get me another half dozen?'

"I say to him, 'Sure, Mr. Hughes.' And I call the hotel interior decorator. The blankets turned out to be a special flamingo pink, and they have to be ordered special. They finally arrived a few weeks later and we sent them up to Hughes. He told us to just leave them in the hall. I forgot about them.

"Several days later, I was in Hughes' room and I see the pink blankets. But they're not on the bed. Hughes has them hanging over the window. To keep out the germs!"

But another possible explanation for the engagement of an entire hotel wing, the personal service, the empty rooms to either side, the blankets hung in the room—and many of the seemingly odd standing orders at Romaine Street—might have been a well-founded fear of industrial espionage. If so, Hughes did not suggest it to Schiller. However this may have been, it is known that Hughes practiced precautionary counterespionage, for, as Schiller said, "One day a 'reporter' came around asking for anecdotes about Howard Hughes. Fortunately, I said only nice things about the guy because I genuinely liked him. I say 'fortunately' because a few weeks later, I learned the 'reporter' was really a private detective sent around by Hughes to find out what his friends thought of him."

A fear of espionage is certainly suggested in the fact that Hughes chose a lonely stretch of desert outside Las Vegas as the site of one business conference. He drove a visiting financier out onto the burning sands in an old Chevrolet, and therein, with the car windows rolled up tight, negotiated his business amid floods of perspiration. And a certain fear of Hughes' use of detectives is suggested in the case of a harried TWA executive roused out of sleep by a telephone call from a Hughes aide at Romaine Street.

"How are you?" the aide said, conventionally enough.

"I won't know until I talk to you," the TWA executive guardedly replied.

Yet in moving throughout his realm of San Limbo, Hughes was not so much awe-inspiring, mysterious, invisible and unapproachable as he was merely undiscoverable. The reason for this is that his empire was so large and his control of its minutiae so close that anyone needing to see him was virtually certain to learn that he was somewhere else, busy on some other matter. For example, while George was having his problems with Hughes Aircraft, Hughes was having his own difficulties with RKO, which in its first year under his management, lost $5,600,000. Moving about between Las Vegas, Hollywood and Palm Springs, soothing George one moment and fretting over TWA the next, Hughes was also busy signing contracts with twelve independent producers to use RKO's facilities, and with making plans to produce thirty-one major pictures of his own.

It's Only Money was finished, but Hughes would not release it because he disliked several of Miss Russell's gowns. He ordered new gowns made, and when he had approved them, ordered the scenes reshot. There was also the real estate in Nevada, the tool company and the new plant, and so when something had to go, golf went. *Vendetta* was finished, and Miss Domergue had gone away and married and had a child and Hughes had sold the Lincoln he had bought from her father but had never driven. Next there was the matter of Gina Lollobrigida. Gina was unhappy, which was unfortunate, but there was barely time in his schedule for Hughes to take her dancing.

In fact Miss Lollobrigida was rather more than unhappy. She was a tall and extremely beautiful Italian actress who was in a towering Italian fury. All had gone well at first, when a Hughes agent appeared in Rome saying that Mr. Hughes had admired a photograph and wished her to come to Hollywood to act for him. But from that moment on, *Magari!*

"Gina was put into the Town House Hotel on Wilshire Boulevard and told not to leave the place unless Mr. Hughes sent orders," the late Jerry Wald, then a producer working for Hughes, said. "He wanted to protect her from the Hollywood mob. A detective guarded her door twenty-four hours a day. A chauffeur was there in case she needed to run an errand, but no one ever saw her. Howard knew what a hot discovery she was."

Indeed she was not only hot but boiling, Wald said. Her English was poor and only by throwing things at her guard was she able to make him understand that she wanted to get out of that hotel room. She wanted to go back to Italy. Her husband was every bit as eager for her to return. He had somehow run afoul of an incredible tangle of red tape, Wald said, and found that he could not obtain permission to enter America with Gina. He kept bombarding Gina with telegrams from Italy. Wald said that Gina simmered down from time to time, and when quiescent would plod through her English lessons, read an occasional script and scream that American food was terrible, but what could one expect of barbarians.

Hughes did what he could to assuage her feelings. On rare evenings, he would come by the Town House, normally after 2 A.M. when the hotel's supper club was ushering out its last customers and closing its doors. Then, Wald said, the orchestra would be retained on overtime to permit Hughes to dance around the empty floor with his Italian protégée, soothing her with promises of a career unequaled in Hollywood. Then the orchestra would be dismissed and Miss Lollobrigida put away in her room again, while

Hughes flew back to Las Vegas. Somehow or other, Wald said, Miss Lollobrigida managed to escape from California. She returned posthaste to Italy and the solace of her husband.

"I was not free in the time I spent there," she explained.

And if it wasn't Gina, it was the British actress Jean Simmons who needed attention. After her triumph as Ophelia in J. Arthur Rank's version of *Hamlet,* Miss Simmons found herself sold to Howard Hughes Productions and en route to Hollywood.

"I didn't know what was happening," she said later. "And I certainly didn't know what I was getting into."

Upon arrival in Hollywood, she went through months of idleness and seclusion before at last threatening to sue Hughes and return to England unless he fulfilled his contract with her. She was thereupon put into three quick motion pictures which a very few people remember. Then she sued, but before the case could come to court, Miss Simmons discovered she had been sold to another studio.

"I guess I'll have to start my career all over again," she said.

Yet Miss Lollobrigida and Miss Simmons were luckier than many other girls who were herded into the Hughes corral by the indefatigable talent scouts of 7000 Romaine Street. A plenitude of young actresses, of young girls who could not act but who hoped to become great stars and then learn, of stage-struck maidens of tender years—all these believed the Texas millionaire had taken a personal interest in their careers. Meanwhile, Mitzi Gaynor, a minor actress, was quoted as saying that other girls could have Hughes' presents but she had his heart.

So in the midst of all his other affairs, there was something else for Hughes to attend to. He was irritated by remarks like those attributed to Miss Gaynor, by the Hollywood gossip columns that suggested the young ladies on his payroll were not really being groomed for careers in films, but for him. His public relations firm sent word around to columnists that Mr. Hughes did not appreciate such unfounded and uncalled-for statements in the press because he was a serious businessman and this sort of news, if news it could be called, adversely affected his relationship with his stockholders.

Another problem was that whenever Hughes left Las Vegas for fashionable California resorts, he was most often the escort of young ladies who were by no means averse to publicity. Thus, blithely ignoring the dark warnings of Hughes' public relations men, Aline Mosby, a bright and prolific United Press reporter, saw no reason not to write what sundry young ladies told her. She filed the following story:

Howard Hughes, the world's most eligible bachelor, had Hollywood buzzing today with four new Leap Year affairs of the heart—Terry Moore, Mona Freeman, Jean Peters and Mitzi Gaynor.

Hughes formerly reigned as the busiest romancer in tinsel town. Tabloid readers used to sigh over communiques that the plane builder and movie maker was courting Katharine Hepburn or Lana Turner in his five o'clock shadow and old tennis shoes.

Recently, though, the multi-millionaire kept any amorous activities under cover, and Hollywood was hard put to know who was getting free rides in his flying machines.

But now comes the news that love has entered his life again, in fact, via a small army of four young beauties.

Miss Moore bubbled that she's dating the wealthy Hughes. But she evaded answering whether she'd get the marriage-shy Texan to the altar. "Of course, I don't know whether I'll marry him or not," she said. "I'll see how I feel in four and a half months when my divorce from Glenn Davis is final."

Miss Gaynor's friends say she broke a two-year engagement with attorney Charles Croyle after she met the forty-six-year-old Hughes. Palm Springs vacationers reported Mitzi and two girl friends were seen about the resort night spots with the fabulous bachelor two weeks ago. . . .

The article went on to say that Miss Peters had pictures of Hughes sprinkled throughout her apartment, that Hughes special-

ized in turning ordinarily beautiful young women into screen im-
ages of sex goddesses, and that he was supervising such a meta-
morphosis for the ingenues Freeman and Gaynor.

The article as originally written was never seen by United Press
clients. While it was waiting in the UP office to be sent over the
teletypes, a Hughes public relations man heard of it and notified
Hughes. Word came back that Hughes wanted to have a personal
word with Miss Mosby. It was now 1952, and Hughes had not
permitted a newspaper interview in years. His availability to the
press at the time of the Brewster hearings and the flight of the
Hercules had been most uncharacteristic. The point was, he needed
the press then. But at all other times he had as little to do with
reporters as a hermit. Far more typical of his view of the press was
his ordering his lawyers to buy out the complete 400,000-copy
issue of a special magazine that had been prepared about his projected round-the-world flight in 1938. He wanted nothing written
about him, his lawyers said.

When Miss Mosby met him, he was, as she later wrote, charming, gallant and attired in "unshined brown shoes and a five o'clock
shadow."

The rewritten version of her story made no mention of Hughes'
friendship with the four young ladies. It was, however, a far more
interesting story than the first, insofar as it represented Hughes'
efforts to set the record straight about himself. He was quoted as
saying:

> I am not a man of mystery. . . . These stories grow like
> Greek myths. Every time I hear them, they're more fantastic.
> . . . I run several businesses, and the people associated
> with me read those stories and do not understand them. . . .
> There is nothing mysterious about me. I have no taste for
> expensive clothes. Clothes are something to wear and auto-
> mobiles are transportation. If they merely cover me up and
> get me there, that's sufficient.
>
> In a Chevrolet, I can go where I want to without being

noticed. I can drive up to the curb without getting the "Hail, the conquering hero."

I've never been to the RKO studio, so obviously I never said "Paint it." If I had an office there, I could not get away from my car to the office without every director and agent with some problem grabbing me. I also want to avoid any ceremony and pomp. . . . I eat in my office or wherever I happen to be because I want to be unobtrusive.

Unobtrusive? Could a man whose holdings were worth approximately half a billion dollars really be unobtrusive even if he hid in a woods? Would not the sheer crushing weight of all that money be at least noticeable in the society that generated it, even if the money were not at work? How could a man who had no time for golf because of his affairs live in obscurity? General George and Gina Lollobrigida might well complain that Hughes was rarely seen —by them—but could they say his influence did not obtrude into their lives? Did it not obtrude into the lives of Eddie the barber and all those young Mormons? Hughes spoke of Greek myths and it might seem as if he were caught up in one of them himself—that of a shy, courtly and well-intentioned prince who wished for a simple life but whose every action, guided by the Fates, inexorably led him farther and farther in the very direction he wanted least to go. San Limbo, indeed! He might seem a shadow, but his shadow covered an empire.

part vi The End of the Dream

29

As the empire's center of gravity shifted from Texas to California, Noah Dietrich moved from Houston and established an office at 7000 Romaine Street.

As the grand vizier for financial affairs within the Hughes empire, Dietrich's interest in the Hughes Aircraft Company was at least understandable, for the explosively successful electronics firm was rapidly becoming wealthier and more important than its parent concern, the Hughes Tool Company. The attitude of the electronics company's management team—George, Ramo, Wooldridge, Eaker and Thornton—was also understandable. It was that they had built up a $200,000,000 business, so who needed Dietrich? Let him worry about the tool company, and they would take care of the electronics business. Ideally the two companies should have been separate concerns, but since they were not, and since Noah Dietrich presided over the parent corporation, a clash of temperaments and opinions was not long delayed.

Trouble first cropped up when the management team wanted to apply the firm's knowledge and experience, gained in the course of work upon defense contracts, toward the invention of devices for popular and industrial uses. "We didn't want to depend solely on the military," General George explained. But Dietrich opposed spending money toward this end, and he won the point with Hughes.

Much more serious was a subsequent violent dispute over what seemed to be a $500,000 shortage in the company books. Dietrich demanded an explanation from George. Investigation proved that the shortage was in the parts inventory. In the company's break-

neck expansion workers had grabbed parts from the storerooms
and rushed them into production without having filled out the
proper requisition forms. Dietrich's attitude was that he neither accepted nor rejected this explanation, and George took Dietrich's
position to be a reflection upon his honor.

"What you have just stated," George said, "is in fact an accusation of fraud, lack of integrity and deceit on the part of certain
principal executives."

The distance between Dietrich and the management team grew
steadily wider. George felt that Dietrich's emergence into company
affairs was reducing his role to that of a mere hired hand; Ramo
and Wooldridge feared that Dietrich's influence would destroy the
company's carefully preserved scientific climate, so necessary for
the growth of pure research.

There were arguments over the budget. George wanted to establish a $35,000,000 revolving credit fund for working capital. Die-
trich cut the fund to $25,000,000. Matters went from bad to worse
until the management team at last sent a personal memorandum to
Hughes in June, 1952, marked "Important Communication." It
said that Dietrich was trying to seize control of the firm, and the
management team demanded to see Hughes at once. A week
passed and there was no reply. But during that week rumors
seethed through the electronics industry that Hughes was trying to
sell his giant young company. The rumors said that Westinghouse
was interested, as were the financier Floyd Odlum and the Lockheed
Aircraft Corporation. The rumors did nothing for George's peace of
mind.

The management team sent Hughes a second memorandum,
pleading that the company's work was being impaired, and since
this work was vitally important to the nation's defense, the nation's
security was being jeopardized. They hinted they would take their
complaints to the Air Force. At this point Hughes sent word that
he would meet with them at his suite in the Beverly Hills Hotel.

They found themselves meeting Hughes the Understanding Father, defending his eldest son, Noah, from the rivalry of the younger
sons; reminding his erring children that Noah Dietrich had a vast

and expert knowledge of finance and enjoyed a pre-eminent reputation among the nation's financiers.

The management team would not accept Hughes in this role, nor would it accept this view of Dietrich. More to the point, they said, none of this sort of talk had anything to do with their specific complaints, nor was it going to help solve their problems. The conversation grew increasingly bitter until Hughes at last burst out with a charge that they were guilty of "Communistic practices." That, of course, was adding gasoline to the fire.

Hughes returned angrily to Las Vegas. Ramo and Wooldridge flew to Washington where, in agonized despair, they told the Air Force of the critical situation at the Hughes Aircraft Company. The Air Force, having its own long, bitter memories of Howard Hughes and his flying boats and interceptors, found their story completely believable. But, the Air Force said, there was nothing it could do; the problem was one for Hughes and his management to work out together.

Hughes asked his management to be patient. Things would change, he promised, and so they did—for the worse. Dietrich assumed an increasing control, and Ramo and Wooldridge promised to quit. Hughes pleaded with them. "Be patient," he said. "I may have a little trouble making up my mind, but once I do I move fast."

A year later, their grievances still unassuaged, Ramo and Wooldridge resigned. They went on to form their own electronics firm that, ten years later, was doing hundreds of millions of dollars' worth of business annually, including much that was vital to the nation's exploration of space. With their resignations, Dietrich moved to Culver City and set up an office at the plant. Whereupon George promptly sent in his resignation. Hughes, thoroughly alarmed, met with George; he accused Ramo and Wooldridge of mutiny and disloyalty and insisted that George stay on.

George replied that the only condition under which he would remain would be if Hughes would establish a five-man committee to govern the plant, and if Hughes stayed out of it. *Fortune* magazine said that Hughes replied, "You are proposing to take from me the right to manage my own property. I'll burn down the plant first."

"You are accomplishing the same effect without matches," *Fortune* said George fired back. "I do not intend to preside over the liquidation of a great company."

With that George quit. So did Tex Thornton. Hughes sent a squad of workmen to their offices at dead of night to remove everything from their desks and cabinets and to change the locks on their doors. Sixteen senior members of the company's advisory council thereupon quit, and company scientists began to drift away, following Ramo and Wooldridge. When news of these resignations reached Washington, Air Force Secretary Harold Talbott immediately flew to Culver City to find out what on earth was going on. He met a furious Hughes, who told him that those who had left were troublemakers, and that he, Hughes, was glad to be rid of them. *Fortune* reported that Talbott found this explanation something less than adequate and said that Talbott replied, "You have made a hell of a mess of a great property, and by God, as long as I am Secretary of the Air Force, you are not going to get another dollar of new business."

"If you mean to tell me that the government is prepared to destroy a business merely on the unfounded charges of a few disgruntled employees, then you are introducing Socialism, if not Communism," *Fortune* quoted Hughes as saying.

"I intend to see that the Air Force contracts are protected," Talbott promised, and on that note, left.

It will be seen that on two occasions, in the heat of argument, Hughes attributed Communistic purposes to those with whom he disagreed. To say that he was dragging a Red herring across the trail would do Hughes scant justice; the issue would seem to be more interesting and complicated than that, and possibly have its roots in the peculiar soil of the time. The voice of McCarthy was heard in the land, and the House Committee on Un-American Activities was looking for Communists in Hollywood.

Now, coincident with these alarms and excursions, and while he was trying to equip and operate an international airline and while internecine warfare threatened to destroy his bright new electronics industry, Hughes had been having rotten luck with RKO. He wondered why he had ever bought it, saying, "I needed it like I needed the plague." Under his sporadic, willful supervision, RKO had lost $4,200,000 in 1949. The following year, Hughes hired Norman Krasna and Jerry Wald, both experienced and successful Hollywood directors, to make sixty films, worth $50,000,000, in five years. Hughes said he would put up 40 percent of the money, and hire the remaining 60 percent from the banks. Krasna and Wald were ecstatic when they signed with Hughes.

"We're going to have the smartest people on our payroll since the Greeks," Wald said. He said he and Krasna would search the world for great stories, great stars, great writers. They would be given free rein, Wald said, because "Mr. Hughes is busy with big war contracts. I mean really big, important contracts."

So Hughes would be too busy to interfere, Wald believed. Of course, it turned out that Howard Hughes managed to find time enough to keep such track of things that Krasna and Wald could not even plaster a poster to a billboard on a theater wall until Hughes had personally initialed the poster. They would buy options on scripts and the services of actors, time would drag along, and the options would lapse before Hughes could decide to approve of his directors' intended purchases. This was not only wasteful of time, but of money. Nor could Krasna and Wald reach Hughes directly. Orders would come to them from Hughes by way of a retired vaudeville actor, Walter Kane; if they wanted to tell Hughes anything, they had to tell Kane what it was. In 1950, RKO lost $5,800,000, but perhaps its most costly loss was self-respect. Hollywood was laughing at Hughes and RKO.

Jet Pilot, for example, was a source of many bad jokes. It was no secret that Howard Hughes intended *Jet Pilot* to be the *Hell's Angels* of the jet age, and someone said, "Why not? The story is just as bad." The script described the love of an American Air Force jet pilot for a Russian woman jet pilot whom he pursued through Palm Springs swimming pools.

Production was begun in 1949. As time passed wits began to say it was a good thing the female lead was supposed to be a Russian, because Russian dress styles hadn't changed in twenty years and wouldn't have changed by the time the film was released. Jokes were made about how anyone who was in *Jet Pilot* had job security; there was speculation that by the time Hughes got around to finishing the film, the actors would be too old to fly, and the aircraft in *Jet Pilot* would be as obsolete as those in *Hell's Angels*. Many of the aerial scenes were stock film footage shot by the Air Force; there was nowhere in the production any evidence of the enthusiasm and passion for aerial detail that had given *Hell's Angels* what distinction it had. The word around Hollywood was that Hughes had lost his touch. And as time went on *Jet Pilot* became less of a joke and more of a source of embarrassment.

Much funnier was the story that Howard Hawks was telling around the town.

"One day I was on the set when a delegation of Hughes' attorneys arrived," Hawks said. "In my film *Red River,* one of the characters uttered the line, 'Draw your gun.' The Hughes men notified me that Howard Hughes was filing a lawsuit against me. He claimed that 'Draw your gun' had been stolen from the script of *The Outlaw.*

"I couldn't believe my ears," Hawks said. "I asked the lawyers if Hughes was serious. They assured me he was."

Hawks said he burst out laughing when the lawyers left, and he laughed again when telegrams began to arrive from other directors. PLEASE BE ADVISED THAT I OWN THE RIGHTS TO "THEY WENT THATAWAY," one director wired. YOU ARE FORBIDDEN TO USE THE LINE "CUT 'EM OFF AT THE PASS," another said. THE WORDS "HOWDY, MA'AM" MAY NOT BE USED WITHOUT PERMISSION. Hawks deleted "Draw your gun" from *Red River*'s script.

Krasna and Wald saw nothing humorous about any part of RKO's situation; it was borne in upon them that their achievements might not surpass those of the ancient Greeks. They received permission to make a comedy called *High Heels,* and Hughes vetoed their choice of leading ladies. He was dating an actress named

Terry Moore at the time, and Kane told Krasna and Wald that
Miss Moore would play the lead. A Jane Russell picture was released. It was called *Underwater,* featuring Miss Russell in a bath-
ing suit. It was the notion of Howard Hughes and press agent Perry
Lieber to hold the world premiere underwater at Silver Springs,
Florida. Columnists and critics equipped with face masks and air
tanks sank beneath the surface to see the fun. United Press' Aline
Mosby subsequently reported she hadn't seen the picture because
she had been too busy trying to keep from drowning. Her colleagues who had seen the film told her she had been lucky.

In the first five years of Hughes' ownership, RKO's balance sheet
showed losses of $20,000,000. The payroll had fallen from two
thousand people to little more than five hundred; the company's
financial condition was so bad that no bank would lend it money
unless Hughes personally underwrote the loan. *Fortune* magazine
piled all the blame at Hughes' door:

"It is impossible to estimate the damage done to RKO by Howard Hughes," the magazine said. "Where is the accountant who can
set a figure on the hundreds of intangible losses that came from
Hughes' inability to produce enough movies? With adequate production, RKO would have been able to develop stars of its own,
rather than buying them from other studios at fancy prices. . . .
the Hughes regime at RKO was about as dismal as it could
be. . . ."

This story of disaster was painfully clear to Hughes when the
House Committee on Un-American Activities arrived in Hollywood
to look for evidence of a Communist conspiracy to subvert the motion picture industry. To the amazement of everyone who thought
he knew Hughes, the shy Texan emerged from San Limbo to play a
public role.

He shut the studio down for three months while he had the loyal-
ties of directors, writers, actors and technicians investigated. He
sought to block the showing of the Charles Chaplin film *Limelight*
in any RKO theater, publicly condemning the film and Chaplin's
politics.

Hughes next stepped to the rostrum to address the Hollywood American Legion Post. He seemed nervous and ill-at-ease as he began to speak:

"I don't pretend to be an authority on Communist influence in the motion picture industry, but I feel I know as much about it as most of the laymen around here, and I think it might be worthwhile for someone in the industry to call a spade a spade."

Gradually relaxing in the warming presence of a congenial audience, Hughes went on:

"There seems to be two schools of thought here in Hollywood. Now, one group believes we have a Red influence in the industry, and the other group, which I believe is joined by the greater number of people in the industry, would have you believe there is no such thing as Communism in Hollywood. This second group would have you believe that the House Un-American Activities Committee has no business investigating this motion picture industry; that it comes to Hollywood for publicity only. . . .

"Well, I happen to be one person who has had some experience in other industries apart from the motion picture industry and while I do not want to draw a comparison, and I do not want to say how many Reds there are in the motion picture industry because I want to be absolutely truthful, still I feel the influence is substantial."

Hughes said many Hollywood people had given money to organizations they believed worthy of support, entirely innocent of the fact that these organizations were actually Communist fronts. But he also said there were many more people "we don't even suspect in the least" who were actively working for the Communist cause. He named no names.

"But I can say one thing," he said. "In spite of all the movement to whitewash the industry, to say that there was no Red influence in Hollywood, to sweep this matter under the carpet and hide it and pretend it does not exist, in spite of that, there is a substantial number of people in the motion picture industry who follow the Communist Party line."

The most remarkable thing about this speech was that Hughes made it. Heretofore he had shown little evidence of a political concern, but even stranger seemed his sudden willingness to speak in public. Yet the shy, withdrawing, self-effacing Hughes to a great extent had always shared the conventional wisdom and enthusiasms of the common man, and his speech was no different from that of many another honest citizen of the time; no different from those of troubled men of good will who, perhaps not realizing the full implications of all they said, carried the burden of their thought as best they could to the forum.

Insofar as a man rarely has just one reason for his action, but more normally several reasons, some of which lie below the threshold of his consciousness, it seems permissible to speculate as to why Hughes should have ascribed "Communistic practices" to scientists whose only concern was the national security; as to why he should imagine that a member of President Eisenhower's Cabinet would be "introducing . . . Communism"; as to why he should have so suddenly erupted as a public champion. A reason already suggested is that the general public, obscurely baffled and oppressed by a sense of drift in the midst of unparalleled prosperity, was willing to think that their vague frustrations could be ascribed to the secret cabals of furtive Communists. Like the nation, Hughes in the flood tide of his fortunes was somewhat in the position of a chef who, trying to create a banquet on three stoves at once, finds every pot boiling over simultaneously. With no intent to minimize the mortal danger that international Communism represents to the American nation, it nonetheless seems permissible to wonder how much the public mood and Hughes' mood merely expressed a disturbed humanity's ancient need of a scapegoat.

Meanwhile something that could not possibly be ascribed to Communists, but rather to capitalism, was added to Hughes' burdens. RKO stockholders, appalled by the company's losses and its virtual non-productivity, filed $30,000,000 worth of lawsuits against Hughes. One of them charged that Hughes was driving the studio bankrupt by putting actresses on the payroll "solely for the purposes of furthering his personal interests." This suit cited, as examples in point, Gina Lollobrigida, Merle Oberon, Ann Sheridan, and Jeanmaire.

Reporters were in search of Hughes, to ask him what his answer would be. They searched in vain, although Hughes was in Hollywood at the time. He had shut himself up in a private projection room. There he sat for three days and nights watching films, sleeping from time to time in his chair, nibbling at trays of food left at the door; one of the richest men in the world the prisoner of himself, alone with his problems.

30

Howard Hughes, said Stephen White, writing in *Look* magazine in 1954, "is so immensely powerful in the various worlds he inhabits —and so thoroughly willing to use his power—that only the boldest man or woman will run the risk of speaking out and incurring his displeasure. Almost invariably, he gets favorable treatment in the Hollywood gossip columns, and in the Los Angeles press. Hughes is quite capable of ruining a man who tries to run him down. Few men, however mighty, willingly take the risk.

"Even if he were disposed to be the most amiable man in the world, the brutal fact of his immense wealth would spread a fear of Hughes," White said. "No one but he knows exactly what his fortune runs to, but . . . it is probable that Hughes could count on something like $500,000,000 in a pinch. To dispute Hughes would seem like challenging the Federal Reserve System."

"You're not dealing with an ordinary guy," one informant told newspaperman Phil Santora, "you're dealing with a feudal baron, the kind of guy who can throw us tenant farmers into the discard."

Mr. Santora, who told readers of the *New York Daily News* that Hughes was "vindictive to an alarming degree, which is the reason so many of his associates and employees firmly refuse to discuss him—even to utter words of praise," quoted one Hughes employee as saying:

"Take a look at those blazing eyes and tell me honestly if you think you'd like to talk about a boss who looked at you like that. The guy scares me. . . . Count me out. Forget you ever met me. I have a growing family, and they're in the habit of eating."

"Hughes gets clobbered with all the bad stories because his ene-

265

mies always talk freely," a Hughes public relations man told writer James R. Phelan. "You could work wonders for his image by telling some of the good stories, but he won't allow it. What he really wants is to have *nothing* written about himself."

Thus, he said, when Hughes once sent an airplane to obtain an iron lung for the polio-stricken daughter of an acquaintance, and one of the public relations staff suggested to Hughes that this was a newsworthy story, Hughes replied "If that story is released, turn in your resignation."

"When Hughes' employees need help, his reaction is swift, dramatic and unstinting," wrote the late Dorothy Kilgallen. "Recently, he learned that the child of a mechanic in his aircraft plant had fallen desperately ill. Hughes dropped everything he was doing at the moment, and within hours, the four greatest American specialists on that disease were flying to the child's bedside.

"Whenever he repays a favor," she said, "he repays it in good measure—but quietly. After his plane crashed into a Beverly Hills house years ago, he was widely censured for not making a big display of gratitude to the Marine and fireman who dragged him from the flames. Actually—and privately—he arranged lifetime incomes for them both.

"He is as liberal a tipper as the most ostentatious South American, but he's got his own system. Like many of the very rich, he carries little cash with him, and his bills are sent to the home office in Houston for payment. He never leaves a tip in a nightclub or restaurant, and waiters serving him for the first time invariably are astounded at being 'stiffed' by a famous multi-millionaire. They are even more flabbergasted some days later when one of Hughes' New York aides, on orders from the boss, distributes $50 to each person who served him on his tour of the late spots. . . ."

"He is one of the most emotional men I ever met," said Faith Domergue. "He can give of himself. He can make you feel as if you were the only girl in the world. There was never a doubt with Howard. He is a man, a real man."

"I hope you murder the son of a bitch," one of Hollywood's best-known stars of the day told Stephen White.

"Why do you call him that?" White asked.

"No you don't," the actor said. "I might have to make a picture for him some day."

A $20,000-a-year physicist, whom Hughes employed now and again to install special telephone equipment, gives us this picture of Hughes in the mid-1950s:

"There'd he be, alone in a big suite, room after empty room. No photographs on the bureau, no books, the closets empty, except maybe for a single jacket on a hanger, and a pair of socks thrown on the floor. Usually on one of the beds there'd be a cardboard laundry box with a couple of shirts in it, and piled around it dozens of manila envelopes. I figured these were his filing system, though I never saw him with a piece of paper in his hand."

The physicist said Hughes had no more of a home, no matter where he was, "than an Indian bivouac."

"Make no mistake about it," a former Hughes executive said. "Howard is a genius. A damned odd one, but a genius."

"I've heard all the stories about his eccentricity," Russell Birdwell told writer Thomas O'Toole, "but my opinion is that they are highly exaggerated and distorted. Just because he doesn't keep in step with all the others, because he sleeps less and works harder and sometimes forgets to shave doesn't mean he's a poor businessman or that he's unreliable."

But, said Mr. O'Toole, "At one point the senior partner of a Wall Street firm—a man known for his icy calm—threw a sheaf of papers toward the sky and shouted 'What is the matter with this man?' "

The object of all this testimony was, in 1953, striving to put his financial houses in order.

Of all his businesses, RKO was the least important by any objective measurement but perhaps the most frustrating and certainly the least profitable. RKO was in fact two separate companies that enjoyed a nepotic relationship. There was RKO Pictures Corporation, which made motion pictures, and RKO Theaters Corporation, which exhibited them. Hughes held a controlling 26-percent interest of 929,000 shares in each. He first sold his share in the Theaters

Corporation to a New York investment counselor for $4,500,000. But then he seemingly turned around in an exactly opposite direction, for he bought 100 percent of the assets of RKO Pictures Corporation for $23,489,478. To do this he had to borrow another $25,000,000 from the Mellon Bank and Irving Trust, consolidating this loan with the $10,000,000 loan he had previously obtained in 1948 to buy Floyd Odlum's interest in RKO. His purpose here was to quiet the litigious stockholders. He paid them approximately $6 a share for their stock, which was $3 less than it had been worth when Hughes took over the company in 1948, but which was $3.25 more than the quoted price on the exchange in 1954. No one seemed to know why he had done this, for wholly apart from the millions that RKO had lost under his management, Hughes' original $9,000,000 investment in the firm was, by this purchase, increased to approximately $27,300,000—and the studio was in far worse shape than it had been when he first bought into it. In any event, RKO Pictures Corporation was now as much his as was his brown fedora.

While Hollywood wondered what meaning there could possibly be in such a purchase, there came to the public ear like a once-charming, but now too-familiar and therefore somewhat querulous obbligato, the piping news that another Howard Hughes picture had run afoul of censorship. The film was called *The French Line,* and Miss Russell, its leading lady, agreed with the censors.

"Of course I realized what the photographers were up to when the first batch of pictures were made," Miss Russell told reporters, referring to the days when she had posed for publicity stills before *The Outlaw* had been released. "Dumb me, I just didn't know how to say no."

But she was saying no now. Although Hughes did not direct the film, Miss Russell felt it was Hughes, behind the scenes, who had insisted on the dance she did and the costume she wore in *The French Line.* The emphasis on her physical attributes was part and parcel of that hateful *Outlaw* publicity, she said. After *that* movie, "It got so I couldn't go anywhere without people expecting me to walk in with five men under my arm and no clothes on. Then

I was supposed to pull a gin bottle out of somewhere and proceed to raise all kinds of commotion. That's what the stinking *Outlaw* publicity did for me."

Miss Russell said she had been struggling for years "to get out of the pig pen" and now here she was in *The French Line,* dancing in a costume that accentuated not only her bosom, but also her pelvis.

"I fought, I hollered and I beefed," she said. "Then when I became emotionally done in, I took off for the beach and stayed there for a week while the picture waited. Finally I accepted the costume I wore, but it actually was a moral victory on my part. You should have seen the others I refused to wear."

She said she did not see the film before it was released, but now that she had seen it, she understood why it was refused a seal of approval—and she thought the censors were right.

"It wasn't the dance so much as the camera angles," she said. "Anyone who knows the picture business knows that you never know how anything will look until you see the film. Where there are usually long shots in a dance of this type, there are closeups!"

From Las Vegas, with something less than his customary gallantry, Hughes remarked, "You never know what she's going to say. No trick camera angles were used to make Jane's dance more suggestive."

If a touch of asperity seems evident here, it might well have derived from a host of sources, not least of which was Hughes' waning interest in films and growing detestation of journalists. In any case, he did not bother to fight the good fight against censorship in the case of *The French Line,* and he has not granted a public interview since 1954.

Frying a far more important fish on a skillet far vaster than any conceivably necessary to accommodate a dozen RKOs and a hundred Miss Russells, Hughes was also at this time somewhat angrily reorganizing his stupendous electronics firm, The Hughes Aircraft Company. He met with scientists who agreed to stay on. He promised them things would be different, and this time they were. If his recruitment programs had offered handsome salaries in the past, they now approached the limits of Babylonian luxury. Fortunately, most of the research and development programs on which Ramo and Wooldridge had been working were fairly near completion when they had quit. New men were hired to begin new projects, and hundreds more joined Hughes Aircraft to help devise weapons systems and perfect the Falcon missiles which one Air Force general called "as vital to our defense as radar."

Hughes persuaded a retired corporate executive, William Jordon, to become general manager in the place of Harold George. A three-man board of directors was established, consisting of Hughes, a company lawyer named Howard Hall and Jordon. Any two members could make a policy decision. The effect was that Hughes remained in Las Vegas while Hall and Jordon made the decisions in Culver City. Within the organization there was also an executive committee of six who were empowered to make the line decisions, implementing those of policy. Production schedules returned to normal, and the Air Force was mollified. The desire for Hughes Aircraft to fare well was not, by the way, confined to the government or to the company personnel. Even the company's rivals in the electronics field patriotically hoped there would be an end to dissension at Hughes Aircraft, because everyone in the industry knew how crucial to national defense the Hughes projects were. Moreover, the scientific community shared a common concern that the team of scientists assembled at Hughes could be kept together, for their mutually supportive efforts were more productive under one roof than their efforts would have been if the scientists had been scattered among a dozen competing laboratories. The point was pressed upon Hughes by both his government and his colleagues.

Six months after Jordon's arrival all was well. Then Jordon quit. He left saying he had agreed to take the job only for so long as required to get the company going again. He assured reporters that his only reason for going back to retirement was the poor health that had led him to retire in the first place, and that his association with Hughes had been nothing but harmonious. The past history of Hughes' general managers made both reporters and the government suspicious, but to their surprise Hughes immediately set up a six-

man management committee composed of himself and five department heads to run the company until a new manager could be
found. There was no problem. The company was running itself,
and doing a good job of it, merely keeping up with its backlog. Late
in 1954, Hughes got Lawrence Hyland, a Bendix Corporation executive, to come in as general manager without a contract. (At this
writing, Hyland is still there.)

Turning back to the ills of RKO, Hughes began a long series of
negotiations with Thomas Francis O'Neil, president of General
Teleradio, a chain of television and radio stations. There ensued a
series of transcontinental telephone calls, at the end of which
O'Neil flew to Los Angeles, where Hughes went to meet him at the
Beverly Hills Hotel. Negotiations continued for three days and
nights. The two men would eat, talk, take a break to watch television, argue, eat, doze and talk again. It was a fantastic experience
for O'Neil, who was flabbergasted both by Hughes' ways of doing
business and by Hughes' knowledge of tax law.

"That man didn't need a lawyer," he said. "He knows more
about corporate law than any attorney I ever knew."

When their agreement was finally drawn up, Hughes refused to
sign it in California. The somewhat bewildered O'Neil followed
Hughes to the Los Angeles airport, where they boarded a Hughes
aircraft to fly to Las Vegas in order that their contracts could be
completed in Nevada. En route, Hughes climbed out of the pilot's
seat, said, "You take over," and left a startled O'Neil alone in the
cockpit. O'Neil, who had never flown an airplane, could only trust
that Hughes had set the aircraft on automatic pilot, or hope that if
the aircraft took a wild lunge toward the earth, Hughes would return to the controls. O'Neil sat at the co-pilot's controls until
Hughes returned, resumed command and drawled, "Well, Tom,
you're a great pilot."

O'Neil was flown back to his Akron headquarters when his deal
with Hughes had been consummated. He went at once to bed, saying, "I haven't had any sleep for thirty-six hours. He's a very clever
man, a very clever man."

O'Neil's experience came as no surprise to one of Hughes' aides, who said, "There's always a plan behind Hughes' seemingly eccentric ways.

"Let's say he had a meeting for three o'clock in the morning, which is perfectly possible," the aide said. "He's wide awake, his mind is razor sharp. The other fellow, he's tired as hell, thinking about nothing but sleep. Hughes is one up on him right there, which is just what he wants. He always wants the chance to tip the scale in his favor."

In the case of the transaction with O'Neil, the arrangement was apparently mutually profitable. Hughes sold O'Neil RKO Radio Pictures, Inc., including its moviemaking facilities, distribution system and library of 740 films, including the still-unreleased *Jet Pilot* and such outstanding successes as *Citizen Kane, Gunga Din* and *Little Women*. For this, O'Neil paid Hughes $25,000,000. What Hughes did not sell, however, was control of RKO Radio Pictures Corporation, Radio, Inc.'s parent corporation, which owned cash and a tax-loss carry-forward. Hughes subsequently merged RKO Radio Pictures Corporation with Atlas Corporation, and the value of the Atlas shares which became Hughes' property as result of the merger was nearly $10,000,000. At this point, Hughes, who had originally bought into RKO for approximately $8,400,000, emerged nearly eight years later with a profit of $7,700,000, escaping $30,000,00 worth of lawsuits en route. But Hughes was now out of the motion picture business which had been so much of his life.

A few months after having sold RKO Radio Pictures, Inc., to O'Neil, however, Hughes bought back his unreleased *Jet Pilot* and another film, *The Conqueror,* from O'Neil for $12,000,000, and paid an undisclosed sum for the original print and rights to *The Outlaw*. He was thus back in the motion picture business again to the extent of at least $5,000,000, which he might hope to recover from exhibition of the films he had bought.

These transactions left Hollywood puzzled, angry and fearful. For ever since the advent of television, Hollywood's motion picture companies had refused to sell their backlog of old films for release to the growing medium that Hollywood regarded as its deadly rival.

This was the first breach in the dike, and O'Neil at once turned it to advantage. In short order, he sold the RKO backlog to a New York television exhibitor for more than $15,000,000. His subsequent $12,000,000 resale of *Jet Pilot* and *The Conqueror* to Hughes presented General Teleradio with a $2,000,000 profit in barely half a year. Since O'Neil had sold nothing but films, this meant that he also acquired the RKO studios and distribution system for nothing.

While these transactions were taking place, Hughes also moved to divorce himself from the most wildly successful of his ventures, the Hughes Aircraft Company—the electronics firm that made no airplanes. The company was separated from The Hughes Tool Company and established as a corporation in its own right. Hughes next established, in 1955, the Howard Hughes Medical Institute in Miami, Florida, under the supervision of Dr. Verne Mason, the physician who had attended him at the time of the XF-11 crash. He then arranged for ownership of Hughes Aircraft to pass to the Medical Institute. To accomplish this a trusteeship was established, with the trustee being Howard Hughes. His critics immediately suspected that Hughes was constructing a complicated instrument whose real purpose would be enabling Hughes to avoid paying income taxes, since the Medical Institute was chartered as a tax-free foundation. But the government was satisfied as to the Institute's *bona fides,* and the result was that profits from Hughes Aircraft were to go, at the discretion of the trustee, to the Howard Hughes Medical Institute. In the meantime. Hughes himself could not touch the profits that Hughes Aircraft earned.

It would seem as if Hughes was presiding over the liquidation of his own empire as he approached his fiftieth year; as if the fire that had once burned so bright was now to be banked against a long winter's night. Was this to be retirement? He had now cut himself off from two old loves—the making of films and the treading of the frontiers of flight. Just as his scientists were showing him the way to the farthest stars, he gave up the company that had once provided him with the swiftest wings man had ever flown.

But he carried with him still certain remembrances of things past. The original print of *The Outlaw* remained in the lead-lined

room, and Hughes would not let Jane Russell go. In 1956 he got
her to sign a twenty-year contract with the Hughes Tool Company,
as an actress, at a salary of $1,000 a week. Possibly, did he imagine
that he was providing for her, out of loyalty, now that he was
through with motion pictures? Perhaps there is something here that
may be explained in the terms a former Hughes aide used in speaking to writer James R. Phelan about the *Spruce Goose*.

Following that first, tentative, mile-long flight, the Hughes *Hercules* was returned to its gigantic, windowless hangar at Long
Beach, and there it remained under heavy guard. It is still the property of the United States government because of the government's
wartime investment in it. Hughes leases it from the United States.
And, through the years, work on the *Hercules* continued. The fantastic flying boat was kept—and is being kept—in constant readiness for flight. Hughes had spent—and is spending—thousands
upon thousands of dollars of his own on an aircraft that no one
(except, possibly, Hughes) believes will ever be flown again. By
1962, it was estimated that Hughes had devoted $50,000,000 to
this monumental aircraft that was so much of his own devising.

"The explanation is simple, if you understand Howard," Phelan
said the Hughes aide told him. "The money means nothing, compared with his pride. He detests failure and even hates the sound of
the word. If he gave up the *Spruce Goose* they'd probably haul the
thing out and chop it up for kindling, and there'd be a lot of pictures in the press. He just can't bear the idea, so the work goes on
and on and on."

31

Ever since the day he acquired a majority interest in Transcontinental & Western Airlines, Howard Hughes had permitted no one else in the pilot's seat while he transformed the company into Trans World Airlines. War contracts, Senate hearings, airplane crashes, motion picture productions, creation of an electronics industry—throughout all these events Hughes also guided the destinies of TWA. Company presidents came and went, some of them without ever having actually seen Hughes but all of them keenly aware of him. TWA was a gigantic property that, in itself, would seem to pose more difficulties than many a corporate executive might be able to handle, but Hughes apparently could operate a round-the-world airline with one hand while juggling half a dozen other multi-million-dollar enterprises in the other. His foreign competitors were national governments, but Hughes met the competition. It had been an early ambition to own an airline, and he owned one; and because he did own it, he ran it.

What was wholly incomprehensible to the aviation industry, however, was how Hughes—a pioneer in aviation in so many ways —had failed to act the instant that jet engines had rendered the world's piston-driven aircraft obsolete for long-distance flight. Here was his own electronics firm manufacturing intricate devices for jet aircraft, and beginning to tread into outer space, while Hughes, in 1955, was buying twenty-five new, improved Constellations for TWA at $2,500,000 apiece. To be sure, the new Jetstream Constellation was a handsome aircraft, but despite its name it was not a jet, and the twenty-five planes he ordered would not be delivered until 1957. Elsewhere in the industry airlines were placing orders for the big Boeing 707 jets, and it was quite obvious that Hughes' major rival, Pan American, would be flying to Europe in hours less time in 707s than TWA would be flying there in Constellations.

If it could be argued that Hughes' attention had been diverted from TWA by the vicissitudes of RKO and Hughes Aircraft during the two years just past, the rebuttal would be that his attention had never wandered heretofore when involved in affairs at least as trying.

Early in 1956, Hughes seems belatedly to have seen the contrails in the sky, for he suddenly decided to buy fifty jets for TWA's fleet. But there was a problem. The jets cost $4,000,000 apiece. One place to obtain $200,000,000 is Wall Street, but to go there is to put oneself into the hands of the bankers. Hughes' seems to have decided therefore to buy the jets himself.

There may be relatively few Americans who would think of spending $200,000,000 of their own money for fifty airplanes, but the idea apparently made good sense to Hughes. There were attractive tax advantages to be realized by purchasing a jet in the name of the Hughes Tool Company and then leasing it to TWA.

But Hughes did not happen to have the cash. True, the Hughes Aircraft Company was doing half a billion dollars' worth of business a year, but Hughes could not touch the profits. They now belonged to the Hughes Medical Institute. The Gulf Brewing Company had, it is true, been worth $12,000,000, but its sales had fallen, the plant had never been modernized despite its executives' pleas, and it was now worth less than $5,000,000. The Hughes Tool Company was worth $250,000,000, but nevertheless it had its troubles. Despite the fact that its profits after taxes were a record $29,000,000 in the year just passed, Hughes Tool would never see such prosperity again, because some of its patents had expired and competitors were happily marketing similar drilling bits. Cheap foreign oil was flooding the country, and there was less demand for any bits, including those of Hughes Tool, and, worse, oil stocks were dropping. Moreover, Hughes had just spent so much money buying those twenty-five piston-driven Constellations that he could not hypothecate Hughes Tool holdings for another $200,000,000.

Hughes had already provided $300,000,000 in cash and credit for TWA in the years he had controlled it, and there was nothing left in the empire that could be taken to the pawnshop. To be sure, the jet aircraft themselves might be considered security for the loan, just as a man may buy an automobile with a bank putting up virtually all the money but keeping the title to the car, but in this event the aircraft would be the bankers' and not something for Hughes Tool to lease to TWA.

Yet Hughes went right ahead and put in his orders for jets, anyway. He called Boeing and said he wanted thirty-three of the new 707s. Next he turned to General Dynamic's Convair Division in San Diego. Convair was the sick child of the many-faceted parent corporation that sold a billion dollars' worth of everything from hardware to nuclear submarines yearly. Hughes told Convair executives that Boeing and Douglas had already saturated the airline market with big jets, and what was called for now was a medium-range aircraft, cheaper to operate, that carried fewer passengers. TWA could use such aircraft for its domestic flights, he said. In fact, he would like to buy thirty of them.

In short, Hughes committed himself to buy sixty-three jets worth some $300,000,000, and the Hughes Tool Company's board of directors, with Hughes as their spokesman, announced the company would somehow find the money.

But how? Surely Noah Dietrich would find a way.

But Dietrich quit. Their relationship had persisted over thirty-two years, but it had grown colder and more distant as the years passed. Dietrich had served Hughes well. It was widely believed that Dietrich, rather than Hughes, was the man who built the empire, much as an emperor's realm might have been carved out for him by a skillful general. Dietrich had always done Hughes' bidding, but when Hughes ordered airplanes he could not pay for, Dietrich was appalled. He could see nothing ahead but the complete ruin of the empire. He tried to convince Hughes to change his orders. Hughes refused. And Dietrich quit—because of this and because, as a former Hughes executive said, the two men had begun "to disagree about more and more things."

At about the time Dietrich left, Hughes was busily discussing the
design and decor of the medium-range jets he wanted Convair to
build for him. The man at the other end of the telephone was Jack
Zevely, Convair's sales manager. Zevely said the telephone would
ring at three o'clock in the morning, and that he would come grog-
gily awake to hear a familiar drawl:

"Gee, Jack, sorry to bother you. If it wasn't absolutely necessary, I wouldn't call. But a little matter has come up . . ."

Zevely said he would still be holding the telephone an hour later,
listening to "the little matter."

Asked why he put up with such treatment, Zevely said, "How
can you stay angry at a man like that? Every time I'd get mad at
him, he would do something so charming, so outlandish, that I'd
forget any grievance I had against the man."

He told of the time that Hughes asked him to meet him in San
Diego.

"I'm coming down to see you, Jack. Can you pick me up at
Lindbergh Field?"

Zevely said he drove to the airport at the appointed time, but
Hughes was not there. The control tower had no report on Hughes'
estimated time of arrival. An hour later there was still no word, and
Zevely was about to go home when a converted bomber slid out of
the sky and put down on the runway.

"Where in hell have you been?" Zevely said he asked Hughes.

"Well, Jack, my plane was dirty and the windshield was all
messed up, and I spotted a little old thundercloud over there in the
mountains," he said Hughes explained. "So I just flew over and sat
there under that rain for a while, taking a bath. Just wanted to get
everything washed off good and clean."

Zevely said Hughes took great pleasure in playing the role of
ladies' man. He said Hughes would send an aircraft to San Diego to
pick up Zevely and two of Convair's top engineers who were working on the new design. They would be flown to Las Vegas, where
Hughes would meet them and then say, "Fellows, I've got some
work that's going to keep me busy a while. But I want you to enjoy
Las Vegas."

The Convair executive said that Hughes' ability to keep going day and night exhausted everyone else. One night, he said, they talked for hours at the Beverly Hills Hotel; midnight seemed to have passed days ago. By two in the morning, he said, his eyes were closing and his body ached, but Hughes seemed not to be aware of Zevely's condition. Hughes kept talking about the new jet's toilet facilities—Hughes' suggested design "was so bad we wouldn't build it." But he said Hughes kept explaining the blueprints he had made until at last he noticed his guest nodding in his chair.

"What we need is some food," Hughes said. He gave an order to a Hughes guard who went to the hotel kitchen to rouse the twenty-four-hour-a-day chef that Hughes had on call. Large steak dinners subsequently appeared, and Zevely said the food did nothing but make him even more sleepy. But he said that Hughes noticed this and tried another idea: "We'll see a movie!"

A Hughes guard trotted off to the telephone to awaken a projectionist; the party drove to a studio and there the weary salesman was treated to a preview of the yet-unreleased film, *Jet Pilot*. Because the sound had not yet been dubbed in, Hughes provided a narrator. Leading lady Janet Leigh was roused out of bed; she threw a fur coat over her nightgown and hurried to the projection room where she described the film as it unrolled.

The eventual Convair aircraft was called the 880. Zevely said it was "not named for the 88 seats it contains, but for the 880 meetings we had with Howard Hughes over its construction." But he added, "To give the Devil his due, he was driven by the unshakable idea that Howard Hughes is the world's greatest airplane engineer. He drove like hell, and his only desire was to have the world's greatest airplane."

32

No one could find Jean Peters. A spokesman at 20th Century-Fox studios said, "We haven't seen or heard from Jean for months." Asked if it were not somewhat unusual for an actress not to let her own studio know where she was, the spokesman said, "Normally, yes. But in Miss Peter's case, anything is possible."

Her telephone rang in an empty house. The studio was worried, and more worried were her friends. Jean was known to have taken trips alone before, but never for four months and never without leaving word as to where she could be found. It was absurd. Leading actresses simply do not disappear.

A newspaperman telephoned Miss Peters' home in Ohio, and asked to speak to her mother.

"Mrs. Peters is away for the rest of the month and I can't tell the press where she is. I have no idea where Miss Peters is," a voice said. The speaker refused to be identified.

"Yes, it is true, but don't quote me," a relative of Howard Hughes told a reporter on the telephone. "I don't dare say anything else."

"The only person who can give you an answer is Hughes, and even we don't know where he is," a member of Hughes' public relations staff said.

Reporters rummaged through marriage license registers in California and Nevada, but there was nothing there. Despite this, a Hollywood gossip columnist wrote on March 16, 1957, that "friends tell me" that Howard Hughes had married the girl he had dated from time to time for nearly ten years. Miss Peters had for a few months in 1954 and 1955 been married to a Lockheed Aircraft

Company executive. The gossip columnist said "I happen to know" that Hughes and Miss Peters had become engaged to one another while sitting in a parked car in "a lovers' lane . . . overlooking the twinkling lights of filmland."

That was certainly more than anyone else knew, and it sounded to other working newspapermen very much like the kind of thing that Hollywood publicists pour out for Hollywood's vision of the reading public—the vision being that of an impressionable shop-girl, reading as she sits alone in a cafeteria over a cup of morning coffee and a breakfast bun. Lovers' lanes and twinkling lights of filmland, forsooth! The fact of the matter is that reporters have yet to find any official record of a Hughes-Peters wedding. Hughes has never said that he is married. The nearest thing to an announcement were the Christmas cards that Hollywood friends received years later, stamped "Jean and Howard Hughes."

"Howard felt that Jean was the only girl who wouldn't marry him for his money," the gossip columnist quoted an unidentified friend as saying. "It was love!"

Another view was expressed by an actress who claimed to have observed the Hughes-Peters romance at a fairly close range. Meow-ing ever so slightly, the actress said, "Jean Peters was one of the first women Hughes had ever met who indicated that he held little fascination for her. If she was only acting, she did it beautifully, because Hughes had to possess, and she wasn't possessable. She wouldn't put up with his orders and foolishness. She didn't even care for his gifts. She didn't dress for him, wouldn't break dates for him, and generally kept him in suspense."

Hughes had told Olivia de Havilland that he would not marry until he was fifty. He was now fifty-two, and Miss Peters thirty, and they slipped off together to no-one-knew-where.

News of the marriage caused intense speculation in the film colony. Miss Peters, whose career had been burgeoning, was one of 20th Century-Fox's most valuable properties at the time of her disappearance. Had Hughes bought out her contract? No one knew. What kind of life could Jean be living now? No one knew that, either, for Miss Peters did not reappear in the familiar places of

Hollywood, nor, for that matter, was she to be seen in Las Vegas. There were rumors that she became ill under the strain of life with Hughes, but these rumors could not be confirmed. There were reports that even Miss Peters' family in Ohio did not know where she was, but these reports could not be confirmed. It was as if Pluto had carried Persephone off with him without the Associated Press knowing it. As Raymond Chandler remarked in one of his Philip Marlowe detective stories, a great deal of money can buy a great deal of publicity—or a great deal of silence. Jean Peters had married one of the richest men in the world, with the result that she left that world as abruptly and as completely as if she had entered a convent.

But Eddie the barber saw her. He said nothing at the time, but in later years he gave this description of family life at San Limbo: "Sometimes his wife, Jean Peters, a lovely girl I used to see around Hollywood, would be sitting on the couch. She'd look up and tell me to cut her husband's hair short, but he never paid much attention. He was always carrying on business. By this time Hughes had become strange. He grew a long beard. I'd walk in every four months or so, and he'd be sitting there looking like Moses. He had a scar on his lip and chin from a plane wreck, so that's why he grew the beard, I guess, to cover them up. I used to trim it down to a Van Dyke, but he'd always let it grow back full."

33

While Howard Hughes was secluded with his bride and the ills of a corporate empire, there appeared in the nation's theaters, like an embarrassing child of middle age, the last Howard Hughes production. It was not only an embarrassing child, but tragically enough, a badly retarded one. It was the motion picture *Jet Pilot,* about which Bosley Crowther, *The New York Times* critic, had this to say—when it was released in 1957: "Wars have been fought and airplane designs have been improved since *Jet Pilot* . . . went before the cameras in 1949. Likewise, John Wayne, the hero, has grown grayer; Janet Leigh, the heroine, has become more blonde, and a good many better motion pictures about jet pilots have gone over the dam. . . .

"If it lacks for aerial interest—outside of a few mild flying scenes—it is probably because obsolescence forced removal of much aerial footage. And if it lacks for dramatic vitality, which it most certainly does, you can blame that on a weak script, poor direction, and indifferent performances by all. . . . *Jet Pilot* is the film that Howard Hughes produced with the idea of making another *Hell's Angels.* It is a dud."

One reason why "they" bothered to release it might well have been that Howard Hughes had paid $12,000,000 for *Jet Pilot* and another John Wayne motion picture, *The Conqueror,* and very badly needed to get this money back, and $300,000,000 more besides. While it is always possible that Hughes might actually have thought *Jet Pilot* was a good motion picture, the economic explanation is the more believable. The picture was so bad that its chances of great success at the box office seemed remote. But any money would be better than none.

At this time, when it was important for Hughes to watch every single million, he nonetheless continued to pour money into the constant care of his flying boat. And, like an upstairs faucet that continues to dribble while a family takes a summer vacation, the girl-watching continued at 7000 Romaine Street. Hughes had sold his motion picture studio holdings, but his talent scouts continued to clip the magazine photographs, offer contracts, bring girls to Hollywood and put them up in hotels, telling them that stardom awaited them as soon as Howard Hughes could arrange it. One of the girls was Gail Ganley, then an eighteen-year-old student at the University of California at Los Angeles, who told the following story:

One afternoon in December, 1958, the telephone rang for her and it was a man who said he was a Mr. White, and that "a certain party" was interested in having photographs made of her.

"Who's interested in me?" Gail wanted to know.

"I can't reveal the party's name," White said, "but I assure you it would be wise to have such photographs taken at our expense."

Gail, who hoped for a motion picture career and already had an agent, suggested Mr. White talk to her agent. The agent subsequently called Gail and said that while he had learned the "party's" name, he had been sworn to secrecy, but to please do what she was told. Accordingly, she reported to the Christy-Sheppard photographic studios in Hollywood, posed for several pictures and left. A few days later she received a $50 check to pay her for the time she had spent posing. Nothing on the check indicated the identity of her secret admirer. A week later White called to say that the person was a very powerful "industrialist-producer" who at that moment was looking at her photographs. Another week passed before White called again. Gail was to receive dramatic coaching and be prepared for a role in a motion picture.

"But who is it?" she kept asking. "Who has all this faith in me?"

"You'll find out," White said.

Two chauffeurs subsequently arrived at Gail's home and took

the excited schoolgirl to the home of a famous Hollywood dramatic coach. There she was told that her benefactor was Howard Hughes.

"I can't believe it!" she said, visions of Jean Harlow and Jane Russell's splendor dancing in her pretty head.

Her instructions were that she should be on constant standby, available at any hour of day or night, in case Hughes should want to see her. She was also to follow a rigid daily routine.

"Every afternoon between three and four," she said, "these two chauffeurs from the Hughes production office would call for me in a company Chevrolet. Their names were Wayne and Argyle, nicknamed Sox. They would take me and my mother to my drama coach's office. There we would work for two hours, and we'd then have dinner at the Beverly Hills Hotel. We were told to order anything on the menu. The bill was paid. After dinner we would go back to the drama coach's house and work until 10:30. Then the chauffeurs would take mother and me home. After about a week everything looked on the up-and-up, so mother dropped out and I went through it alone."

A month later Gail began to fret about expense money. She notified her agent, who in turn called Walter Kane and told him that Gail wanted a contract. Kane later called back to say that while the contract had been drawn up, Hughes was unavailable to sign it. In the meantime Kane urged that Gail continue to study and eat at Hughes' expense. But Gail had had enough of both school and food, and told her agent that the deal, if there really was a deal, was off.

She was working with an orchestra in San Diego when the Hughes office next called—two years later. They wanted to send an airplane down for her to bring her to Los Angeles. Gail said she would drive herself to Los Angeles when her engagement in San Diego was completed.

"I soon learned it was the same old run-around," she said. "They wanted me to take new pictures, but this time there would be a contract and expenses, and a picture to shoot."

Gail was given a script, *Pale Moon,* to read. She thought it was terrible, but was told it had cost $50,000 and was being rewritten. The dramatic lessons began again. Gail said she would go to her lessons without escorts this time, and that she would have dinner at Perino's instead of the hotel. At that time, Perino's restaurant was one of Los Angeles' most exclusive tables, where dinner for one could easily cost $25.

At first the routine was pleasant enough. Waiters and captains would crowd about, suggesting the steak Diane or the trout amandine. There was no check to sign; no tip to leave.

"The Hughes people told me practically every day that my screen test was coming up and I would meet Mr. Hughes," Gail said. "I felt I was so close to meeting Hughes that I bought an expensive red dress and kept it in the car, just in case the meeting came up suddenly. I carried it around so long that I started calling it 'the tired red dress.' "

It suddenly dawned on her that she was a prisoner. "I ate at the best restaurant in town, but I had to eat alone, and I could have no social life," she said.

She was also told that on no account should she mention to anyone that she was undergoing grooming by the Hughes organization.

There was still no contract. Hughes would sign it the moment he found the time. Meanwhile, Gail needed expense money. It was delivered to her by White. But one day she was told to meet White in front of 7000 Romaine Street to receive her money.

"White honked his car horn three times and called up to a guy named Harry, who eventually poked his head out the second story window," Gail said. "Harry looked around cautiously, then lowered a string with a white envelope clipped to the end. White took the envelope, signed a receipt and clipped it back to the string. My expense money was in the envelope. I was almost hysterical, but the Hughes men played their game with a straight face."

In the months that followed Gail was permitted to go after her own money. Once a week she would drive to the building, honk her horn three times and Harry or someone else would appear at the window. The money would come dancing down on a string, Gail would sign for it, the string would go up again and the window would close.

No less curious than any young woman, Gail wondered what went on inside that building. She walked around it. It seemed deserted. Paint was peeling off the sides, and the shrubbery needed trimming. All the doors were tightly locked. Gail tried to question the men at the window.

"Is Mr. Hughes up there?" she cried. "Are you hiding him?"
The window came slamming shut.

By this time, Gail had memorized every part and every line of dialogue in *Pale Moon*.

In April, 1962, four years after the Hughes men first approached her, Gail was called to Kane's office. There she was told that Hughes had decided not to do the picture and that Gail would be released from her contract.

She burst into tears.

34

The executive's visitor, a journalist, could see no way out of the mess, for everywhere he went throughout the Hughes empire the signs of impending disaster were very plain. The one man who might be able to explain matters was Hughes. But Hughes had not granted an interview in the past four years, and none of Hughes' associates would say where he was. Indeed, it seemed as if they were telling nothing but the truth when they said they really didn't know. Still the reporter persisted, talking to members of the Hughes organization in the perpetual hope that one of them might shed some light on a murky situation. He apparently made himself a sufficient nuisance to rouse Hughes out of seclusion.

When the reporter returned from the interview, he had quite a story to tell his friends. He said that Hughes had given him an off-the-record, not-for-attribution, but solely-for-background interview. He said he was given a date and a late hour, and told to drive at that time to a certain intersection of Olympic Boulevard in Los Angeles, blink his lights a certain number of times and wait.

He said he did this. Presently an old, battered automobile appeared and he was ordered into it. He was driven to the Los Angeles airport and down a runway to the side of a Boeing 707 jet that bulked dimly in the darkness. He went aboard and found Hughes alone at the controls. Hughes took the aircraft aloft, and for an hour the two men flew through the night sky over California. Hughes freely answered the reporter's questions. They returned to Los Angeles where on landing Hughes fled down the steps into a waiting automobile and vanished once again. No reporter has seen him since.

The reporter honored his pledge of secrecy to Hughes. The only thing he would say was that Hughes should never be underestimated.

But the external facts, obvious to all in the aviation industry, were these: TWA's piston-driven aircraft were taking a bad beating from their competitors' jets, and the company was losing money; TWA's management record was terribly weak, what with presidents coming and going more rapidly than football coaches at a university whose teams were unsuccessful; Hughes had a choice of bankrupting his empire or going to the bankers for a loan—and the bankers would think long and hard before lending any money to Hughes.

The financial world's view of Hughes was fairly stated at the time by *Fortune* magazine, which reported:

"His personal resources are still extensive; his properties are sound; and the debt that presses so heavily upon him is for jet aircraft, which themselves are valuable assets and should become big money-makers. The trouble is that Hughes is temperamentally incapable of fitting himself into orthodoxy. Suspicious and withdrawn, elusive to the point of being almost invisible, he is loath to give anything up, loath to admit error. His calling in outside help is tantamount to his acknowledging publicly the magnitude of his problems and perhaps a certain want of foresight; and the terms on which that help might be forthcoming could mean, further, his relinquishing the absolute control he has so far exercised over his properties. There is one other aspect of his character about which his former associates are agreed: he abhors making a decision."

Hughes, *Fortune* said, was no Henry Ford, for: "It would be hard to point to anything in the Hughes holdings that has been the product of creative insight or driving purpose on the part of the proprietor. Nevertheless, an immense pool of wealth has come into being under his auspices" and "like Ford, Hughes regards his properties as wholly his own." What Hughes wanted, the magazine said, was a banker willing to let him run his own business, but what the bankers wanted was to convert the Hughes empire into public properties.

The essential trouble was not that TWA was losing money. Despite its current difficulties, the airline was a half-billion-dollar property that could earn money under proper management. Nor was the problem that Hughes could not borrow against his holdings. It was, *Fortune* said, Hughes' own narrow, grasping, suspicious character, his desire to be beholden to none and to do as he pleased.

If ever there was a time when Hughes needed Noah Dietrich, that time was now, but Dietrich had gone. It would seem that Hughes would have to try to sail between Scylla and Charybdis all by himself, but he attempted to steer an alternate course. If the bankers were loath to lend him money, perhaps the solution to this problem was to make them more agreeable. To that end, Hughes persuaded Charles S. Thomas, a former Secretary of the Navy, to accept the presidency of TWA. Thomas was a man of immense business and personal prestige, and his presence in the firm was certain to impress the careful men in the gray flannel suits who dwelt in the paneled offices of Wall Street.

And so it did. With Thomas in the president's chair, negotiations were begun for a group of New York financiers to advance $165,-000,000 to TWA. But before this transaction could be completed, Thomas resigned. The bankers' story was that Hughes had no real intention of going through with the loan, and at the last minute got Thomas to resign so that the deal would fall through. The Hughes version is that the bankers persuaded Thomas to step out because *they* had now decided to back off the loan and needed an excuse to do so. In any event, Thomas quit, the New York financiers pulled out and Hughes was once again faced with his original problem.

Now in the deepest seclusion of his life, Hughes moved like a phantom from one place to another in San Limbo, meanwhile barraging Boeing and Convair with nocturnal telephone calls. He called Boeing to cancel part of his order for 707s; called Convair to hold up production; called them back to order more 880s; called Boeing to say he needed more 707s. He made a partial payment on the first 707s, and arranged for Hughes Tool to lease them to TWA at a reported $2,500 a day. Unforeseen delays began to plague production at Convair. As is customary between airlines and manufacturers, TWA inspectors watched the Convair assembly line. Convair complained that Hughes would call the inspectors off their jobs, one by one, so that work could not proceed. At other times TWA test pilots were not available to accept finished aircraft. What with one thing and another, Convair's 880s were not forthcoming until a year after their due date. Convair then had the problem of delivering them, for Hughes sent no one to take possession. There the completed aircraft sat on the company field—signed for, sealed, but not yet delivered. Hughes was meanwhile trying to find some other airline to take them off his hands, having no money with which to pay for them. And Convair now had problems of its own, for they hesitated to begin production on eleven 880s that United Airlines had ordered until they found out whether Hughes was going to pay for those they had built for him. While Convair delayed, United canceled its order and went to Boeing to buy the medium-range jets that Boeing was now producing to compete with Convair's 880. The result for Convair was stark disaster; the company lost $27,000,000 in 1960 and $40,000,000 in the following year, in the course of which the structure of its parent corporation, General Dynamics, was shaken and so were the careers of several executives.

As 1960 drew to a close, Hughes was backed against a wall. Several banks offered to lend him the money he needed, but only if Hughes would put up a part of the tool company and his $100,-000,000 in real estate as collateral. Hughes refused. He would not part with any of his holdings.

So the bankers said, in effect, "Very well. Goodbye."

But then the men in Wall Street had second thoughts. A consortium of lending institutions, the Equitable and the Metropolitan insurance companies and the Irving Trust Company and Dillon, Read Company, told Hughes that they would finance his jet purchases on just one condition. The condition was that he put his TWA stock in the hands of a three-man voting trust. Two of the three would represent the lending institutions; the third could be a Hughes man. The trust would control Hughes' stock for ten years.

In other words, the bankers were saying, "Look, Howard, you go away somewhere for ten years while we see what we can do with your half-billion-dollar property."

The men who believed they knew Hughes best swore he would never accept such an arrangement. But it was really the only possible way out.

The lending institutions appointed Ernest Breech, former chairman of the Ford Motor Company, and Irving S. Olds, former chairman of United States Steel, to represent them on the voting trust. Hughes appointed a vice-president of the Hughes Tool Company to watch over his interests.

The announcement of Hughes' capitulation raised eyebrows in board rooms across the nation. Financiers could not believe that Hughes really meant to stay away for a decade from the one venture he loved the most. Therefore, the men in the board rooms speculated, Hughes must have still some higher, hidden trump to play.

But he had none. He could only watch, from wherever he was, while the voting trust installed a new management at TWA, bringing in Charles C. Tillinghast, Jr., a former Bendix Corporation executive, to be TWA's new president—its sixth in the past fourteen years.

In December, 1960, as he turned fifty-five, Hughes could reflect that he had come a long way back to where he had been thirty-five years ago. Then he had come to California, a rich young man with his motion picture enterprises, his aircraft company, his electronics company and his world-girdling airline all in his future. Now, a graying man and, a friend has said, an ill man, all this was in his past. He had given up motion pictures, had given away his electronics concern, and the money men had taken his airline away from him. Seen nowhere in the glittering places he once frequented, Hughes more than ever seemed to fit the epithet that *Fortune* applied to him, The Spook of American Capitalism. Small wonder that the Gail Ganleys of Hollywood never saw him; the incredible thing is that, adrift on his sea of troubles, Hughes had the Ganleys come to Hollywood at all. Could he really have believed that one day he might begin anew in the motion picture business with a fresh, new star? Was this a wistful belief, akin to the notion that one day the *Hercules* would fly again? Or did Hughes even know that Hughes Productions still existed at 7000 Romaine Street? One fact of which he certainly must have been aware was that he was an enormously rich man who had gained an empire—and lost a world.

35

In late 1961 a wealthy Los Angeles financier named John Zurlo put his French Regency mansion up for sale. It stood atop a hill in the fashionable suburb of Bel Air, and its price was $500,000.

"Shortly thereafter," Zurlo said, "I got a telephone call from a well-known real estate woman named Virginia Tremaine who specializes in renting homes for celebrities. She said she had a client who wished to remain anonymous and who wished to rent my house. I laughed, because nobody could afford to pay the kind of rent I would need. The house is full of priceless antiques, and I would have to be sure it was a respectable tenant, and a very, very rich one.

"She then mentioned a sum, a fantastic sum, and I thought it was a joke. But she said she was not kidding. Her client wanted the house, provided that his identity could remain strictly secret. To this day I don't know for sure who lives there. All I know is that each month a check arrives signed by Miss Tremaine. I can't get into my house, but I am assured by her that my furniture and my house are being taken care of properly."

The twisting road that leads up the hill terminates at the ornate gate of the high fence that surrounds Mr. Zurlo's property, and in 1961, before the gate, pleasant-looking muscular young men sat in old Chevrolets. The young men would not open the gate for anyone whose description, automobile, automobile license plate and time of arrival did not tally with the written notations the young men consulted. Similar young men in similar automobiles could also be seen at the end of a road on another hilltop—this one in Rancho Santa Fe, a rich man's resort fifteen miles north of San Diego, five miles inland from the coast. The house that crowned that hill was an enormous, rambling structure built in a style that someone called "anonymous fortress modern," and it commanded all approaches. There, one of the young men before its gate sat in an automobile, learning Spanish. Similar men sat on the front porches of $100-a-day bungalows in the garden of the Beverly Hills Hotel.

At times lights would be seen in one or another of these residences, and this phenomenon would be taken by the nearest neighbors as evidence that someone was at home. While they all suspected that the someone was Howard Hughes, no one could be certain. For example, the Bel Air police force—a private service for the millionaires of the area—told reporters they knew nothing of Hughes' presence. Many a Bel Air neighbor spent many an hour sitting in his rose garden with field glasses, but none of them ever saw the tenant. Once a reporter went up the hill to the ornate gate and engaged in conversation with a polite young man whose manner was as firm as his smile was amiable.

"I want to see Mr. Hughes, please," the reporter said.

"Who is Mr. Hughes?"

"Mr. Howard Hughes."

"Mr. Howard Hughes doesn't live here."

"Oh, I was told that he does. Well then, where does he live?"

"I don't know."

"Why are you guarding the house?"

"I don't know."

"Who do you work for?"

"I don't know."

"Who lives here?"

"I don't know that, either."

"Does Mr. Hughes ever come out?"

"I don't know."

"Can I go inside?"

"No."

From time to time luxurious automobiles were passed through the gate after scrutiny, and the occupant of one of them subsequently returned down the hill to tell her friends that Jean Hughes enjoyed playing with her black cat, Nefertiti, and had taken up art. She said that Jean had done a somber black and white portrait of herself.

"Her life is a lonely one," the friend said. "But she has apparently adjusted to it. She genuinely loves Howard, and despite his strange ways, theirs is a good marriage. She would like him to come out of his shell; she wants the world to know of her husband's greatness, rather than of his eccentricities. But he doesn't listen to her. She's learned to please him and to accept his reclusive way of life."

On the other hand, she said, Jean seemed anxious to hear talk of places and people she had known; she was delighted to hear gossip of the studios, of who was planning what sort of film and who would be the actors.

It was from the hilltop mansion, or at any of his residences, that Hughes sought by telephone to recover control of TWA, and, incredibly enough—in view of his tangled financial situation—to gain control of Northeast Airlines and merge it with TWA. His first action, in May, 1961, was to inform the Securities and Exchange Commission that he was considering legal action against the TWA voting trust and the lending institutions which had appointed it. But before he could file such a suit, TWA's management struck first. They sued Howard Hughes and the Hughes Tool Company for $115,000,000 damages, charging that Hughes had mismanaged TWA, had damaged it; and they petitioned the court to force him to sell his stock and get out of TWA forever. Their suit charged Hughes with violation of the Sherman and Clayton antitrust acts.

Here was a paradox for lawyers. How could a man sue himself? After all, Hughes still owned more than three-quarters of TWA's stock, even if he had signed away his voting rights. How could TWA sue its owner?

Hughes' answer was to file a sixty-three-page countersuit, demanding $336,000,000 in damages from the men who controlled TWA. He charged the lending institutions and the management with conspiring to violate antitrust laws in airline financing, and with conspiring to perpetuate their control over TWA beyond the ten-year limit. He asked that his tool company receive $231,000,-000 in damages, and that $135,000,000 in treble damages be paid to TWA. Finally, the suit asked that the voting trust be dissolved and that the voting rights of his stock be restored to their rightful, injured owner, Howard Hughes.

"Any assertion," TWA's management replied, "that TWA is controlled by persons or interests other than by its independent board of directors is, of course, completely ridiculous. The fact is that since January 1, 1961, TWA, for the first time in many years, has not been a captive of Howard Hughes and has been operated solely in the interests of its stockholders and the public."

All of the bulky documents were dropped in the lap of the United States District Court in New York, which appointed a special master to take pre-trial depositions from the warring parties. In one or another of his houses, Hughes meanwhile made his telephone calls seeking acquisition of Northeast Airlines.

Northeast was a small, struggling trunk line that served the Boston-New York area primarily, but had temporary permission to fly the lucrative New York-Miami run. It was Hughes' notion to merge Northeast with TWA, which would, by adding the East Coast run to TWA's cross-country routes, enable TWA to serve more principal cities than any other United States airline. It so happened that he could acquire Northeast because the Atlas Corporation, the giant holding company presided over by Floyd Odlum, owned 56 percent of Northeast's stock. And Hughes, through his RKO stock trade and later purchases, was a large stockholder in Atlas. He thereupon bought out Atlas' 56-percent interest in Northeast for $5,000,000 cash, and assumed $16,500,000 worth of notes owned by Northeast. He then advanced Northeast nearly $12,000,000. How was this possible? The point of the matter was that while Hughes could not have raised $300,000,000 to buy TWA its jets, he could afford to raise $33,000,000 for Northeast, particularly inasmuch as the lending institutions that had taken over TWA had paid for the jets that Hughes had ordered, and were trying to recover their loan out of TWA earnings.

By coming to Northeast's aid, Hughes sought to convince the

Civil Aeronautics Board that Northeast's temporary permission to
fly the New York-Miami run—the only route that kept Northeast's
operation profitable—should be made permanent. Eastern and National Airlines, both of whom owned permanent rights to the New
York-Miami route, immediately complained. They said Hughes
had no right to own both Northeast and TWA, even if TWA's ownership was in dispute. But the CAB, after lengthy hearings, ruled in
June, 1962, that Hughes was entitled to own interests in both airlines.

Hughes' personal sky began to brighten. But TWA's management was equally optimistic, for they believed they had found a
terribly simple way to win their suit against Hughes: get him in
court and have him try to explain to the special master just how he
did business. There he could be asked, perhaps, to explain the
rather complicated way in which he received his money. The way
was this:

While Hughes drew no salary, once a month the Hughes Tool
Company in Houston would transfer funds to Hughes Productions,
Inc., the inactive motion picture company at 7000 Romaine Street,
which in turn would place funds in the account of the L. M. Company at the Bank of America in Los Angeles. "L. M. Company
isn't really a company," said Lee Murrin, who in 1963 was general
manager of Hughes Productions. "It's just—well, I don't know." In
any event, Hughes' bills would be sent to Murrin, who would pay
them out of the L. M. Company account.

To TWA's astonishment—and to the court's—Hughes could not
be found. San Limbo is a vast and mysterious emptiness. The airline hired private detectives to try to serve subpoenas on Hughes.
Thousands of dollars were spent in this futile activity, for the detectives were everywhere confronted by the muscular young men in
the old Chevrolets who disavowed any knowledge of Howard
Hughes or whoever it was who lived in the houses they guarded.
Newspaper reporters, joining the hunt, did succeed in drawing from
a guard who sat in front of a Beverly Hills Hotel cottage the admission that Hughes paid the rent on the cottage.

To a reporter the guard explained that it was his job to see that nobody went into the cottage, not even to clean it, because he'd been told Mr. Hughes liked things left just as he had left them; if Mr. Hughes had perhaps dropped a piece of paper beside a red chair, then he expected that paper and that chair to be there if he should return ten years later.

It was all very frustrating for the reporters and the process servers. Everywhere they went, the answer was the same; no one had seen Howard Hughes in the last five years. Anyone who wished to talk to him could, however, try to do so. All he had to do was pick up a telephone and dial OL 2-4500 in Los Angeles. A polite young man would answer in the building at 7000 Romaine Street. He would advise the caller to state his name, telephone number and the nature of his business, and would say that when Mr. Hughes called in the message would be given to Mr. Hughes. Years ago Hughes left orders at 7000 Romaine Street that no one there was to call him in any circumstances, presumably not even if the building caught fire and burned to the ground. And the young men at Romaine Street said that Father had not called them in years. One man who said he had seen Hughes in 1960 said that Hughes had not then seemed well. But now the telephone calls had ceased entirely. And although lights might burn in the mansion in Bel Air, who was to know, really, if Hughes was there when they did? Hughes had committed no crimes. No warrant could be issued for the search of his house; a man's house is inviolate against search without a warrant.

When all of this was duly reported to the Federal District Court in New York, legal tempers grew choleric. It appeared as if Hughes were making a mockery of the court—here he was, suing for a king's ransom, yet not deigning to appear in person. To this Hughes' lawyer, Chester C. Davis, somewhat wistfully said, "Of course it would be a challenge to *meet* the man. At times, I admit, it would be helpful to see him face-to-face. Communication *is* a problem. I'd be less than candid if I denied that. So far, however, the telephone has been adequate."

Then, somewhat angrily, Attorney Davis said, "They are trying to get him on the witness stand so they can embarrass him for two or three months. But if he ever does appear to testify, he'll knock 'em from here to breakfast. This is a phony lawsuit; it's nonsense, and both sides know it.

"There's a hell of a lot of mystery being thrown around here when there's really not. Howard Hughes is brilliant and unusual. He knows what he's doing. He has very good reasons for what he does and for what he does not do. If he doesn't want to see somebody, why the hell should he?"

In the spring of 1963, the court's decision was that Hughes had lost his suit against TWA by forfeit, and that he would have to pay his own airline $135,000,000 in damages and sell his stock. Hughes' lawyers replied that the court could make no such ruling because the whole controversy was not properly within the jurisdiction of the courts, anyway. It was, they said, a matter that the Civil Aeronautics Board would have to decide.

While the legal bickering went on and on, the CAB, ruling on another matter, announced that it was taking away from Northeast Airlines permission to make the New York-Miami run—the only route that had kept Northeast in the air and the only reason Hughes had wanted Northeast in the first place. It would seem that at the eleventh hour a hard-beset and furtive Highes was destined to lose all, at every turn.

In the midst of these torments, while reporters and process servers searched for her husband, Jean Peters began to live a somewhat more public life. Whereas the elegant Beverly Hills shops had once sent gowns to her for inspection, now she began to shop herself, driving into town in a nondescript Chevrolet station wagon. She began to make recordings of books for blind people. In 1962 she appeared twice at concerts at the Hollywood Bowl—but in a box well screened from public view by a mass of shrubbery. She saw a performance by the Comédie Française at the Greek Theater, and for the first time since 1957, talked briefly with a reporter. She was still beautiful at thirty-seven, swathed in an enormous black mink coat, a purple scarf at her throat.

"I haven't been ducking the press," she said. "It's just that they aren't interested in an old married woman any more."

She smiled.

"My husband and I don't go out very often," she said, as if to explain her attendance alone at the theater.

Mrs. Hughes said she was confident that her husband would regain control of his aerial dominions.

No, she said, as she walked toward the black Cadillac limousine where two guards waited, she did not believe she would ever return to the Kleig lights, the cameras and the microphones of the sound stages of Hollywood.

"Not unless it was a dream role," she said. "And those don't come along any more."

36

Indeed, now in 1966, in Hughes' sixtieth year, it would seem that Mrs. Hughes was quite right. No dream role has come along for her save as that of consort to a deposed king. There is no role at all for her husband, save that of a monarch in exile, watching from a distance as his kingdom prospers under other princes. There is evidence that Hughes still dreams of returning to power—several million dollars' worth of evidence, in the form of the legal fees he is paying out to regain it. But it would seem that his chances of success are most remote, for as writer John McDonald put it in the May, 1965, *Fortune* magazine, Hughes' lawyers, and TWA's, are playing with a legal can of worms sufficient for them to fish with for several years. Given the glacial movements of corporate lawyers and the courts in cases involving millions upon millions of dollars, the bickering may go on until Hughes' death makes matters moot.

The management's accusation is that Hughes wrecked the airline through his capriciousness. Management can point to the last year of his control, when TWA lost $39,000,000, and then point to 1964, when TWA profits were $37,000,000. By this simple measurement, matters are quite clear: with Hughes out of the cockpit and Tillinghast in it, the company changed course 180 degrees.

On the other hand, there is reason to believe that Hughes was forced out just at the moment the harvest was ripe, and that TWA's current prosperity may be directly attributed to Hughes' earlier husbandry. For during the profitless years, Hughes had established the long intercontinental routes; it was he who thought of the inflight motion pictures that gave TWA an edge over its rivals in transoceanic passenger preferences. Under his management the company commissioned the late Eero Saarinen to build the soaring Flight Center at Kennedy International Airport. The Kansas City maintenance base and the TWA training programs are models for the industry, and these, too, were established under Hughes. If the switch from piston to jet aircraft seemingly found Hughes asleep, he at least did not buy the prop-jet aircraft that other airlines did in the course of their conversion to jet service. The other airlines are now phasing out those expensive compromises, and what seemed to be Hughes' original error may now be TWA's advantage. For, as TWA rapidly phases out its last piston aircraft, it seems certain to become the world's first major all pure-jet airline. This is a matter of crucial importance, for the pure jets are far more efficient and economical than any other aircraft, as well as having far more appeal to passengers.

An irony of Hughes' situation is that he, as majority stockholder in TWA, is indirectly financing the company's suit against him while directly financing his suit against the company. Another irony is that even if he lost and had to pay millions in damages, the money would merely move from Hughes Tool, which he wholly owns, to TWA, of which he owns 77 percent. Practically speaking, he would be shifting money from one pocket to another. But what is really at stake is not money, but power.

A further irony is that Hughes has grown richer while the lawyers squabble. Thanks to a rising economy, a remarkable increase in long-distance passenger travel since 1960, and to Tillinghast's lucid management of TWA, Hughes has gained approximately $215,000,000 through an increase in the market value of his airline stock. In addition, he converted $30,000,000 worth of TWA debentures into stock, and thereby gained another $45,000,000. *Fortune* today estimates Hughes' worth at $1,432,000,000—he is one of the handful of billionaires in the world. And, as a billionaire, he is not without power.

But what are the permissible uses of power? An airline is in the nature of a public utility, and there are limits to what any manager may do with one. Economic laws have much to do with whether any airline can make money no matter who is in the pilot's seat.

But again, money is beside the point. If it were the point, Hughes could simply make peace with TWA's management, take his billion dollars and do something else with it if he wished to resume an active role in the world. If he intends to remain a hermit, why should he care who runs the airline? Why does he wish to recapture his kingdom? Is there some pride that drives him on and on?

At one point in his life Hughes spoke of himself in terms of Greek tragedy, and the parallel has occurred to others. Mr. McDonald put it this way:

"In the well-ordered and codified world of modern large-scale business, Hughes is a distracting legend, and the TWA conflict a Greek spectacular with a chorus of fifty lawyers from ten law firms with a million and a half documents chanting versions of its mysteries while the central character himself remains invisible."

The image summons up a memory of an ancient play performed on another stage, involving the story of a king who, through a fatal flaw, fell into the grip of remorseless Fate and was destroyed. At the end of it, the chorus chanted, "Count no man fortunate who is not dead."

Perhaps so.

One wonders what the view from San Limbo must be.

About the Author

JOHN KEATS is the author of innumerable magazine
articles and many successful books, including
*The Crack in the Picture Window, Schools Without Scholars,
The Insolent Chariots, They Fought Alone,* and *The
Sheepskin Psychosis.* Keats, his wife, and three children
live in Philadelphia, but they spend their summers
in the Thousand Islands.